TORO BRAVO

STORIES. RECIPES. NO BULL.
OR, THE MAKING, BREAKING, AND RIDING OF A BULL

JOHN GORHAM & LIZ CRAIN
PHOTOGRAPHS BY DAVID L. REAMER

CONTENTS

FOREWORD

LIZ CRAIN

I met John Gorham for the first time in 2008, while interviewing Portland chefs for a story about their tattoos. To put it plainly, John wasn't a dick. He was the nicest and smartest of them all, and I liked him immediately. There wasn't any throat-clearing or posturing with him; we walked around the block for our interview, laughing as we talked, especially when he told me about one of his favorite tattoos—a chicken shitting out his sous chef's name on his ass. I thought, *This guy is crazy and really fucking funny.*

The first time I ate at Toro Bravo was late in the summer of 2007, not long after it opened its doors in May. Even newly opened, the sixty-seat restaurant—on the ground floor of a two-story turn-of-the-century building in a low-foot-traffic area of Northeast Portland—was already packed. My boyfriend at the time had designed the restaurant's logo, a fighting bull, and inked it on John's forearm, so we got a big smile and a nod of recognition from John—cooking on the line—when we entered.

Inside, it was dim and loud and all the chunky crosscut tables—two-tops, four-tops, and the long communal table across the room from the bar—were crowded with arms, elbows, drinks, and plates. There were just four people in the kitchen, where oxtail fritters were getting golden in the fryer, drunken pork was spitting on the grill, and paella was crowding the burners. John, 130 pounds heavier than he is now, orchestrated it all.

Tyler and I ordered a couple of martinis and a plate of bacon-wrapped dates for the wait, and were seated an hour later. We ate a lot of big-flavored foods that night: salt cod fritters, manchego fritters, seared scallops with romesco, radicchio salad (I still have to get it every time I visit), and the coppa steak. And, of course, when we thought we could eat and drink no more, John sent us out after-dinner glasses of slightly salty Manzanilla sherry that made us never want to leave.

I've loved Spanish food since I was a teenager, when I spent a spring working on a farm in Spain and, when work was over, traveling through the Southeast. I loved the simplicity of Spanish food—jamón thinly sliced and served at room temperature with olives, griddled langoustines, served with heads and shells intact with a wedge of lemon. I loved how everything tasted older and better, how most foods were tangy and grassy with olive oil. In Spain, the meat seemed to have more funk, the vegetables had more bite and flavor, and the seafood was both sweeter and saltier. Everything seemed more steeped in history, more *storied*.

That's the kind of food John brought to Portland: food that's three-dimensional, robust, and rich with personal history. The food at Toro Bravo adopts the simplicity and comfort of Spanish cuisine: it's served in cazuelas and unfancy plates and bowls, all family-style. But John's food isn't strictly Spanish. It's a little brighter and fresher, more layered and complex. Since opening Toro Bravo, John has opened Tasty n Sons and Tasty n Alder—a neighborhood brunch spot and steakhouse-inspired eatery, respectively—which, along with Toro Bravo, have become a few of Portland's most perpetually slammed restaurants.

Now that I've spent the past two and a half years working with John on this book, I can tell you this: John is extremely loyal, generous, passionate, occasionally bullish, deeply curious, and always learning, and constantly over-the-top busy. John takes care of the people he loves. Stay on John's good side, and you won't know a better friend or boss. (Fail to, and, well, you're fucked.) I'm lucky to know him, and Portland's lucky to have him.

Another thing you should know about John is that he's relentless: always wanting to push harder, *be* better. If he takes a trip to Spain, it's a guarantee you'll find new items on the menu as soon as a week later: from the rabbit fideos inspired by a trip to Barcelona just before the restaurant's opening, to the *cocido madrileno* inspired by the trip we took to Spain together in September 2012.

About that trip: when we were wrapping up this book, John took a group of us to Spain—me, Toro's chef de cuisine Kasey Mills, charcuterie manager Josh Scofield, our photographer David Reamer, and our McSweeney's editor Rachel Khong. We had just five days to spend in Madrid and Barcelona, but we still managed to consume far more than five days' worth of food and drink. On our trip we divvied up pharmaceutical sleep aids over cocktails in the Philadelphia airport, ate a cheese in Madrid that John described as tasting "like licking a goat's asshole" (in a good way), went to one of the last bullfights of the season (and watched a matador get gored), and spanked bewildered Spanish men (okay, only *I* did that). The trip was—in keeping with Toro Bravo style—nonstop. We must have averaged about three hours of sleep a night. We wanted to see, eat, drink, and do everything we could. What I've learned, so many stories, recipes, and insights later, is that running with the Toro Bravo bulls is always an adventure. If you want to keep up, you've got to open your heart, and run like hell.

INTRODUCTION

JOHN GORHAM

On May 18ᵗʰ, 2007, Toro Bravo opened its doors at 120 NE Russell Street and served its very first meal. But it was in the works well before that. The story starts in Washington, DC, with my mother, who had me when she was just a teenager. When I was four, my mom married Gene, my adopted father, and that's when the moving began. Gene worked for Kroger, the grocery chain, opening new stores in different locations and never staying in one place for very long. Our moves went like this, through Georgia, North Carolina, and Virginia: Savannah to Greenville to Charlotte to Shelby to North Myrtle Beach to Myrtle Beach, back to Savannah, back to Greenville, and up to Newport News. By the time I graduated from high school, I'd gone to twenty-one different schools.

All of this moving really took a toll on my mother, and she battled deep depressions her whole life. There were weeks she couldn't get out of bed at all. I learned to cook at a very young age. I learned how to flip eggs in first grade. In second grade, I bought a cast-iron pan at a garage sale so I could make better French toast. Learning to cook not only gave me the feeling that I could survive, it also made me feel that I could do anything.

All the moving meant that I never felt I belonged anywhere. Once things started to feel settled, we'd be up and off again. For all the drawbacks of my itinerant childhood—the chaos, the constant feeling of never belonging—I can't imagine it another way.

During the holidays—regardless of where we were—I'd visit my grandfather, who lived in DC. He loved a party, good food, and friends. Whenever I visited Granddad Gordon we'd eat at steakhouses, old German restaurants, and crab shacks on the Chesapeake Bay. We'd go to European candy stores for the best licorice, or hunt down the city's best burger. We'd watch Justin Wilson, the Cajun chef, together. He'd never let me order off the kids' menus, and always pushed me to try something different. We'd pass our plates so we could try as much as we could. Those times spent with Granddad Gordon taught me that good food was worth seeking out, and that sharing good food could make everything—at least momentarily—better.

When I was fourteen, I got a job washing dishes at Teco Taco. It was my first kitchen job, and I loved everything about it: the camaraderie, the practical joking, the hard work. For the first time in my life, I felt right at home. My next job was at a barbecue pit called Parker's, and I felt it again: that feeling of belonging, that feeling that cooking was exactly what I was supposed to be doing.

I still cook corn the way I learned to do it at Parker's (page 150). There's a lot of that, in this book. I peel asparagus the way Jean-Pierre Moullé taught me in my twenties; the coffee cake I bake today wouldn't be the same if I hadn't first made it, at age seven, for my mother. It's the places we've been, the people we've met, the shit we've been through—good and bad—that makes each of us unique. For anyone who cooks, all that shows up in our food: the people we've encountered, the places we've lived, the choices we've made, our travels, our curiosity, our obsessions. Something that appealed to me when I first started studying Spanish food was its diversity and variety. Spanish cuisine is influenced by centuries of trade and travel. It isn't any one thing. It's all over the place, and anything but straightforward. That was something I knew more than a little about.

I got to Portland in 2001, and in 2004, when my daughter Ruby was born, I knew that I'd be calling Portland home. There were great ingredients to work with, and a young chef could make enough money to buy a house in the city. For years, opening a restaurant had seemed like such a pipe dream, but all of sudden, in Portland, it wasn't. In Portland, it was possible. The restaurant I'd wanted to helm since I first started eating with my grandfather, since I was cooking for my mother, since I was a fourteen-year-old kid biking to a Mexican restaurant to wash dishes—that restaurant was finally going to become a reality.

Toro Bravo opened on May 18th, 2007. Portland loved Toro Bravo right away, and who knows why. We were loud, different, and hard to pin down—a "Spanish" restaurant, but only sort of. But you could come—whoever you were, wherever you'd come from, whatever your personal history—to get full and maybe get drunk, shoot the shit with your friends and laugh as loud as you wanted. Meanwhile, it was everything I'd ever wanted, and what I'd craved growing up: a space to cook in and a community of people to cook for, to eat and drink and have a good time with.

There isn't a day that I don't feel grateful to be able to work with all the people that make Toro Bravo what it is, and bring their stories—their unique histories—to the table. And I'm grateful to everybody who comes in, every night, to pass our plates of food. You make this possible. I hope this book inspires you to cook a meal, invite some friends and family over, and pass your own plates.

Only a few will understand this, but the real title of this book is *Choo! Choo! Fat! The Train Ride to Flavor.*

TB STANDS FOR

TRAILB

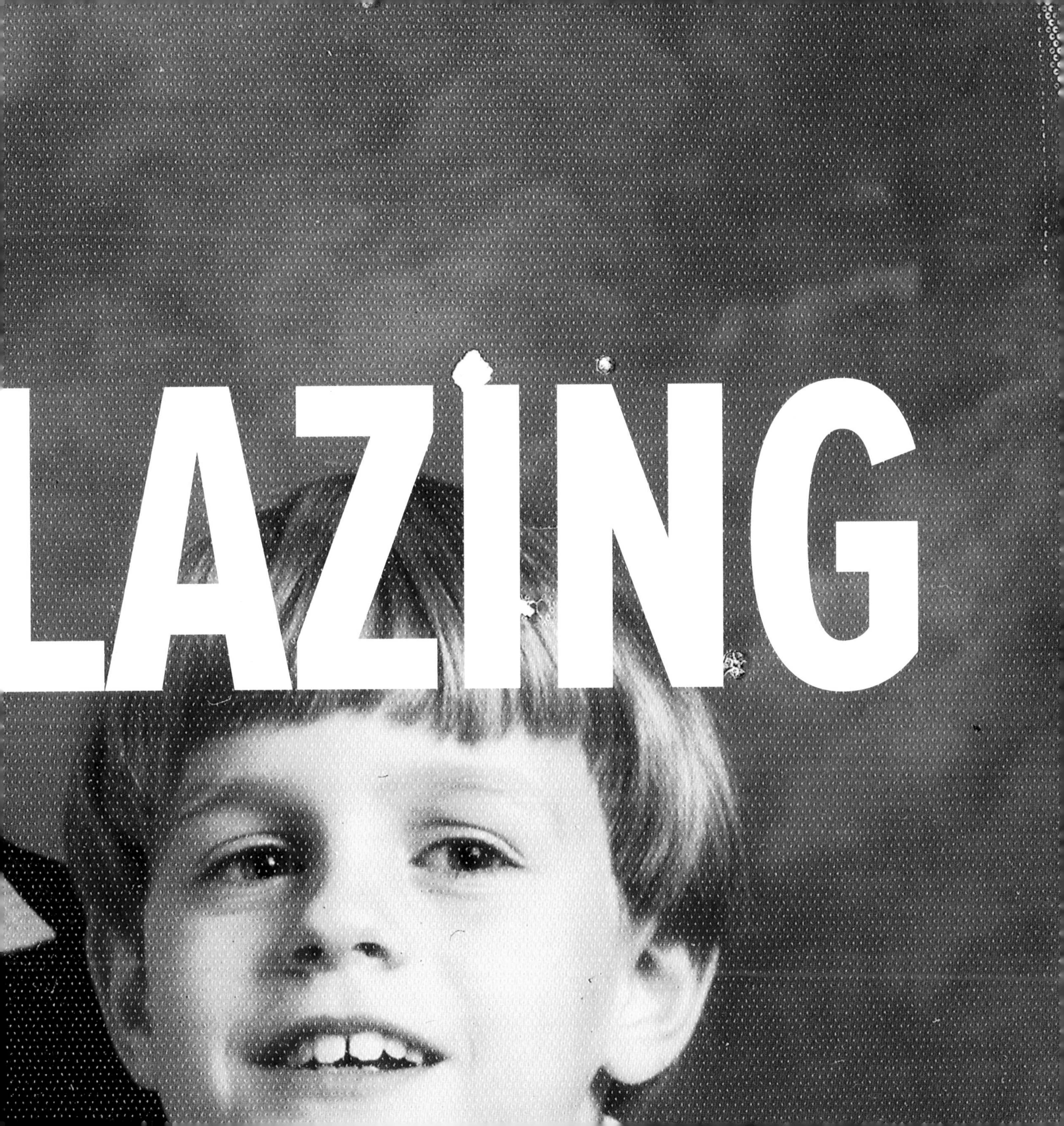
LAZING

WASHINGTON, DC

NOVEMBER 14, 1972

My mom was fourteen when she became pregnant with me. Soon after her parents found out, they kicked her out of the house. In order to pay for the delivery, she worked as a live-in maid for six months for the doctor who would deliver me. The original agreement was that the doctor and his wife would adopt me once I was born. When the time came, though, my grandparents couldn't go through with it. They decided they wanted my mother to keep me after all, and accepted her back into their home.

My grandparents had all daughters—my mom and her three sisters—and I was their first grandchild. I don't think it hurt matters that I was a boy. My dad was twenty-one at the time and he'd come around now and then, but he wasn't—and never wound up being—part of the picture.

I was two when Mom met Gene. She was sixteen and Gene was twenty-seven, married with two kids, and in the navy. My mom told Gene that if they were going to get serious, he had to get divorced, so he did. Not long after that, my mom and Gene were out on a date—joyriding in his souped-up Mustang— when a car T-boned them on the driver's side at a two-way intersection. Gene was fine, but my mom— who was driving—was seriously injured, and had to be flown to the hospital. She came very close to dying. Because of the accident, she had chronic back pain for the rest of her life.

VIRGINIA BEACH, VA

1975–76

A few months after the accident, Gene—who was heading to Vietnam to work on aircraft carriers—convinced my mom to move in with his ex-wife and kids. Some of my first memories are of living with my mom, my stepsister Michelle, my stepbrother Brian, and their mom Toby, in Virginia Beach. We'd all go to the beach and get soft-serve ice cream after. That was our thing. My mom and Toby—who was probably twenty-five or twenty-six at the time—got along well enough, but it obviously wasn't an ideal situation.

Here's an example: my mom had a poodle that Toby's daughter Michelle didn't like. Once, when my mom caught her beating the dog with a stick, my mom went out, took the stick, and started beating Michelle. Our family still talks about it.

JACKSONVILLE, FL

1976–77

After Vietnam, Gene was stationed for the navy in Jacksonville. My mom and I went with him while Toby, Michelle, and Brian stayed behind. Gene was on the USS *Dwight D. Eisenhower*: a pretty famous aircraft carrier. They'd go out for various missions for three to four months at a time, so I remember that time in Jacksonville as being mostly my mom and me together.

In kindergarten we went on a field trip to a nearby restaurant: a steakhouse chain called Bonanza. We daisy-chained there and toured Bonanza, and got to

Mom

My mom was in and out of rehab my entire life until she died at age fifty-one. She had two main issues: depression and chronic pain from the car accident. Chiropractors prescribed her pain pills, which she needed, but always went too far with. According to the coroner's list, there were twenty-two substances in her body at the time of death.

Growing up, there were so many nights my mom was depressed that we had a name for what that meant in terms of dinner. We called it "fend for yourself" night. My daughter Ruby is eight now, and by the time I was her age no one took me to school. Half the time I washed my own clothes and cooked my own dinner. But even though cooking was a means of survival, there was pleasure in it as well.

I cooked for my mother when I could. Cooking wasn't just a way to take care of myself—it was a way to show her that I cared for her, too. Despite all of my mom's difficulties I was very close to her and loved her a lot.

When I was sixteen, and my mom was managing a drug store, she got caught going behind the pharmacy counter and skimming from the top. It was a small town and everyone knew about it. She was humiliated and ended up having a nervous breakdown. She felt like she couldn't go home—couldn't face everybody—so she checked herself into the hospital.

My mom returned a couple months later but she basically said screw it. After that, we'd see her really fucked up, using heavily and openly and doing crazy shit. In the end, my mom and Gene decided that they were too embarrassed to stay in North Carolina. That's when Gene quit Kroger, took his stock options, and bought a house in Virginia. In Virginia, my mom began seeing a psychiatrist. For a while, she seemed to be doing pretty well. I was seventeen, and dating this girl, April, whose best friend was my mom's psychiatrist's daughter. One day my girlfriend was over at our house, and while my mom was in earshot she talked about how her friend, my mom's psychiatrist's daughter, had had an abortion.

I didn't learn this until years later, after my mom died: when my mom overheard what April said, she went to her psychiatrist—who was a strict parent, and very Catholic—and said, *I will tell everyone that you got your daughter an abortion if you don't give me whatever the fuck I want.* For a couple years my mom had access to anything she wanted. She was doing things like not getting out of bed two days at a time, nodding out, wrecking cars.

Not long after, I got a phone call at the restaurant where I was working. My mom was in the hospital. The psychiatrist that my mom had blackmailed into giving her pharmaceuticals ended up paying someone to beat the tarnation out of her. He just wanted the problem to go away. He'd been playing with something illegal and wanted out. My mom was black and blue all over with serious head trauma and was hospitalized for several days. The guy who did the job for the psychiatrist told her that if she said anything to the cops about it, he knew her kids and would do the same to them. I know the psychiatrist and a few times over the years I've wanted to say something to him to at least let him know that I know, but I never have. Probably because I know, if I'm honest, that if I had been him, I might have done the same thing myself.

Helen

In Greenville, there was a woman named Helen, a family friend who lived on a small farm, and whose husband had recently, tragically passed away. He was electrocuted underneath their house while working on some piping. He hit a live wire and died instantly. Helen didn't find out until a few hours later.

After Helen's husband died I visited her regularly, sometimes with a friend or with my brother, and I'd mow her lawn. I mowed people's lawns for money—I'd been doing that since I was twelve—but I never charged Helen.

Helen lived far enough away from my family that she would always pick me up from home, have me mow her lawn, and drop me back off later that night. Every time, after we were finished with the lawn, she would invite me and whoever came with me in for a home-cooked dinner. She cooked everything: tuna casserole, green bean casserole, meatloaf, fried chicken, and baked ziti. Dinner usually came with a salad or two, and big cold pitchers of lemonade and milk. Everything was always family-style—we'd pass plates and share. I remember thinking: *This is how a family should feel.* I'm still the happiest and most comfortable around a dinner table like that.

watch the cooks in the kitchen. Afterward we had chopped steak for lunch. I remember thinking, then, that cooking seemed pretty cool.

SAVANNAH, GA
1979–80

When I was six, we moved from Jacksonville to Savannah, where Gene and one of his good friends started a pin-striping business together. We went to a lot of big fish fries at churches and community centers in Savannah: you paid a small amount, grabbed a plate, and then it was all-you-could-eat fried fish, straight up. There were usually french fries and fried shrimp, salad, and tartar sauce, cocktail sauce, and lemons to go with the seafood. There was always plenty of sweet tea to go around.

Hurricane David, which hit Georgia in early September of 1979, was devastating—especially to our neighborhood. Our house was okay but a lot of our neighbors' homes were destroyed. We couldn't drive out of our neighborhood until a week after the hurricane, because trees and debris blocked the road. There was no electricity and no water, so we'd walk to various nearby relief areas for supplies every day.

I remember my mom being very nervous about the dry ice that we'd been given for our food. She was scared that I would touch it and get hurt. She was nervous about everything during the hurricane, but Gene, on the other hand, was very relaxed. He actually grilled outside during the eye of the storm. It was sunny and beautiful and the eye probably lasted at least half an hour, from what I remember. We'd gone fishing that week, so Gene got the grill stoked and

Gene

Gene wasn't home a lot because he worked so much, but when he was it was a police state. Growing up, if I ever left anything of mine in the living room, Gene would put it in the trash. I knew the rule, but my little sister was too young to always abide by it. She'd go into my room and take out things of mine to play with and then forget to put them away. She didn't know any better because she was so young—just a toddler. It happened all the time: Gene would find whatever it was and throw it in the trash. I took the eye-for-an-eye approach. His hobby was restoring old cars and on weekends he'd work on everything from old '50s Impalas to Chevy pickups. There was always a car in the garage that Gene was working on and restoring to make into a show car. Every time he'd throw something of mine away, I'd go to the garage, take one of his tools, and throw it away, too.

One of the first times I sought revenge like that was when my sister got my Star Wars action figures out while I was asleep and took them into the living room. She forgot to put them away, and

when Gene came home he stepped on one, broke it, and threw it out. I was heartbroken—I was really into Star Wars then—so later that night I snuck out to the garage and tossed one of Gene's wrenches in the trash. Another time I was by myself in my room listening to music when Gene came home, thought my music was too loud, punched my stereo, and broke it. I threw away his floor jack that night.

I remember Gene sometimes almost like a cartoon character with smoke coming out of his ears, running around and screaming things like, *Where's my fucking wrench?!* These days I try to rein it in and not be too vindictive when I feel wronged but it's still sometimes difficult. When I was younger, if you pissed me off I rarely took it without a fight.

The summer after first grade, when my sister was born, was an especially difficult time for me. My sister was born in June and I went from getting all the attention to none of it, and dealing with my stepdad all the while. My mom would make her and Gene's bed every morning, so one day I unmade it, took a jar of honey, spread the honey all

over the sheets, and then remade it. It was my first real practical joke. My stepdad came home tired from work, and went into their bedroom to take a nap. He was a really hairy man, and a couple minutes later he came running out into the living room with the sheet stuck to him. I was laughing so hard I could barely stop, but I managed to get out, *I didn't do that.* Of course, I got in a lot of trouble.

Gene did his best to isolate our family by moving us around constantly. There were plenty of times that he could have opened and then managed Kroger stores in one area for longer than he did. I think he wanted us to be dependent on him. He continually moved us to new cities and towns where we didn't know anyone and had to start again from scratch.

One of the cool things that Gene and I did together, though, was we had a vegetable garden. In Charlotte, we had a great big backyard, probably a quarter acre or so, and we grew our first garden in it. We grew all kinds of vegetables in mounds: cabbage and broccoli, tomatoes and zucchini. I remember everything did well.

cooked up some of our catch. I remember him finishing the fish just as the wind started back up again, so we took it back to the hallway to eat. That's where we stayed throughout most of the hurricane.

Hurricane David destroyed a lot of the company's pin-striping equipment—after that, Gene started working for Kroger.

GREENVILLE, NC

1980–81

Greenville's where I had true North Carolina barbecue for the first time. On our second day in town we went to Parker's Barbecue Restaurant, which years later ended up being one of my first cooking jobs. The only barbecue I'd had before was the sauce-smothered kind. I remember thinking, *Where's the sauce?* and hating it. I went up to the counter and asked for real barbecue. Of course, they told me, *This* is *real barbecue.*

CHARLOTTE, NC

1981

We lived in Charlotte for a few months, and it wasn't a great time for me. I did really poorly in school because there were no walls. I could always hear and see what was going on in all the other classrooms around me, and it was impossible to concentrate.

One afternoon, my friend Scott and I went to the park and started playing on one of those metal springy animal things. Scott was on the front and I was on the back, and we were rocking back and forth really fast. Too fast. I fell off, and then Scott got flung underneath

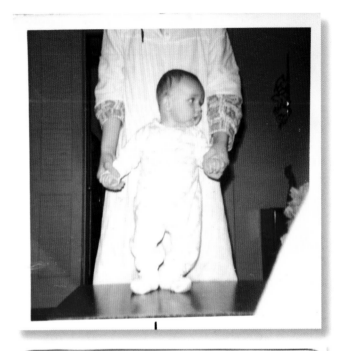

and it kept on rocking as fast as it had been and completely smashed in his face. In a heartbeat he was unconscious and covered in blood. It looked like he had no nose because his nose pretty much got smashed into his head. I took off running to his house, which wasn't far, and screamed at his parents, "He's dead! He's dead!" because I honestly thought he was. By the time we got back to him he was in and out of consciousness and the ambulance had arrived to take him away.

Scott went through numerous rounds of reconstructive surgery for his nose and face for months afterward, and his parents blamed me. I was shunned by the neighborhood. His birthday was two months later, and his parents bought him a go-kart; everyone was invited to ride the go-kart except for me.

Here's a happy story from our time in Charlotte. My aunt Vicky was getting married and asked me if I'd be the ring bearer. I said yes, of course. So we went up to Virginia for the wedding, and as a thank-you gift for being the ring bearer my aunt's husband-to-be, Carl, who worked in a car lot, took out a brand new Trans Am—the exact one that was in *Smokey and the Bandit*—and took me to the drive-in in it. I've always been a bit of a car geek. He let me sit in the driver's seat and watch the second *Smokey and the Bandit* movie that had just come out, *The Cannonball Run*. After the movie we did doughnuts in the parking lot. That was one badass night for eight-year-old me.

SHELBY, NC
1980–1981

You know that HBO show, *Eastbound and Down*? Shelby, North Carolina, is the main character's

hometown. It's a really redneck area and a lot of crazy shit went down when we lived there. My godparents Helen and Walter—an older black couple who were in their fifties then, and who had been in my mom's life for a long time—came and stayed with us for a few months because their son had moved to Shelby and gotten in a car accident that killed his wife. He was left to take care of the kids, so Helen and Walter moved from Virginia Beach to help out. They stayed with us for three or four months while their house was being built and twice, we woke up in the middle of the night to crosses burning in our front yard: big wooden KKK crosses. Gene went out both times and put them out. The people who'd set fire to them were never to be seen. We also had our windows smashed in once while Helen and Walter were staying with us. At school I was called "nigger lover" and made fun of. It was a crazy place.

Helen and Walter were really great cooks, and I remember Walter teaching me how to make tuna salad his way. His tuna salad was much better than my mom's. Hers was basically just a bunch of mayonnaise and tuna whipped into a mush. Walter diced onions, pickles, and parsley, and added paprika and fresh lemon juice.

I went to three schools in third grade because we moved around so much while we were in Shelby. But at one point, we lived right next door to the grandmother of Richard Petty, the racecar driver. Whenever he raced in Charlotte he'd park his racecar in front of our house, and once he let us sit in it. That was right around the time I started regularly visiting Granddad Gordon on my own.

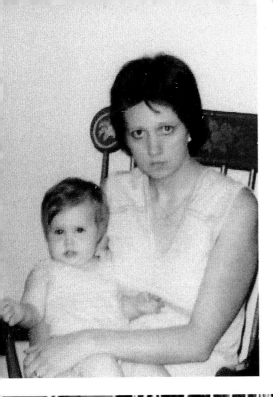
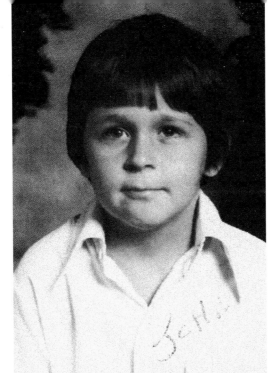

Granddad Gordon

Growing up, we visited DC
twice a year. During that time
I would always stay with my
grandpa. I called him Granddad.
His name was Gordon.

The first time I flew in an air-
plane was on my own. I was seven
years old. I was flying from Virginia to DC to visit my grandpa.
I wasn't scared to fly, just really
excited. I got dressed up in a suit.
At the airport they bumped me
up to first class because I was a
seven-year-old in a suit.

Granddad Gordon lived right in
the heart of DC, and looked like an
older Frank Sinatra: tall, white hair,
always dressed up in suits and hats,
blue eyes. We ate out every meal.
My family went to restaurants from
time to time, but on that trip we
did things like go to a steakhouse
in downtown DC, and a German
beer hall in Baltimore with a polka
band playing. Afterward, we always
danced. My grandpa's first wife died
when I was three, but his new wife
really liked to dance. My grandpa
had a deep love of food, dining, and
entertaining, and I was happy and
excited to share that with him.

I remember trying raw oysters with him for the first time
on that trip. I didn't like them—
they tasted bad to me—but it was
exciting to try them. Back then
there were still a lot of taverns that
you could take a kid to, so I'd go
with my grandpa to them after he'd
finished up with work. He'd have
his drink and I'd sit at the bar with
all of the old guys. I remember a lot
of *This is what it's like to be a man*
and *Your word is your honor* talks.

My grandpa had invested in a
crab shack in Baltimore as a silent
partner. It was a huge space with
a nightclub, bar, and restaurant
all connected. We went in one
night during that first trip and
got a bushel of crabs, and the next
time we went there, same trip,
I remember eating so much peel-
and-eat shrimp that I got sick.
The nightclub was twenty-one-
and-over but my grandpa snuck
me backstage and we got to watch
the dancing for a little bit. When
we went into the kitchen after our
meal, a really big, busy kitchen,
I remember thinking for the first
time: *I want to do this. I want to be
a part of this. I want to be a chef.*

At that point in America, there
weren't celebrity chefs like there are
today. But my grandpa had spent
time in Europe, in the military dur-

ing World War II, and knew that
chefs were respected over there.
Maybe it wasn't like that in America yet, but chefs were respected in
other parts of the world, and they
would be in the States soon enough.
Every conversation we had after that
night at the crab shack was always,
*Are you still going to become a chef?
Are you cooking? Are you reading
about food?* As soon as I started getting jobs he was always asking me,
*What are you cooking? Are you mak-
ing good food?* He saw that I loved it
at that really early age, and wanted
to support that ambition.

For years after that initial trip,
I visited my grandpa in DC for
three to four weeks every summer
and for a few days every Christmas with my family. He'd come
visit us too, and he and I would
always break away on our own
because he and my stepdad didn't
get along. They were very different types of men.

I stayed with Granddad Gordon the
summer before he was diagnosed
with cancer. I was fifteen. He'd
just moved down to Boca Raton,
Florida. We went deep-sea fishing
and caught a mahi mahi. All of my
grandpa's friends came—we grilled
the mahi mahi and had a big, cele-

bratory night of it. That was my last big dinner like that with him. I'm happy that my grandpa got to see me start to make my way as a chef, although I wish he had been able to eat at one of my restaurants.

When he passed away several years later, he didn't want anyone to see him looking sick, so he asked to be cremated. He was always a very proud, big guy. For the funeral he'd said that he wanted us all to continually donate to the American Cancer Society in his memory. He died when I was twenty-three, and I didn't have much money then, but I emptied out my bank account and put everything, literally every penny, that I had toward the American Cancer Society.

Whenever I eat mahi mahi, I think of Granddad Gordon. I also think of him whenever I eat black licorice, which we both loved and would hunt down at candy stores. There was always a lot of hunting down food with my grandpa. He'd say, *This is where you go for the best burger,* and so we'd go get burgers there. Or, *This is where you go for the best steak,* and that's where we'd get steak.

MYRTLE BEACH, SC

1982–85

I was nine when we moved to Myrtle Beach, where Gene opened four Kroger stores. I never stayed in one school more than a year there, because we kept moving south, toward Murrells Inlet.

There were peaks to my mom's happiness—times when it was fun. In Myrtle Beach, she had the coolest job in town. She was the sales rep for Hawaiian Tropic and Ray-Ban sunglasses. Her job was to drive the strip and sell the two things that everyone on the beach wanted most: suntan oil and sunglasses. At the end of every summer, my mom got to keep the sales case for that year's Ray-Bans, which meant one of each type of sunglasses. She always let me choose one pair as a gift for my teacher.

I'd taken French starting in second grade, and in the seventh grade, for a project, I made crepes for everyone in my class. I'd never even eaten a crepe before, but I'd studied them in library books. They turned out great, and I remember thinking, *I can make anything.* That's been my mentality ever since: it might take studying and practice, but if someone else has made it or is making it, I can too.

SAVANNAH, GA

1985

When we moved back to Savannah, to the same neighborhood where we'd lived before, I got myself kicked out of the school bus system. My friend John had a bunch of firecrackers, and decided to start setting them off by throwing them into the back of the bus. The bus driver pulled over and kicked us off in the middle of nowhere. We both had two-liter bottles of soda, and we sprayed the driver with them as we got off the bus.

We were thirteen, and in the mood to make trouble, so we walked into the first neighborhood that we came to. We saw a trampoline in one of the backyards, so we hopped the fence and started jumping on it. We lit more firecrackers as we jumped and they ended up setting the nylon on fire. We took off running and someone saw us and called the cops. The cops brought us home, and the next day the school called our folks about the school bus incident. Shit hit the fucking fan. I did community service—cleaning a park—for a couple weeks, and was banned from the school bus for life.

After that I had to be very creative about how I got to school, which was twenty miles away. (I lived in the white part of Savannah, and even though there was a school right next to my house, they bussed us to the black part of town so the schools would be racially balanced.) My parents were pissed and flat-out refused to take me to school. They wouldn't pay for me to take the city bus either. A mom of one of the kids that I skateboarded with worked at our school, and I could get a ride with them if I woke up really early and skateboarded to their house, forty-five minutes away. If I had money I'd just take a city bus, but when I didn't I skateboarded or figured out another way to get there.

I got my first restaurant job not long after. I found out I could get a worker's permit when I turned fourteen, so I did. I showed up at the busiest restaurant I could ride my bike to—a Mexican restaurant called Teco Taco—and asked to wash dishes. I told the owner that I wanted to be a chef, and that I had to start somewhere. They hired me and I was immediately hooked. I loved

Mickey Spillane

When we lived in Murrells Inlet, we lived just down the street from Mickey Spillane, the guy who wrote the best-selling Mike Hammer detective books. There are still a lot of Mickey Spillane fans out there. My brother Brian and I had to go through Spillane's side yard to get to the beach, where we liked to net fish; that's where the oyster beds were. We got to be really good friends with him. Back then Spillane was doing a series of ads for Miller Light, and he had a Miller Light bar in his front yard that was always tapped with cold beer. Before shucking our very first oysters, we went to his front-yard bar and snuck ourselves a couple pints to wash the oysters down with. From then on we'd pour ourselves pints of Spillane's beer to drink whenever we shucked oysters on the beach.

The oyster beds that we harvested from were behind Spillane's house. There were a shit ton of oysters out there, and we'd wear Converse low tops to go out and harvest them. The shells were like razors if you slipped or fell. We'd get our knives and screwdrivers—usually screwdrivers—and just pop the oysters off. On the same beach in the evenings we'd take raw chicken legs and throw them out to the areas where the crabs were and hundreds would scramble like lunatics to get them. We'd get our nets and scoop the crabs up and into our buckets. We had crab pots too, but rarely needed them.

When Brian visited in the summers (he also visited his dad most Christmas holidays), we went shrimp fishing off the beach. We'd use a big net, walk it out for a bit, and then walk it back in to see what we got. We usually caught a couple flounder along with the shrimp, and that was just fine with us. We did a lot of grilling—Gene really liked to grill—but when we caught flounder we usually panfried it. We also caught a lot of little salt bream. Every now and again we'd get a big bass. I got a lot of practice gutting and cleaning fish.

Growing up, my favorite seafood was always fried flounder with tartar sauce. The best way to cook flounder—and any seafood—is the simplest way: flour, butter, panfried. One of my favorite North Carolina restaurants that I always visit when I'm back there—that has a horrible name—is Sanitary Fish Market, on the pier in Morehead City. Sanitary serves very simple sea fare: fried oysters and fried flounder with tartar sauce, hush puppies. They do it right: plain and simple.

In Murrells Inlet we also had a lake right behind our house. There was this one tree that went over it that I would climb up, getting out onto a limb to fish for sun bream and big-mouth bass. I've always loved to fish; most of the men in my family do. The fishing we did was primarily coastal fishing—pier and beach fishing. We caught the shallow fish. In the Southeast, we had a bounty to reel in: blue crabs, Carolina shrimp, rock crab, rock shrimp, and flounder. Fishing was a big part of growing up. Every now and again I'll go fishing, but it's never the same.

the camaraderie. I loved the energy of nighttime rushes. I had the feeling that finally I belonged somewhere. And then just as Gene always seemed to do, right when things were going well and I was starting to feel a part of something, he told the family that we were moving—just three weeks after I'd landed my first job.

GREENVILLE, NC

1986–88

When we moved back to Greenville, North Carolina, I wanted to get back into a kitchen as soon as possible. But the rules in North Carolina were different from Georgia's. I'd have to wait almost ten months. When I turned fifteen, I landed a job at a barbecue pit called Parker's (it's still open).

Again, I got the feeling that I *belonged* in a kitchen—that this counter culture of people was its own sort of family. These were the people that bought beer for me and my friends on the weekends. They taught me tricks to make me a faster, stronger cook. They even shared their grown-up problems with me and invited me to their homes for meals and drinks.

NEWPORT NEWS, VA

1990–91

My culinary program was in Williamsburg, Virginia, and was essentially an apprenticeship—non-stop hard work. It was too expensive to live in Williamsburg, so I made the commute back and forth from Newport News every day. Newport News is the armpit of the United States—the worst fucking place ever. There are military outposts all around it so it's basically a bunch of people in one shitty place learning to fight. It's very white trashy; there's no culture and nothing to do. It's strip-mall hell with no cuisine. Everywhere else that we lived had some sort of special local dish or food, something, but there was absolutely nothing in Newport News. The day I arrived I started thinking about how the hell I was going to get out. I really put my head down and worked.

GREENVILLE, NC

1992

Back in Greenville, I lived with college kids and had a lot of fun. East Carolina University is there and it's a big party school. I wasn't going to school, but I went to all of the parties. We had a huge old farmhouse in the black part of town, because it was cheap as hell. It was a four bedroom for $350 a month. We each had our own room and mine was off of the kitchen, without any heat, so when it got cold I'd camp out in the living room. We did a lot of grilling out, but we didn't cook too much in the kitchen, because it sucked.

NEWPORT NEWS, VA

1992

After Greenville, I moved back to Newport News to help open a country club called Kiln Creek, with the chef who'd been in charge of my apprenticeship. I was a grunt and did a little bit of everything: banquets, fine-dining cooking, grilling for the golfers. I don't think there was a position that I didn't do. Because it was near the Chesapeake Bay, we were cooking a lot of crab, seafood, and steaks. All of the members were part owners, so they sort of owned *you*. You could never refuse any request no matter how crazy it was. If a member came in and asked for something that wasn't on the menu, you just figured out how to make it happen.

Up until that point I'd never had great beer. We had Bass on tap at Kiln Creek and we all got really into it, and into the other microbrews and imports. That was when I learned that beer wasn't just Budweiser.

One day at the end of summer, I found out that my mom had been severely beaten up. My chef had read about it in the paper and told me that she was in the hospital. When I visited her, she was so drugged she was pretty much unresponsive. I knew that she was embarrassed. I knew that she didn't want anyone to see her like that. It was a pretty big turning point for me. That's when I decided I had to leave. I wanted to go west. I got a job in Snowshoe, West Virginia, working in a ski resort kitchen, and from there I kept moving west.

SNOWSHOE, WV

1993

I'd met Courtney in Newport News. Her brother was my roommate while I was doing my apprenticeship. Courtney and I became good friends, started dating, and moved to Snowshoe together. She got her first serving job there; I cooked at the same restaurant.

The restaurant was part of a resort—a grill with simple scratch cooking: a steaks, burgers, and chicken sandwich kind of place. I learned how to handle big pushes there. It was the busiest restaurant that I'd ever worked at. We were the most approachable of all the restaurants up on the mountain, and that meant a lot of table turning. There was an Italian restaurant, one that was trying to be fine dining, snack shops, and us. We had a big bar and were mid-priced. It was a resourceful kitchen. When the snow melted, rain would filter down through the ventilation hoods, so we had to put tarps up, monitor them, and take them down and empty them out all through the day.

After our contract was up, Courtney and I spent six weeks traveling through Kentucky, Tennessee, North Carolina, West Virginia, Georgia, and Pennsylvania in our '69 VW Bug. We'd met so many people working at the resort that, all along the way, we had friends to visit. Our Bug was acting up when we left Snowshoe, and by the time we got to Lewisburg, West Virginia—this little town of hippies—it needed some work.

The mechanic thought we'd put bad gas in the car, so I siphoned the gas out and while doing so swallowed a shit ton of it. I'd obviously never siphoned gas before. I went to a nurse and she told me to drink milkshakes. Right afterward we went to this amazing Chinese restaurant, but I couldn't eat a thing because my stomach hurt so much. We ended up staying in Lewisburg for four or five days, and then we set off again.

We were headed to Wyoming ultimately. We'd been waiting for our bonus checks, which we were having sent to my parents' house. A week or two before we were planning to leave for Jackson Hole, I called Snowshoe and asked when they were going to send our checks. They told me our checks had been cashed a month ago. My mom had stolen our money. All of it. We hadn't budgeted at all and we'd expected that money to take us to Jackson Hole. We ended up having to sell our Bug and take a Greyhound bus to Wyoming. It was a three-day-long bus ride. It was horrible. We saw the country through the Greyhound bus windows.

JACKSON HOLE, WY

1994

In Jackson Hole, we worked at the Grand Teton Lodge Company. The food was way better than at Snowshoe. No one could have kitchens because it was a national park, but fishing and hunting were allowed, and if you brought us your trout or game we'd clean it and cook it for you. People would often give us cooks a trout or two to take home.

There was a lot of game meat, of course: buffalo and deer. That was the first time that I got to work with game like that. The chef there, Chef Walton, was a really nice guy, and he lived at the resort during the year but had a house up in the mountains. For Courtney's birthday he let us take a big group of friends up there to have a feast and camp out at his house for a couple days. I remember making fresh pasta and roasting different meats. We were still traveling, when we could: we'd take trips to Utah, Wyoming, and Idaho.

EUGENE, OR

1992–95

I was twenty when we pulled into Eugene on the Saturday night of its Eugene Celebration, a three-day annual event downtown. It seemed like everyone was out. Until then, all the town festivals I'd been to were usually military based or rowdy with drunkards, but Eugene's celebration had a real feeling of community: just people in the street, having fun. I loved it. The next morning we woke up and went to an artisan bagel shop. I got an onion bagel, and it was the best bagel I'd ever had.

I'm sure now it wasn't even that great of a bagel, but I'd grown up eating Thomas's Bagels out of a bag—most everything came from the grocery store in a bag—and here I was, at a bagel shop, having a fresh bagel that had been baked. I thought: *Maybe I could live here.*

In 1996, when I was twenty-three, Courtney and I got married on the beach at Cannon Beach, Oregon. Our officiant was this guy named Bill, who owned a bookstore and had a church called the Cowboy Rastafarian Buddhist Church.

In Eugene, we did a lot of hitchhiking all up and down the I-5: we traveled to Portland, Seattle, San Francisco, and Tahoe. We always tried to start at rest areas so we could choose our rides—people it looked like we might get along with. Once, when we were at a rest area outside of Olympia, having just gotten dropped off from Seattle, a woman came up and asked us if we wanted a ride. She said she was bored and she had this brand-new Mazda rally car of which there were probably only two hundred made. She'd just taken her boyfriend with his rally car to go to Europe to race. This was a full-on street-legal racecar. She asked if we minded if she drove fast and we said, *Hell no.* We went 130 miles an hour down the I-5 in this souped-up, crazy rally racecar all the way back to Eugene.

GHANA, AFRICA

1995

In Eugene, I befriended a Malaysian woman whose husband was living in Ghana. She asked if I'd go over and help him open a restaurant in a casino that he'd already opened. How could I turn that down?

All of us—everyone who was working at the casino—lived in the former president's palace. It was in the same compound as the casino, and surrounded by a huge fence topped with broken glass. There were a shit ton of dogs in the compound (which was about the size of a city block) that you didn't want to mess with at all. They were mean-looking dogs. There'd been a coup and that president had been ousted, and the top floor of the palace had been bombed and was completely gone. He'd been the first post-apartheid president in Ghana. The palace was in serious disrepair. On the concrete-bunker-type entryway, in huge letters, someone had spraypainted STOP SPEAKING ENGLISH.

We didn't have washers and dryers in the compound; there were Africans who hand-washed our clothes for us. Every item of clothing had to be ironed so that it wouldn't get maggots. Maggots liked to live in the elastic, and once they got in there they'd burrow into your skin. I lived with fifteen Chinese people who had never been out of China before and two Africans.

Next to the palace was the casino. The casino was on the ground floor; the second floor was going to be the restaurant and the third floor, the nightclub. The kitchen was makeshift: all propane and open fire. Not a conventional kitchen in any sense. A Chinese woman cooked breakfast in the mornings for everyone in the compound while everything in the kitchen was cov-

ered in mosquito netting. We had congee in the mornings, and I liked to put diced pineapple in mine, and every now and again scallions and chicken. We'd get these lobsters at the beach and she'd do this Chinese pineapple-fried lobster, almost like a General Tso's. She'd pick the meat out, batter and fry it, and toss it in sauce. We'd beg for that. But probably my favorite dish in Ghana was groundnut stew from a restaurant near the airport: a chicken and peanut stew with hardboiled eggs, hot sauces, and pickles.

There were open markets and street carts. All the expat communities brought chefs over to cook their homeland cuisines. I ate some of the best French, Italian, and Indian food I'd ever had. Most importantly, I learned not to waste food. There were a lot of hungry people all around us. The entire country understood what passing a plate meant.

EUGENE, OR
1996–98

Back in Eugene, I was hired as a daytime line cook at Café Zenon, where Bill Hatch was the chef. Zenon was where I fell head over heels in love with food. The res-

THE BEST OF EVERYTHING

I traveled all around Ghana by car, and picked up a lot of hitchhikers until someone told me I was going to get killed if I kept it up. At one point a friend and I wanted better weed, because all we were getting was brown. We met some Rastas out in the farmland and we bought a plant from them. They were all in their teens and twenties, and they liked good food and were vegetarians. They grew a lot of vegetables in addition to weed, and we had tea and ate lunch with them: a really good vegetable stew. I had long hair then and that was enough to make me good in their book. We chopped down a huge pot plant, wrapped it up, and strapped it to the top of the car to cure it ourselves. We were looking for the best of everything.

Bill Hatch

Bill was a skinny chef who drank coffee every day until he shook. He was like a surgeon, though, because the moment you put a knife in his over-caffeinated, shaky hands they'd immediately steady up. At the same time Bill was offered the chef-owner position at Zenon, he was also offered the editor-in-chief position at the University of Oregon's *Northwest Review*, a prestigious literary journal, which he ultimately turned down. That was always a huge worry for him: whether or not he made the right decision.

Bill had a master's degree in literature, and reading and writing were important to him. He was an insatiable reader and researcher and instilled that in me. He'd tell me what cookbooks to buy and how to research cuisines and cultures. I'd write down all the questions that I had throughout the day while cooking and then go home, pull out my books, read, and take notes. It's not so much that way anymore, now that you can look up anything so quickly on the Internet and gain knowledge so fast.

Thanks to Bill, I was reading books and cooking from them and developing my own style. I realized that with cooking, you could learn the rules, the techniques, and the science, but once you'd absorbed those things—once you were at ease with the basics—you could make food your own, make recipes of your own.

So that's what I learned from Bill. Bill also used to say, *Routine maintenance is the only defense against the onslaught of chaos.* Ask anyone at Toro Bravo. They're still words I live by.

taurant had lines out the door from eight a.m. till midnight every day. We'd break down three pigs and three lambs a week. We made everything in house: breads, terrines, ice creams, you name it. We saved all our scraps for the very pigs we slaughtered weekly. We had a regular diner who owned a cattle ranch who would bring us cow heads that we made into *fromage de tête*. Farmers would drop off their produce and talk to us about what we were going to do with it.

At Zenon I learned how to use a band saw and how to break down animals, how to use a sausage caser, how to put pâtés and terrines together. But maybe most importantly, I learned how to research. That was all Bill Hatch.

BAY AREA
1998–2000

When I was twenty-six, I went to Berkeley to stage at Citron restaurant for Chris Rossi (whom I'd replaced at Zenon when he left for Citron). When I showed up, I was told that Chris was out for the night because he was getting a hot tub installed at his house. The cook said, *Here's the menu, here are your dishes, prep. If you have any questions, ask the guy beside you.* We were slammed that night. Chris came in an hour into service and said, *All right, you're hired. If you want the job, come on down.* So, a month later, that's what I did.

Citron's kitchen was tiny, and that's where I learned that you don't need a massive kitchen to put out a lot of food. The menu—which was French-bistro-style—completely changed every two weeks and always included a lot of charcuterie. We got truffles in from Italy and France. There were always pounds and pounds of foie gras in the walk-in. We were working with very high-quality and exciting products. Chris's brother was a hunter, and he'd bring in ducks that he'd shot; we'd serve them in the restaurant even though they weren't USDA approved. We did what we wanted to do.

After Citron, I took a month and staged six days a week at twenty to twenty-five different restaurants in the Bay Area. I learned so much in a day, and saw a wide range of ways a kitchen could be run. Toward the end I staged for the a.m. sous chef position at the Fifth Floor when George Morrone was there. It just so happened the day of my stage was the same day they were named one of the top ten restaurants in the world by the *New York Times.*

George had gotten into a fight the night before with the sous chef that I was staging to replace. George was a screamer and ran a very intimidated kitchen. I remember at the beginning of my stage, while I was doing a bunch of knife work, the kitchen felt good, and as soon as George came in, everyone stiffened. Part of the a.m. sous chef's job was to set the line up and then expedite on slower nights until George came in for the pop. I was expediting with George, and the guy on pantry was so afraid of him that when he ran out of raw steak for the tartare he went back and pulled scraps of tenderloin from the trash. I walked in on him when he was doing it and he had this look of fear in his eyes; he motioned for me to get the hell out. He was too scared to tell George that he'd run out. I

remember thinking, *I never want to work in a kitchen like this, or run the sort of kitchen with cooks so nervous and intimidated they'd go to these lengths in order to please me.* George never found out, and someone that night ate trash tartare.

I worked at Restaurant LuLu for about a year with Jody Denton. I liked LuLu a lot. It was scratch, Provence, family-style food with two wood-fired ovens and grills, a wood-fired rotisserie (we went through a cord of wood every two days), and a really great seafood program with a lot of shellfish and whole fish. LuLu was a massive restaurant with several kitchens. The year that I worked there, the *San Francisco Chronicle* named it the best French restaurant in the Bay Area.

Most importantly, I learned how to expedite at LuLu. We were doing a thousand covers on a Saturday night, and there was only one expediter. You wore your headset and worked five different kitchens. It was insanity.

THERE'S NO PLACE LIKE

When I moved to Portland in 2001, I knew a few people in town—some friends from Eugene, and a few cooks from the Bay Area—but that wasn't why I chose it. I moved to Portland because I felt it was ripe for the picking. When I was cooking in Eugene and in the Bay Area, all my pigs, all my lamb, all my mushrooms, and a lot of my produce was coming from Portland. The farmers up here, I knew, were leading the way. And I knew that because there were such amazing products available all the time, chefs would eventually take notice and come here to be a part of it. I could feel the momentum. It felt like something big was about to happen, and Eugene had always felt too small.

Portland was sleepier then, but that pioneering spirit was there, and it was already obvious. The timing couldn't have been more perfect. When the housing market opened up in Portland in the mid-to-late '90s, that was really special for the restaurant industry, because Portland became the cheapest sizeable city to buy a house in along the I-5 corridor. You could buy a house, take out a home equity loan, and open a restaurant fairly easily—and that took away the need for investors. When I started cooking in my teens, the dream of owning my own restaurant seemed impossible. I remember thinking for a long time in my life: *How will I ever do this?* In the Bay Area, if you wanted to own your own restaurant and didn't have heaps and heaps of money, you had to get with one of the hotel groups. You could team up with a hotel group and they'd give you a restaurant that they owned and back your name up but you'd be a slave to them—crunching numbers for the rest of your life. I could afford to buy a house in Portland in 2001, and I did.

I was all about charcuterie and meat fabrication by the time I got to Portland. Vitaly Paley of Paley's Place was just getting started, and by 2003 I was doing meat fabrication for Vitaly and others around town. I did a lot of whole spit-roasted animals for Vitaly—mostly pigs and lambs—as well as sausages and roasted holiday hams. I helped him out with meat and charcuterie for various events.

Viande Meats & Sausage in Northwest Portland was one of a handful of places in Portland butchering and doing the sort of charcuterie I was interested in, not just Styrofoam- and plastic-wrapped steaks and chops. Viande had been owned by a husband-and-wife team, but when they divorced, the wife, Mary Kay, kept it. Mary was a good businesswoman but struggled with the butchery and charcuterie, so she decided to throw in the towel. She asked me if I'd buy it—she trusted me to turn it around.

At that point I was thinking about owning my own business and wanted a commissary-type place. My thinking was, I could buy Viande, get it going, and then spin a restaurant off of it. You know, fabricate the terrines, sausages, and meats at the shop and then send all of that off to a restaurant. I liked the idea and asked my friend Ben Dyer—now owner of Portland's Laurelhurst Market, Ate-Oh-Ate, and Simpatica Catering and Dining Hall—to move up to Portland from Eugene and be my partner. In October 2003, we bought Viande.

In the summer of 2004, bored with just butchering, I wanted to start something of my own. That's when Brooke Storer—who was a server at Paley's Place at the time—and I launched Simpatica (now Simpatica Catering and Dining Hall).

Simpatica was a roaming supper club. We ran four to eight dinners a month at friends' homes, backyards, and restaurants after hours, as well as at local farms and markets. We let whatever space we wound up in dictate the dinners. When we were on a farm, we'd do pig roasts and whole-roasted lambs. When we were in more restaurant-like spaces, we would do courses, though everything was still always family-style. One of the first dinners we did was at Bridges Café. We served smoked duck with a phenomenal roasted cherry salad, a New York strip loin that we carved up, an avocado risotto.

Our cedar-planked salmon was the dish that really put Simpatica's stake in the ground as a catering company. There was a lot of technique for that one, learned through trial and error. We used a really great marinade that wasn't overpowering for the salmon. We'd soak the boards overnight and cut them down every time, since we charred them to hell. We pulled the salmon off rare to mid-rare and put it, still on the plank, into these boxes. The cedar boards were still hot, so the salmon would steam and finish off in the box. That cedar-planked salmon was amazing.

Unlike other supper clubs, Simpatica wasn't at all exclusive; it was affordable (usually $20–$30 a dinner). We found a home for it at the end of that summer in La Luna—the old rock club in Southeast Portland—because by then we wanted a permanent kitchen. The building was an old warehouse, and we built a really cool kitchen in the basement. By the time we were fully loaded and turning out meals, a lot of chefs in town wanted to guest chef there.

The only rule I had with other chefs when collaborating on those dinners was that they could not cook what they made for Simpatica at their own restaurants. Simpatica was a big experiment in pushing our limits as cooks—in finding out what other things we were interested in learning about and getting out of

The Pink House

Ben and I met in Eugene. He lived five houses down from me in what we called the Pink House. A lot of my friends lived in the Pink House: Dana Mason, Dave Sag, Dave Schlageter. It was pretty much all restaurant workers living there. After work, everyone would go to the Pink House to party and play pool on the living-room pool table. We'd do these big dinners on Thursday nights: a group of us would read cookbooks together and go to the grocery store to get ingredients so that we could cook together. One night we might cook German food, another night Oaxacan. I remember fried catfish, duck spring rolls, chili verde. We really geeked out on those Thursday night dinners. There was a convenience store across the street from the Pink House, and at two thirty in the morning, a local donut shop would deliver fresh, still-hot apple fritters. Many of our nights ended with those fritters.

our respective comfort zones. I wanted the chefs that collaborated with us to push their limits too. I didn't want Cory Schreiber—who cooks Pacific-Northwest-style dishes at his restaurant Wildwood—to come do traditional Northwest cuisine at Simpatica. I wanted to see what else he had up his sleeve. Tommy Habetz of Bunk Bar, formerly of Ripe Family Supper and Gotham Tavern, cooked Mexican food with us; Andy Ricker of Pok Pok did Peruvian food. We never wanted to get stuck in a rut with the same style dinners.

Travel fueled us too. Those dinners got attention from some TV folks. We were asked to do a PBS show called *Endless Feast*. The show itself wasn't very good, but they flew us to farms all over the country to host farm-to-table dinners. If I went to Boston, I'd come back and do a northeastern dinner at Simpatica. If I went to Phoenix, when I returned we'd do a southwestern dinner. If I was reading a Spanish book, then you knew there was going to be a tapas dinner soon enough. We were experimenting with food—just doing whatever the hell we wanted—and our interests educated us.

By then, at Simpatica, we'd release an e-mail about a dinner and several minutes later we'd have a 300-person wait list. It was crazy and it was fun and it was a rush, and I still feel that way today when there's a big group of people standing outside one of my restaurants, waiting to get in. There's an energy to that that's probably the same as what musicians get when there's a crowd waiting for their show. *All these people want to be here.* It's an exciting feeling.

I got obsessed with Spanish food. I researched and made my first salbitxada for our first tapas dinner and served it with spring onions and roasted potatoes. For those tapas dinners, we'd make open wood-fired paella with mesquite, salt cod fritters, different croquettes, and Spanish tortillas. Our dinners were always family-style, but we really bombarded people for the Spanish ones: sending out dish after dish after dish.

In 2006, during our fifth tapas dinner, the food writer from *USA Today* came in. He named the Spanish tapas meal he had at Simpatica that year's number one meal in the world. That's the moment that I knew I was onto something. I thought, *This town needs a Spanish restaurant, and I think I can get the money and energy together to do that.*

I went to my business partners, Jason Owens (Simpatica) and Ben Dyer (Viande), and said, *Look, I want to do a restaurant. I don't want to cater anymore; I want to open a restaurant. It doesn't have to be without you. It doesn't have to be with you. I don't care.* They were nervous for the regular financial reasons, but also because we were having a lot of personality clashes at that point, which wasn't a surprise: we were three strong personalities wanting to go in three different directions. They told me I should do it by myself, but that they'd buy shares—which turned out to be ideal. Who knows what Toro Bravo would be like today if things had gone differently.

I sold my shares in both businesses and took a little time off to travel and wrap my head around things. I'd already bought tickets to Barcelona when I saw our future building listed on Craigslist. Right away I thought, *That's it. That's where Toro belongs.* We got pretty deep into negotiations for the space while I was in Barcelona. I came home to the restaurant and we started construction two weeks before we even finished lease negotiations.

I had $50,000 to put into the restaurant, Ron had $25,000, and then we went around and did something

ANYTHING WAS POSSIBLE

n Portland, in 2001, it felt like anything was possible and, honestly, it still feels that way. Someone
opens a food cart and if this person says that they're
going to make the best fucking popcorn that you'll
ever eat, they'll have a line twenty people long the
day that they open, because people want to believe
them. Portland will give you a shot at proving yourself. It's a place for people who feel like they have
something to prove, and do.

Another thing about Portland is chefs here
can open what they want. When Naomi Pomeroy
and Michael Hebb started up Ripe Family Supper, there was nothing else like it. And you can't
leave out people like Vitaly Paley, Greg Higgins,
and Cory Schreiber, who were the forerunners in
terms of celebrating Northwest ingredients and
sharing them with the world. In Portland you can
break the rules and do it your way. And that's not
just tolerated, it's celebrated. If you come to Portland and eat at our restaurants they feel real. They
don't feel like restaurant catalogs. They feel like
people's homes.

a little different. Instead of getting investors, we got lenders. We patched together several $20,000 loans and guaranteed our lenders not only their money back, but gift certificates too. We paid off all of our loans within six months, and within six more we'd put that much more money into it.

Toro's building was built in 1907, by WOW, the Woodmen of the World. Back then, it housed the Prince Hall Masons, an African-American Masonic Lodge. WOW halls went up in many different cities as showpieces for the organization. Before we got a lease on the building it had been the home of a nonprofit arts organization called Disjecta that used to throw big roller-skating parties in the ballroom upstairs. When we moved in, there were 200 pairs of rollerskates piled in the basement.

Toro Bravo served its first meal on May 18th, 2007. The opening staff was just Kasey Mills, Ryan Bleibtrey, Ben Meyer, Ron Avni, and me. Toro's menu was pretty small at first—especially compared to what it is now. We had the Coppa Steak (page 192), Scallops (page 202), Potatoes Bravas (page 136), Lamb Ragu with Eggplant (page 230), Fried Anchovies (page 130), Salt Cod Fritters (page 124), Radicchio Salad (page 116), Sherry Chicken-Liver Mousse (page 174), and the Bacon Manchego Burger (page 240). But we made our own charcuterie, brined everything ourselves, and processed so much every day.

It was nuts, but it didn't matter: Toro was everything I'd been fighting for my entire life. I was at the restaurant twenty hours a day, and the four hours that I slept I dreamt about being back. The only feeling I can think of that compares is getting your driver's license: that exciting independence. It was this feeling of, *Yes, let's do this. I finally get to go where I want to go.*

Those first few months were all about figuring out how to address what I was unprepared for, or fix what I'd fucked up. Our original business plan showed that if we did $2,000 in sales a night—about eighty covers—we'd be okay. We had about four times that.

Portland loved Toro Bravo right away. We were busting at the seams and unprepared for it. In the beginning, we had no walk-in, so we were bringing in small amounts of food from farmers and processing that food immediately. We were scratch cooking from zero every day, and just couldn't process what we were using in one night fast enough. We needed more space and we needed it fast. I lost sleep over how to rebuild within a building and still keep things rolling.

Another thing that I fucked up from day one was I designed a horrible bar. I thought I knew how to put a bar together, but I had no idea. And then, the cocktail craze was right on my ass and I didn't even know it. I wasn't in tune with that as much as I should have been. So a couple weeks in we put a lot of energy into working out new systems and improving the bar program, and then we redid the bar itself a couple years later. Mindy Cook, our bar manager, came on, thank god, eight or nine months after we opened, and she was in tune with all things libations and caught us up.

The first major change was getting the POS system—the network that allows the front of the house to enter and store orders in a computer that then prints them out on easy-to-read tickets for the kitchen. We'd been handwriting tickets for weeks, which was ridiculous. Servers would handwrite every new item with one copy for the table, one for their records, and one for the kitchen. Let's just say there were a lot of lost orders.

BY ANY MEANS NECESSARY

We mined our resources pretty heavily. When you're putting together a restaurant on a tight budget, you have to be scrappy and at times pretty fucking opportunistic. We couldn't afford designers or architects, but that didn't stop me from calling up every restaurant designer and architect I knew and asking them to meet with me. During our meetings I'd ask, straight up, *What would you do here, with this space?* No one was going to just hand over all of his or her best ideas, but just about everyone was willing to give me a little bit. So I'd listen and nod and say, *Good idea, yeah maybe.* In the end I took a lot of their ideas, put them to mine, and there you have it: Toro Bravo.

The store that we bought our lights from had a lighting engineer, and he agreed to do our lighting schematics for free. When we were hunting down restaurant equipment, we found out that if we bought most of our equipment from one particular store they'd do our blueprints for the health department.

Tim Lundholm made all of our tables. I didn't pay him enough but it was also his first commercial job, so we were each doing the other a favor. He'd done a lot of catering with us at Simpatica and, at the time, was working on odds-and-ends welding jobs. When we met in the Bay Area, Tim was a diesel mechanic for the Green Tortoise, that hippie bus that goes across the country. Prior to that he'd gone to school and gotten certified to make ceramic teeth for people who'd lost theirs.

Tim's a genius in his own right; I've always known that. We're still using Tim's tables today:

custom-sized, three-inch-thick, reclaimed-fir tabletops with an all-natural finish, welded, heavy-steel leg posts. Those tables are the face of Toro Bravo, and they're bulletproof. We refinish them from time to time, but that's really all the maintenance they need.

Tim was building the tables in a warehouse in Beaverton, outside of Portland, so I didn't get to see any of the progress. He and his guys were working around the clock, and so were we. The tables showed up at around ten o'clock at night, two nights before we opened. They came in a big box truck, and when they opened the door and I saw the tables it was like the Holy Grail coming out. They were the coolest fucking tables in town. So many people have copied that look by now, but I won't copy it, not even in my own restaurants, because I want them to be special. If you've been to Toro you know those tables.

We wanted the kitchen and bar to feel like a bullring—in that you could see all of the action from any seat—and my friend, welder/woodworker Matt Cartwright, translated that into a sort of fencing for those areas with nice materials. Every step of the way we invested in reclaimed materials; we put the feel of an old building back into the building. It was completely gutted and at studs when we started working on it and the only thing now that's original is the floor.

Build-out was fifteen weeks from studs to opening. I know: it's stupid fast. Granted, what we opened with looked very bare compared to what it is now. We've rebuilt Toro again and filled in the blanks: especially with the prep kitchens, the walk-in, the computer system. We had two shelves behind the bar when we opened and now we have twelve.

Team Ron!

In 2005 and 2006, this older Israeli guy named Ron was always eating brunch at Simpatica. He would come in with an Armenian cucumber, an heirloom tomato, his own saltshaker, a tea bag, and a newspaper. Ron would always order a big brunch, and at the end of it ask for a cup of hot water and a plate, and then he'd cut up his tomato and cucumber, salt them, and eat them as his dessert while drinking his tea and reading the newspaper. That's Ron.

After being a Simpatica regular for a couple years, Ron came to me with a request. He said, *Hey, I just finished culinary school, and I don't really need any money. I just want to see what you guys are doing here. I'll mop floors, clean up tables, whatever you want me to do. I just want to work for you guys this summer.* I thought, *Okay, he's a crazy old man who's decided he wants to cook and he probably has a lot of student loans and doesn't really care.* So I said, *Sure, why not?*

One night, while Ron was mopping floors at Simpatica and I was sitting at a table with Michael Hebb of Ripe Family Supper and Gotham Tavern, Mike turned to me and said, *That's one of my investors from Gotham who's mopping your floors right now.* He laughed. I had no fucking clue.

Simpatica needed a new HVAC system at the time, so a couple days later I sat down with Ron and said, *Hey, I hear you're an investor for Gotham. Would you lend us some money for Simpatica's HVAC?* I paid him back rapidly, and after that he always said, *If you ever want to do something else, just talk to me first before you talk to anyone else, because I'd really like to work with you.* When I sold my shares of Viande and Simpatica, I called up Ron and ran the idea for Toro Bravo by him. He came on as a 30 percent partner, and while I was in Europe he was in Portland brokering the deal.

For the restaurant's first few months, Ron was one of two dishwashers. He wore sweatbands around his forehead and wrists during his shifts, and that's when we started calling him "Team Ron."

In the early days Ron did a little prep too. I'm pretty sure that it was crostini that he burnt into coal-black chunks. Ron said simply, "I think I overheated these." That quote is used to this day in the Toro kitchen for burnt food.

Now, I'm a clean freak in my kitchen and I'm especially adamant about nothing being on the floor. That's a big one. If you spill something, it's a *You're going to get it up before it hits the ground* kind of thing. It's week one of opening. It's about five p.m. on a weekday night. It's crazy busy and we're working our asses off when I look over and see cartoonish footprints of flour everywhere. All over the restaurant. What the fuck is going on? Why the hell is there flour everywhere? Ron pipes up and says, *I spilt some oil and thought that flour would absorb it.* He'd opened a bag of flour and dumped the entire thing on the floor over the oil. Team Ron!

Please let it be known that back in the day Team Ron worked as a software engineer for a subcontractor of NASA. He was part of a team that developed software to analyze test data from space shuttles. We always make it a point to ~~fuck with~~ tell new employees that Ron was responsible for blowing up the space shuttle *Challenger* in the '80s and that's why he left NASA and got into restaurants. People just don't know how to react to that. After Ron worked for NASA for three years,

he opened a software company that's top-selling product was a software package that automated shipping and receiving for companies like Microsoft and Intel. So, yeah, Ron has shifted gears a bit. Nowadays he does a little Toro Bravo office work, computer work, and one of his favorite Toro things is to take the cooks out to lunch and update the recipe book.

I think of Ron as the dad I always wanted. He's so fatherly to me. I can go to him and tell him anything. Ron always gives good advice and he never judges. He'll say, *Take care of yourself, man, come on.* Ron's the kind of man that you can talk to about anything. He's one of the most kindhearted people I've ever met. He also holds a penny tight, and constantly challenges me to do things on a dime, which is good. It's part of the success of our company.

One more thing to know about Ron is that he is very by the book. Any time he takes something from the restaurant he adds it to one of his many ongoing handwritten lists that he usually writes on the back of an old menu. In his chicken scratch he'll write things like *2 cinnamon sticks, 3 bay leaves, 1 cup of olive oil.* Ron's really upstanding like that even though we've told him a more than a few times that it's kind of difficult to calculate the cost of one bay leaf.

45

In week five or six, right after we got the POS, we had our first major robbery. One of the scariest things after getting the phone call from the alarm company and walking into the building was seeing our brand-new POS hanging by wires on the ground. I was honestly more upset that the POS might be broken than that we were robbed. We'd just gotten it programmed and figured out, and it had cost us so much money. $10,000 and change. It was our savior, and our savior wasn't looking so hot. In the end the POS was fine, as in no harm done at all, and that's when I thought everything else would be all right. We rehung the doors and got back to work.

You know that sound of a needle scraping across a record in a show or movie—that point just before something important is revealed? I just did that. All right, so I left something out about that first robbery that you should know. I'd bought this fireproof

file cabinet with strong locks, but like a dumbass I decided right after buying it that the locks weren't strong enough. So I drilled into it and added a dead-bolt. After that I wrote in permanent marker in big bold letters—DON'T FORGET TO LOCK. What a fucking dumbass move. I was basically shouting—

→ **"MONEY HERE!"** ←

—and pointing to it with big bright flashing arrows.

The thieves that got in that night had a crowbar. They climbed up the basement wall to put enough pressure on it to get into the cabinet. There was even a footprint on the ceiling of the basement where one of the thieves had to brace himself to pry it open just enough so that the other thief could reach in and grab the bank bags. They got $3,500 in cash that night.

Two weeks after that, early on a Saturday morning, Kasey and I were coming back from the market. (At that point, we were having to go to farmers' markets constantly because we didn't have a walk-in.) We'd just gotten our asses handed to us during dinner service the night before; we hadn't gotten off until two a.m. and we were fucking exhausted. Right as were walking into the restaurant with all of the produce for that night, I heard it: this steady *shhhhhhhhhh*.

We looked around and couldn't figure out what was wrong. When I opened the basement door it was louder. I turned on the light, looked down, and saw that water was already up onto the first step. There were six inches of it flooding our two-thousand-plus square-foot basement. I ran down as fast as I could to check on the POS. Water was shooting out from the main line and missing the brain of the POS by about six inches. No exaggeration. The POS was intact and fine. Again.

Unfortunately, nothing else down there was. We lost all of our linens, flour, salt—basically all of our dry storage. The plumbers had done a botched job and our main water line had come apart. It had been blowing water full force onto our dry storage all night long. I called up to Kasey and when he came down he almost started to cry.

One of my big philosophies is to always treat purveyors really well because, of course, they're good, salt-of-the-earth, hardworking people and also for a much more self-serving reason: when you need a favor, they'll jump. I called every last one of them and said, *Look, I have a disaster and I need your help now.* They all pitched in. Everyone always does.

It's a good thing that there was a working-order sump pump downstairs, because it turns out that a main water line puts out a fuck ton of water. We squeegeed the water into the sump pump, got rid of all of the ruined supply, and—several hours later—opened for dinner. We always open.

In May 2008 I had my first gallbladder attack. I thought it was a heart attack. Basically, in the most simple terms, your gallbladder secretes nutritional bile that breaks down cholesterol. When you have a gallbladder attack you usually have a lot of gallstones, and just like kidney stones they need to get passed. When they get passed, that's an attack. My first gallbladder attack led to months of craziness: being sick and not knowing what was wrong with me and losing a ton of weight. I'm six foot three. At my heaviest I was 320 pounds. I lost 130 pounds when all was said and done. My biggest worry was that the public would find out that I was sick and think that I was weak. There were rumors, I think, that I had cancer. I had a lot of meetings with the staff, telling them

to not let anyone know what was going on. I wanted to keep up appearances of being strong and having everything under control. It felt like a very dangerous time for Toro Bravo. Throughout that time, my twelve-year marriage was falling apart, too.

Halloween 2008, all of my cooks and I decided that we were going to shave our heads to look like Ron. You know, do the bald thing. But the night before Halloween I was hospitalized again, and that's when they determined that I had gallbladder disease. At that point I was having gallbladder attacks every two to three months. They were debilitating, and would often end with me in the hospital. Every time I had an attack I felt like I was dying.

On New Year's Eve, I went under the knife to have my hernia repaired, and my gallbladder and a foot of intestine removed. It was a five-hour surgery, with two days of rest in the hospital afterward followed by ten more days of recuperation at home. After the surgery I felt like something was missing, because it really *was*.

2009 was a busy year for the restaurant, and an incredibly hard year for me personally. Courtney and I got divorced, and my mother died. That same year, I started really exercising. I did my first triathlon.

I was introduced to Team in Training by my friends Allison Blythe (of Mitchell Wine Group) and Pascal Sauton (formerly owner of Carafe and now owner of Milwaukie Kitchen & Wine). Pascal, in particular, was looking out for me. He wanted to see me in shape. He was worried about my health and so were a lot of my friends and staff. Team In Training is a nationwide initiative of endurance events that raise money and awareness for the Leukemia &

Lymphoma Society—a cause that was especially important to me because I'd lost Granddad Gordon to cancer. I started training for a local Team In Training triathlon in February—a month after my surgery. It was just what I needed with all of the chaos that I was going through at work and at home: something regimented and good for me that I could focus on from February all the way through until the triathlon in June.

We worked out five to six days a week, and Saturdays were our big group workout day. Ruby, who was now in preschool, was with me Fridays, Saturdays, Sundays, and every other Monday. Sundays and Mondays were my days off, and on Mondays I'd go for bike rides with Ruby on the back of my bike. Then we'd grocery shop and spend the day together. Tuesday I'd get a morning run in before work. On Wednesdays, before work, I'd go for a swim. Thursdays we'd train as a team. Every day I was getting up early to do all different types of endurance training and then I'd go to Toro Bravo. Despite the crazy schedule, training for the triathlon—especially the swims—really helped with the stress. That spring it gets even funnier: I got hit by a car.

I was training for the triathlon and riding from Northeast Portland to Rocky Butte when I got hit on the Rocky Butte run. I was going really fast through 82nd and Fremont, where it's really flat. I'd go on these speed sprints on straightaways with no stop signs a lot and I was going twenty-five miles per hour—just flying—when this car came up and turned in. By the time I hit the brakes I'd clipped his rear and slid in the street. I tucked into a ball. It was so scary.

As I was sliding down the street I remember thinking, *Wow, this helmet is really working.* I had good bike gear on. The driver took off and I got up and went running down the street after him. I was pissed, and probably in shock, and yelling, *You really hurt me! I'm doing the triathlon, and you've really hurt me!*

The impact shredded up my gear and crumpled my front tire. For the next year I had major hip problems and a hernia because of it. There was a little pet store

ICE SCOOPS

Courtney was my first wife and Toro's first front-of-house manager. We weren't right and we hadn't been for a long time. We had a good life and a beautiful daughter but neither of us was happy. We never fought all that much but that was part of the problem: there wasn't much passion there. I started not wanting to go home at night. We were both looking for ways to get happy, and both of us had started to see other people. I was seeing Renee, my wife now, who at the time was also working front-of-house at Toro Bravo. For a while, the three of us were working together, and that was tense, to say the least. Renee was managing five days a week and Courtney was managing two days a week.

We were using these cheap glass Ikea pitchers and the metal ice scoops would click on the edge of the pitcher and the next thing you know broken glass would be everywhere. That wasn't okay, of course. Renee came to me and said, *I have a solution. We should buy plastic ice scoops. We'll have less breakage that way.* So I put the metal ice scoops in the basement to use with dry storage and I went and bought all-new plastic ice scoops.

When I got to work the next day, there were brand-new metal ice scoops. Courtney had pitched the plastic ones and bought new metal ones. From there on out, if Renee was managing, the staff would bring up the plastic scoops, but if Courtney was managing they'd bring up the metal ones.

there at the intersection, and the lady at the pet store was sympathizing with the guy who hit me because I was so livid. I thought, *Are you fucking kidding me? This guy just fucking hit me!*

I was scheduled to work at Toro that night but called in. I'm always guilt-ridden when I call in—even when it's to my own fucking restaurant.

We always try to anticipate when something is going to bite the dust (*Routine maintenance is the only defense against the onslaught of chaos*, like Bill Hatch always said) but we can't always. We have a big white dry-erase board in the basement that we call the Magic Board. If the kitchen needs anything, they put it on the board, and we get it for them within a week. If you break a whisk, or a wooden spoon, or you think a sauté pan is about to be RIP, you write it on the list and every week someone does the equipment rounds with that list.

Sometimes the Magic Board is completely full and sometimes there are only four or five things on it, but there's never been a week with nothing. For the first four years I did all of that weekly hunting down myself—mostly at restaurant supply stores. One day, in spring 2010, I was getting ready to do the rounds when Kasey came downstairs and said, *I have a little problem. The fryer is on fire.*

Drew had cleaned it out the night before and when Kasey started it, it kept catching on fire. I went up to check it out. It was a really poorly designed fryer and they'd scraped out all of the carbon, but it had gone down to where the jets were and it was catching on fire. The cooks put a little baking soda in there to put it out, but that didn't work. So I said, *It's going to burn out eventually—just turn it on let it catch on fire and then immediately turn it off and keep doing that over and over until the carbon is all eaten up and it'll be good to go.*

So I went on my weekly equipment run and Kasey did what I said and eventually he thought that he'd burned all of that flammable carbon out. Every day at four p.m. all of the cooks go downstairs to the walk-in and prep kitchen to bring up their mise en place for the night. They thought the fryer situation was cleared up, so they turned it on to get it up to service temperature and went downstairs for their mise. A few minutes later a server came running downstairs to Kasey and announced that the kitchen was on fire.

Kasey did the smartest thing he could have done: he grabbed the Ansul hose—the emergency water sprinkler—and pulled it away from the fire so it wouldn't go off and then they tried to fight it. The extinguishers didn't make a dent in the fire though, and it got to the point where they thought the oil was going to catch fire. They called 911 and got out of the building. At that point Renee called me and I could hear the fire trucks coming down the street when she said, *I have bad news. The restaurant's on fire.*

Renee gave me the rundown and I said, I'd be there in fifteen minutes with a new fryer. I had just gone to a restaurant supply store and I'd seen a fryer I wanted, so I hightailed it back to the store and bought it.

As soon as the fire trucks left, the staff started cleaning up. Everything that had been out in the open was lost. Thirty minutes after the phone call with Renee, I was back at Toro with the fryer and Bob was there to install it. At this point it was four fifteen or four thirty. Toro usually opens at five p.m. We called the health department and our scores were so high that they said, *Just clean up. We trust you. You can reopen.* So we finished cleaning up, installed the new fryer, put a WE'LL BE OPEN AT SIX P.M. sign up on the door, and wrote our fire-day menu, which was maybe a third the size of our regular menu. It was one of our busiest nights.

Chickenshit Mills

Kasey Mills was nineteen years old and living in an apartment with friends in South Dakota when he decided that he wanted to have manicotti for dinner. He cooked manicotti for himself, even though he'd done next to no cooking up to that point. He had a great time making it and got really into how it tasted and thinking about what he could do to make it taste better. Four days later his next-door neighbor came by, listened to him talk about this manicotti for a few minutes longer than he probably wanted to, and then said to Kasey, *I'm a chef in town. Do you want to come work for me?* A few days later Kasey was doing just that at the Silverado-Franklin Historic Hotel in Deadwood, South Dakota. From there he moved to Portland for culinary school and several short years later—at twenty-five—he was Toro Bravo's sous chef. Kasey is thirty-one now. In 2010 he became part owner of Toro Bravo.

Kasey once made the mistake of ordering cucumbers instead of zucchini. He got up on line and was ready to cut them before he realized his mistake. I said, *How the fuck do you not know the difference between a cucumber and a zucchini?* and that was when one of the first Kaseyisms was born. Kasey's answer: *I'm from South Dakota.*

Kasey proudly tells the story of how he was named after Casey Kasem, of the American Top 40. Kasey used to call demitasse spoons "debutante spoons." Kasey still—to this day—after a dinner service will ask, *Was everything okay? Did they like everything?* He is a shining example of a chef and Toro absolutely could not run without him. He also has excellent teeth—his dad's a dentist. Everyone has their own Kaseyisms, but Kasey has more than most.

1. "Nip that in the butt."

2. "So I don't mean to put a monkey in your wrench." Kasey often uses this one when our food runners are having a bad day and he wants them to do something.

3. "You can teach a man to fish, but he'll never catch any fish." Unfortunately, I've only heard him say this once.

4. "You can't blame me, I'm from South Dakota." I'd like to add that we do, however, hope that this book sells in South Dakota.

5. "Don't pass the puck, man." He says this all the time.

KASEY: In early 2009 John and I were in the office, and John was talking about wanting to get a funny tattoo. I said, *You could get my name on your ass,* and he said, *That's a good idea. I should do that.* I thought I knew John pretty well, at that point—we joked around a lot—but I hadn't learned how serious he can be about things once he says he wants to do them. So we're joking and I said, *Well, I'll name my first kid after you if you get my name tattooed on your butt—that's fair.* Then he said, *I think you should get your own name tattooed on your ass.* We laughed about it for a bit and then we went upstairs for service.

The original tattoo that John thought up that day was KASEY MOTHERFUCKING MILLS with a corn dog underneath it. John wanted us both to get that on our asses. So John went off line in the middle of dinner service that night and ame back a little while later and said, *I just made us appointments.* And I said, *For what?* And he said, *For our tattoos. Yeah, we gotta leave right now.* I said, *Are you kidding?* and he said, *No, we've gotta go now.*

At first I thought, *Hell yeah, I'll do this and it'll be really funny.* Word spread to my girlfriend Dori at the time, my wife now, who was working a catering event upstairs, above Toro. We'd just started dating at that point and she came downstairs and said, *Kasey, you need to think long and hard about what you're doing here. I don't know if you really want to do this. You're never going to have to see it, but I'm the one who's going to have to look at a corn dog on your ass.*

I had my mind set on it already, so John and I finished up and headed over to the tattoo shop. They weren't quite ready for us by the time we got there and told us it was going to be a while. I had some work that I still needed to do at the restaurant so I said to John, *Let's go back, have a drink, I'll finish my orders and then we can come back.*

So we went back to Toro and at that point Dori said to me: *You shouldn't do this.* And so yeah, I pretty much chickenshitted out, I just bailed. I thought, you know, maybe I *don't* want my name on my butt. This might not be the best idea.

JOHN: So a little while later I asked Kasey to draw me a chicken and I didn't tell him why. That's what I took with me to Sea Tramp for my tattoo. Kasey Chickenshit Mills.

KASEY: That was when I learned how literal John can be. Now I know that I better be careful about what I say because I'll end

up getting my name tattooed on my ass. John wound up getting the chicken that I drew tattooed on his ass shitting out the word *Mills.* Literally, Chicken Shit Mills. So yeah, I was Chickenshit Mills for a while in the kitchen. New cooks come up to me all the time and ask, *Does John really have your name on his butt?*

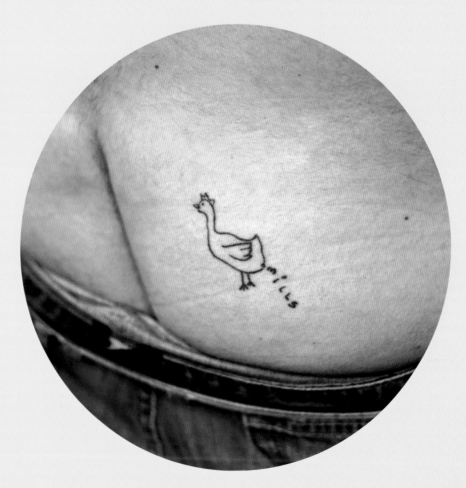

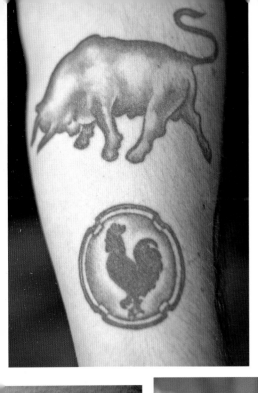

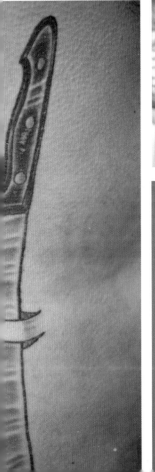

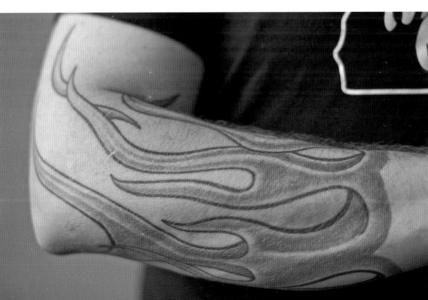

A "SPANISH" RESTAURANT

We get a lot of complaints from people who've been to Spain, or know a thing or two about Spanish food, and want to point out what is and isn't Spanish on our menu. Yes, the restaurant's inspired by Spain, and Barcelona in particular. Many of our vegetables are Spanish varietals. We import about 30 percent of our ingredients from Spain, including our anchovies and octopuses. And nowhere in the world makes jamón that tastes like Spain's—it's dirty, almost.

But to set the record straight: we're not offering "authentic" Spanish food, whatever that means. Spanish cuisine, itself, is a vibrant mix of hundreds of years of trade and exchange, and that mixing hasn't stopped. What I love about Barcelona is how open-minded and untraditional it is. If there's anything we've imported, it's that: that Spanish culture and spirit of excitement and open-mindedness and let's-enjoy-life-ness. And what we're importing is Spanish culture—what *I've* experienced and understand of Spanish

culture. We're also importing my childhood in the Southeast, what I learned in Ghana, Eugene, the Bay Area. It's all of that.

One of my favorite Barcelona restaurants is Cal Pep, by the

Picasso Museum. It's a total zoo. If you want to get in you have to line up a half hour before they open. Once you're seated, they ask if you want red or white wine, and once you've gotten that they ask whether you prefer more fish, meat, or vegetarian dishes. Then they start serving you food based on that—plate after plate of delicious things until you say, *Stop, we can't eat any more.* It's brilliant.

When I was dreaming up the restaurant service and design for Toro Bravo, Cal Pep was a big influence. At that point I had a grasp on what our menu would be, but I didn't fully understand what made a Spanish restaurant tick. I found that out quickly in Barcelona. The answer: a ton of energy. Most great Barcelona restaurants and tapas bars are a constant, relentless party, and all the restaurants are essentially bars. Even Cal Pep. It's a Michelin one-star restaurant and even *it's* really a bar.

These spots are as much community centers as they are restau-

Pastel en forma de hamburguesa elaborado por **Patricia Schmidt** -pastelera brasileña- utilizando 5 tipos de masas de azúcar especialmente diseñado para el restaurante TICKETS

rants. Patrons are drinking coffee all day long, hanging out, meeting friends, then having a couple of drinks, some food, drinking more coffee, more drinks. You generally don't go to these spots to just eat a meal and get out. The food's important, of course, but there's also the community and socializing. Toro is a busy tapas restaurant— and yes, we tend to have a very long wait—but you can't look at the experience of coming to Toro Bravo as starting when you take your seat. It starts when you arrive at the restaurant. If you do it right, you go to the standing table while you wait to be seated, you get some sangria, have some drinks, and order some tapas. Eventually you move to a table and continue to eat, drink, and enjoy yourself. In Spain and at Toro Bravo, it's not just about being seated and having dinner. It's the whole experience.

The other day, we opened up for service and all of the sudden all the people at table nine stood up: a preacher, two witnesses, and a man and a woman. They got married right there in the restaurant. They didn't say anything to us, no announcement. They just stood up, said their vows, sat down, and started feasting. We sent them champagne, of course.

1 €
Unidad/Piece

Ruby

I never wanted to be a father. I thought that being a chef was all that I could handle—that being a father on top of it would be too much. The other worry was that my family had been so dysfunctional, I worried that would rub off onto mine.

The irony of my work worries is that in a lot of ways having my daughter Ruby in 2004 kick-started my career. As soon as I found out that we were having a baby, I bought Viande Meats & Sausage in Northwest Portland. Up until then I'd always worked for other people, but I thought, if I'm going to be a father—if I'm going to have that responsibility— I want my financial fate in my own hands. Prior to being a dad, my career entirely consumed me: I'd eat, cook, repeat. That's a path to burnout. Having kids makes you stop, think, and look at things from a different perspective. Things that can seem like a big deal in the kitchen aren't actually a big deal. As a dad, I use my time a lot more wisely. Having Ruby and my second daughter, Royal, has ultimately brought balance to my life.

62

I'm a little less pissed off with my parents as time goes by, but for the most part they were struggling with their own shit, and weren't there for us. My mom had her issues. Gene was "Dad," but I can remember maybe three or four times that we actually had fun together. He'd come home from work and everyone would go into their rooms and hide. There was always a lot of fighting and chaos in the house and, of course, all the moving. Discipline mostly involved fear tactics. We got spanked, beaten, screamed at, and yelled at.

Ruby is growing up very differently than I did. I lived in so many cities and went to so many schools. I was determined to keep Ruby in one city for her entire childhood. I don't know that I would've done my own childhood differently—all that moving made me who I am—but it's always seemed romantic to me to have a core group of friends your entire life—to grow up in one neighborhood, and to live in one city your whole life.

I take time out every day—usually a half hour to forty-five minutes—just to talk with Ruby. In spite of all her issues, my mom did the same thing with me until I was about fifteen. She always made an effort to take a breather, a little time out every day, to talk with me. I always appreciated that.

My main parenting philosophy is this: treat your child like a person and don't talk down to him or her. Kids have stresses and all sorts of things that they worry about, just like we do. To adults, children's worries might seem small and insignificant but to the child they're enormous. For that reason, they should be taken seriously.

Ruby is very art-minded and loves performance—especially acting and dancing. She's always been comfortable in her own skin. When she was three or four, when we were out, she'd sometimes slip away. We'd usually find her nearby with another family, charming them, trying to join in on whatever they were doing. She's like me in a lot of ways: we both have a certain amount of seriousness, but we both want in on the fun, too.

Ruby's first food was pho and the second was barbecued ribs. I grew up always wanting to try everything—it's another one of the ways that she and I are alike. I didn't necessarily love all of the more adventurous foods I tried as a kid, but I always wanted to taste them. We love going out to dim sum as a family—Ruby's favorites are shrimp dumplings, sweet tofu, and all of the noodles—and on our last visit Ruby tried chicken feet for the first time. She doesn't always love what she tries, but she'll almost always give it a shot.

When I'm cooking at home, I always try to cook for Ruby within the realm of what Renee and I like to eat. We like really flavorful, spicy foods, but Ruby is sensitive to spice, so if I'm making a spicy red sauce I'll make the red sauce without the kick and put some aside for Ruby before making ours the way we like it. I want Ruby to eat—if not what we're eating—at least a version of that. I don't want to be a short-order cook.

One of our favorite things to make and eat together is gnocchi. We'll make the dough and roll it out. We often make gnocchi for Sunday dinners, which we've done for years now: informal dinners at home on Sundays with friends and family. One of the main reasons we started hosting Sunday dinners was to give Ruby a regular ritual: the experience of being around a table and sharing food, stories, and good conversation with people you love who love you.

TORO BRAVO

RU

ALWAYS SHARE

Family-style became my MO when I was living in the Bay Area, where I was part of a group we loosely called the "sous chefs club." Basically, it was a bunch of chef friends that got together once a week to go out and eat lunch. There would usually be fifteen to thirty of us—from Citron, Chez Panisse, other Bay Area restaurants—getting together. We went to a different restaurant every week; we'd order one of everything, fill the table, and share it all family-style. We never ordered our own entrées; we always ordered so that we filled the table with food, and passed things around, trying everything. We ate our way through a lot of different cuisines that way. We were all in our mid- to late-twenties and we knew that we were going to be chefs—that in the future, we were all going to be big deals. We were cocky enough to think that, and that bonded us.

One of the sous-chef-club meals that I remember vividly was at Vi's, this Vietnamese restaurant in Oakland that everyone was saying was the best Vietnamese food on the West Coast. I hadn't had a lot of experience with Vietnamese food at that point, and I remember that meal blowing me away. We probably had five different phos and vermicelli bowls, and wings, and all the Vietnamese foods that I now love.

There was the hole-in-the-wall Jamaican restaurant where we shared rotis, Johnny cakes, and curries. Another time we went to a Hong Kong—style Chinese restaurant, and it was the first time I'd ever had abalone. We probably ordered abalone eight different ways there and feasted on it all morning. We didn't bother with moderation. We wanted to try as much as we could. It was an education, and we thought, *What's an education worth?* When I go out to eat now, you can't bring me too many share plates. If you're not a good sharer, don't come to Toro Bravo.

ALWAYS HUSTLE

Visiting Barcelona opened my eyes to the importance of everyone in a restaurant working their asses off. You don't see Barcelona restaurant managers schmoozing, and there's no guy in a monkey suit in the corner buttering up the "important" people. Everyone is busting their asses and everyone is firing together. At Toro Bravo, you'll never have just one person serving you. We all help one another out. We're here to throw the party, but we're not here to be a part of the party.

Toro Bravo has some of the best servers in town, and for the most part they're not noticed. That's the point. We want our service to be very flexible and fluid. But that takes a while to learn: we put out more plates and silverware per person than the average restaurant.

We also have a long wait and a bar upstairs, so our staff has to put up with a lot of drunk people, who come down from the bar starving and with low blood sugar. They've waited way too long to eat and now the server has to charm and win them back from their drunk frustration. We also have an insanely fast table turn time. People come in at five p.m. and the kitchen starts getting tickets at 5:03. No joke. Some people know what they want right away and order quickly. Serving at Toro takes its toll, no doubt, but there's really no place to hide. You can go in the basement and cry but it's a long flight of steps.

On a normal weekday we'll have a host, food runner, three servers, and a bartender on the floor. On the weekend we add another host,

but that's it. We like our servers to know and work the entire service cycle, so they all take turns doing the door and food running in addition to waiting tables.

The dining room on a Friday or Saturday night is like Nascar. I'll be cooking and I'll look down for a second and when I look back up, a just-vacated table will be completely cleared, wiped, reset, and about to be sat in about one minute.

Serving, like cooking, is a craft. Here in the US, people are just catching onto that. My hope is that everyone does. It takes our servers a good year of working at Toro to get the hang of it. In Europe you'll see servers who've been doing what they do for forty years, more: it's their life, their career, their passion, and they're still stoked to be there.

SATISFACTION GUARANTEED

At Toro Bravo, if you don't like your order—for any reason—we don't charge you for it. Even if we bring out something you asked for and then you say you no longer want it, it's coming back to the kitchen and off of your bill. We don't want your money if you don't like what you paid for. Often it's just a matter of personal taste and preference when someone dislikes a dish, but if you've never had whole fried anchovies and you take a bite and just don't like them, we take them off your bill. We never argue and never judge: that's our policy. We think it's a solid way to get behind our servers. It allows them to recommend dishes and get people out of their comfort zone without the fear that their table will dislike the dish and get pissy.

IF YOUR LIGHTS GO OUT

We call 911 more than any other restaurant in Portland. I think it's all the overstimulation at Toro Bravo that often makes people who've had a few drinks just drop and hit the floor. People pass out so often we have a policy about it: we get them into the hallway so that the ambulance can deal with them in the back. And no matter what they say, if they go unconscious, we call 911. It doesn't matter if the passed-out person wakes up. There have been way too many occasions where we've had someone pass out and

wake up, insist they're fine, only to hit the floor again. We always take them out to the back, where we have chairs. We lay them down, shut the door, and let the EMTs do their thing.

We've seen it all. There was a couple that was sitting near the kitchen. I noticed he was nodding out, but not like he was falling asleep. He was fainting. He'd get up and seem all disoriented and then he'd take a bite of food and faint again. And finally, after this happened a few times, I was like, *We better call 911.* The couple was trying to keep it together, and I think they were embarrassed. But I could see that she was getting antsy and didn't know what to do: he'd get back up, take a bite, and go back down. We also had a woman who had a heart attack. In retrospect, her husband probably had Alzheimer's. He was really, *really* liking the food. She was back in the hallway with the EMTs and he was still at the table eating. We'd tell him, *They're taking her to*

the hospital; maybe you should go. He'd say, *But this is so good,* take a bite, go check on her, sit back at the table, continue eating, go check on her again. Another time we had this skinny-as-a-rail teenage girl who passed out, then got back up. We thought she was okay until she fell backward in her chair and started having seizures.

If your lights go out at Toro, even temporarily, we pick up the check. It's not your fault—not exactly—so we pick up the meal. We've got it.

73

WORK HARDER, PLAY HARDER

Every Fourth of July we rent a U-Haul and pull out all of the furniture in the dining room, lock it up, and a crew comes in to refinish the floors. The same folks that originally laid the floors have it in their contract to refinish the floors every year. Since we have to close the restaurant for that refinishing we always have a big Fourth of July staff party for all of our employees.

We used to go white water rafting but it got too crazy. At the first July Fourth, Courtney, Renee, and I had a big falling out for all the staff to see. At the second, I got a

call the morning of—I literally had a pig on my shoulder, that I was about to start roasting—telling me that my mom had died. That last time when we went out on the Deschutes River someone broke a toe and another person got really beat up on the rapids. People drank a little too much and got too rowdy so we had to switch that up to an in-town Fourth of July barbecue with our marching band.

One year we teamed up with Andy Ricker and had a joint Pok Pok and Toro Bravo Independence Day party. We took over Irving Park in Northeast Portland and probably had 250 to 300 people. Tasty had just opened and the staff there had no idea what they were getting into with our brand of partying. I was roasting pigs and Pok Pok had different foods planned too but we didn't know until the day of that they'd recently taken the power out of the park. We had to go knocking door to door around the neighborhood to get extension cords to reach to the

park so we could roast our pigs and cook our food.

That same night, one of our servers, Heather, got talked into pounding a liter of Gruner Veltliner and ended up passed out in the back of the Toro truck. Someone's friend got in a car accident so people borrowed the truck to go to the hospital. They didn't know Heather was in the back and after they'd driven around town for about four hours they found her there, still passed out. When they dropped her off at our house, she was in shambles. She also had to work the next morning. Rough.

FOUR DAYS ON, THREE DAYS OFF

My cooks work eleven to twelve hours a day for four consecutive days, followed by three days off. That means that the cook working sauté is never sautéing food that somebody else has prepped for him. All of my staff has three consecutive days off every week, unless there's a vacation or something weird. When there's a vacation slated we just shift to the five-day work week temporarily. When you have three days off you get to take that first day off easy and just rest and recoup. Then once you're rested you can have a real weekend and be human.

Katrina had a whole side business going while she was at Toro Bravo. She made these ornate cloth button flowers that she sold all over the country. Josh has a full charcuterie kitchen set up in his basement where he makes all sorts of cured meats (page 162). Lots of us cycle, and there's always someone about to join a triathlon or do something health-and-fitness conscious. There's a lot of partying too, of course, but with three days off you can go party on your Friday and have a hangover and still have a full weekend. And you can get yourself ready for another four-day pounding once you're back.

For the most part my staff comes to work wanting to be here. Not every day, of course—I'm not delusional—but most of the time. When people finally burnout with the bull they know that it's time to go. You can't be at Toro Bravo forever and be happy. Well, some can and some can't. There's usually an expiration date and when it starts to stink everyone smells it.

I'm a firm believer that everyone is giving their best to the restaurant and therefore they get my best. Our policy is to never say no to vacation requests for anyone in the front or back of the house. I've sent people on trips as well—bought the ticket and sent them on their way with my American Express card mileage. I've paid for Kasey and Amber to go to Spain to explore the food over there and visit the restaurants, and I paid for Renee to go to New York to do the same as well. Since opening I've wanted to keep our employees connected with the Portland food scene. Every Christmas we do a gift certificate exchange with all sorts of Portland restaurants and other local businesses. Our entire restaurant staff each gets a packet of fifteen to twenty-five gift certificates from local businesses. In 2010 we exchanged about $30,000 in gift certificates and in 2011 about $50,000. I want our staff to see what other people are messing up and what they're doing really well. It helps generate new ideas, gets them excited, and is a great way to strengthen relationships with other local businesses.

THE MAKEOUT ROOM

The Makeout Room is this small four-by-twenty-foot closet-like space at the front of the restaurant to the right of the entrance. There's enough seating for six, although we've squeezed up to sixteen in there. It was the original entrance to the building and since it's the main support for that wall the city wouldn't let us do anything with it. At first we thought we'd make it a closet, then for a little while we thought we could put the bar up there and that space could be the inside of the bar. What the hell do you do with a little room like that?

During build-out someone said, offhandedly, *That'll be the makeout room.* That's what we've called it ever since. My landlord at Simpatica—Kenton Wiens—said, I could see a big mural going inside that room. My friend Michael Paulus ended up painting a Don Quixote mural on the makeout room wall. So thanks, Kenton. If you get caught making out in the makeout room, we'll buy your cocktail. We've always said that if anyone ever gets caught fucking in there, your dinners are free.

79

TCHEN

READY, SET, COOK

Expect fuck-ups. Cooking is like any kind of craft or art. If you try woodworking and you want to be a master woodworker right from the get-go, you're going to be disappointed. There are specific rules I could give you, like be conservative with the salt and heat when you're just starting out—you can always add more salt later (though you've got to be sure to salt *enough*), and you can always add more heat. But when you're learning to be great—in cooking and in other crafts—there is as much failure as there is success in the beginning, and that's okay.

Use all your senses. I just compared cooking to other crafts, but that doesn't really do it justice. With cooking, you get to work with all your senses. That's one of the things that makes cooking special—there aren't too many other crafts like it. When I first started at Zenon, I worked mornings, setting up breakfast. I was the first one there at six in the morn-

ing; no one else would show up till seven. I remember wanting to wear my headphones to listen to music, and Bill telling me, *No, you can't do that. You're listening for the sizzle of the bacon.* Cooking engages your whole body; you need to be in tune—not just with the way food tastes—but with the way it feels, looks, smells, and sounds.

Eat what you cook and love what you eat. If I have a chef working for me who just doesn't like a dish, it's hard to force it on him because he won't put the love there. That's why I make a case

for seeking out foods, traveling to try them. Kasey and I were working on fried sweetbreads, but I couldn't get a consistent sweetbread from him because he hadn't ever had the best sweetbreads—he just didn't get it. When we were in Madrid, we went and got sweetbreads—simple, fried sweetbreads with wedges of lemon—and he said, *Oh, I get it!*

So a lot of times it's taking my chefs out and going and experiencing it. I think that's why travel is so key, so important: you're exposing yourself to all the stuff you wouldn't otherwise get. Once you finally encounter the thing, it's like, *Okay, now I get it. I want to make it myself, like that or better.*

Back at Zenon, we had waffles on the menu. We had cast-iron waffle makers, and they took some finesse. We always had them seasoned, but you had to have enough oil—not too much—put the batter in right, know when to flip them over. It wasn't easy to make a great waffle off these irons and one cook, in particular, struggled with them. One day I said, *Lawrence, let's go grab breakfast*. We got a waffle. And he said, *Oh my god, this waffle's so good!* From that day on his waffles were perfect.

Actually cook. If you're just starting out and don't know how to cook something, look it up. There's so much information on the Internet. And you're going to have to *actually cook*. If you want to learn to bone a fish, bone some fucking fish! You gotta do it, and do it again, and do it again. You're probably going to fuck up a few times, but that's part of the deal. There's nothing more rewarding than succeeding, and finally mastering what you've set out to do.

Enjoy cleaning. The media's turned chefs into rock stars, but so many people now see the glamour and don't realize how hard and unglamorous cooking can be. Half the job is cleaning up: washing, cleaning, scrubbing, wiping. Enjoy that too.

COUNTRY CROCK OF SHIT

Gene working at Kroger meant our house saw all the food trends of the '70s and '80s come and go. When margarine was popular, we had it. My mom would pour Country Crock on popcorn, which invariably wilted it and made it soft and disgusting. We had all kinds of Kroger brand products that were never as good as the name brands. Since the Kroger brands were so much cheaper, that was usually what Gene brought home. I was maybe twelve and I wanted Heinz ketchup and my mom said, *No, we're getting Kroger ketchup.* I remember thinking then and there, in the aisle: *when I grow up I'm never fucking eating generic.* I'm a man of my word. At

a certain point, when I was pretty young, I resolved to not eat shit. It started with: I don't want margarine on my popcorn; I want butter.

Right around my twelfth birthday, Gene took me out, bought me a lawnmower, and told me to never ask him for money again. I lived in Myrtle Beach at the time and pretty soon after I was mowing ten to twenty yards a week at $10 a pop. At age twelve, I was buying my own food. If I wanted a bottle of Heinz ketchup I bought it myself.

Another habit my lawn-mowing job supported was going out to eat. We were twelve- and thirteen-year-old kids going to restaurants, and at first nobody took

us seriously. After a while they realized we were good kids and we always paid our bill and tipped. Well, I always paid because no one else had money. Which was fine: I never begrudged anyone for that. I've always loved treating people. When we moved to Savannah, I fell in love with gyros, which were kind of exotic at the time. I loved feta cheese and big Greek salads. There was a mom-and-pop Italian restaurant called Baldino's where I'd go and eat big plates of manicotti. It was owned and run by a family that had moved there from New York.

Anyway, point is: always get the good stuff. Don't skimp. Country Crock is shit.

SOLID GOLD INGREDIENTS

Honey

We use a lot of local Hood River honey. We use it more often than sugar to sweeten. Honey gives you a layer of flavor that you don't get with sugar. When we need granulated crack, I'm particular to using only cane.

Saffron

We use a shit ton of saffron. Iran is the world's biggest saffron producer, but America's bad relationship with Iran makes it really expensive. Still, there's no better saffron than Iranian. Every time we've tried saffron from another region we've been burned. You can feel, touch, and smell the difference in quality. Over the years I've had a lot of people tell me that they can get me cheaper saffron, but the thing about cheap saffron is that, yes, it does cost half the price, but you'll use three times the amount to get a similar saffron flavor. So it's ultimately not cheaper.

Paprika and Dried Chilies

Toro tears through paprika. Paprikas are always dried and ground chilies—some are sweet, some are smoky, some are spicy. At Toro we use sweet Hungarian sweet paprika (referred to as "paprika" throughout the book) and Pimentón de la Vera Dulce, a smoked, sweet Spanish paprika (referred to as "pimentón" throughout the book). We now ship in a spicy pimentón (Pimenton de la Vera Picante) and a dried Calabrian chili, too. We also use a dried and ground espelette chili from Viridian Farms.

Oil-Cured Calabrian Chilies

These are a staple in Italian cooking, but we use the shit out of them because I think they're one of the most flavorful and delicious chilies around. They're right on the edge of being too hot but they never cross over that edge. They're slightly pickled with an acidic sting, and the flavor is unlike any chili I've ever had. If I had to compare them to something, African piri piri is as close as it gets. I first tried them when I was in the Bay Area helping to open the Italian restaurant Via Centro. We got some in and I immediately fell in love. We'll suggest substitutes but I think you should order them online if you can't find them at your local Italian grocery.

Salt

At Toro Bravo we generally use kosher to cook with and fleur de sel to finish. Unless otherwise specified, all recipes in this book call for kosher. From time to time I'll give suggestions for how much salt to use, but they're only suggestions. In the end, it's *your* food, and you should be constantly tasting what you're cooking and adjusting the salt to your liking.

TOOLS OF THE TRADE

Don't buy crap. I know at the time it'll seem like you're saving money by buying the cheap piece of equipment, but you're not. In the short run, you are, but in the long run you're not. Be smart: do your research, buy something that's high quality and will last you the rest of your life instead of shit from Wal-Mart that you'll have to buy every year, forever. When you add it up at the end of a lifetime, the Wal-Mart shopper will have spent five times as much as the person who bought the nice thing once. So save up if necessary and always favor quality so that you don't buy crap for the rest of your life. Obviously it's also wasteful and terrible, environmentally, to buy the cheap stuff and have to throw it away.

Less is more when it comes to kitchen equipment. You shouldn't bother scouring food media's best-of lists at the end of the year and purchasing gimmicky things like hot dog cookers or meatball formers, but you'll be a happier home cook if you invest in quality items like a reliable blender and countertop deep fryer.

Thrift stores, antique stores, and estate sales are where I've found some of my favorite kitchen equipment. Craigslist is also a great place for kitchen stuff. Just look up "restaurants for sale" and you'll score. You'd be shocked at what you can get for next to nothing when it comes to quality used kitchen equipment. And if you check out restaurant auctions, you won't leave empty handed. At the very least, there'll be a beat-up-but-still-kicking Cuisinart. It might need a new bowl and a new blade for $60, but the Cuisinart will cost you $10 and will last you the rest of your life.

Be resourceful and you'll end up with quality, reliable kitchen equipment at a fraction of the cost. When Matt Johnson, Toro's building owner, bought the restaurant's building, a café had recently shut down, and he bought their big commercial coffee grinder and gave it to me. I'd recently gotten a ton of coffee beans for Christmas, so I thought I'd take the grinder home and use it to grind them all at once. (I know it's heresy, but I don't care about grinding my coffee right before I brew it. You have to pick your battles. That's not one of mine.) Around that time someone broke our pepper mill at Toro and a light bulb turned on: we could use that big commercial coffee grinder for our pepper. It's our workhorse pepper grinder to this day.

Pots and Pans

At Toro Bravo, all of our kitchen pots and pans are heavy-lined stainless steel, with cord bottoms. They treat us well. Stainless is a good conductor and it's safe. Fuck aluminum. Aluminum is good for boiling water and that's about it. If all you want to do in your kitchen is boil pasta, be my guest: buy a shitty aluminum pot and have at it. For anything else, you should invest in stainless steel. Stainless

doesn't change the flavor of your food like aluminum does and it lasts forever. Copper is very nice too but that's a gift to yourself; it isn't cheap.

I'm sorry, All-Clad, but it's always better for the home cook to go commercial with pots and pans. They last twice as long and cost a lot less. Restaurant supply stores have all sorts of brands that will get you All-Clad quality for a quarter of the price. A good stainless sauté pan will cost $20 and last you a lifetime. (Well, it'll last Toro two years, but it'll last the home cook a lifetime.) If you're going to be cooking paella you'll want a paella pan too.

In my own home, I'm a minimalist. I have a cast-iron pan that I've had for years that's completely seasoned and works as a griddle more than anything else. That pan is all mine and seasoned from years of use. Whatever is cooked in it contributes to that seasoning, so that it's essentially the flavor of my cooking. There's a personal history to it. We also have small and large sauté pans, eight inches and twelve inches, and a paella pan. We have ten-quart and twelve-quart pots. I like having a nice nonstick egg pan, but remember with those that once that layer of stuff—whatever

it happens to be—starts coming off, it's trash.

A good knife

I like Japanese steel knives because they're soft and easy to sharpen. My chef knife is a hand-forged Japanese steel Nenox knife. They cost a lot, but you can get good mid-ranged Japanese steel knives by Mac that are great too. I have a lot of Mac knives at home. But for any chef out there who wants to go spend some money on a knife, get my Nenox. It's awesome.

All of the Solingen stuff (the German city known for its cutlery)—J. A. Henckels, Wusthof, etc.—is extremely hard steel. If you can get and keep those knives sharp then they'll be the sharpest you'll ever use.

Regardless of your knife, sharpen it every use or every other use. What happens with a knife is that when it's super sharp the blade will bend as you cut. If you look at it under a microscope after using it, the blade will be crooked. A sharpening steel straightens the blade back out. If you don't sharpen your knives on steel, then the blade will roll. Once it rolls it has to be rolled back out on a stone.

Every home cook should have a good eight-inch chef knife (contrary to what other chefs say, you don't need anything bigger than that), a serrated bread knife, a paring knife, and a boning knife. Those four will pretty much get you through everything. If you're going to do any chopping of bones then you'll want a cleaver too.

Mortar and pestle

I love all of my different mortars and pestles and use them all the time, both at home and at my restaurants. The key is to have a few different ones of varying materials and sizes for different projects. When cooks arrive at Toro Bravo, they usually don't know how to use a mortar and pestle properly. I always ask them if they do and nine times out of ten they look at me like I'm insulting them, but I'm serious: there's more to it than just banging two rocks together. It's all about the grind. Move the pestle circularly, putting a consistent amount of weight into it, and never smack what's in the mortar. This is the best technique for releasing oils and flavor. It's also much better to do several small batches of something rather than one batch that's enormous and unwieldy. A lot of cooks who don't know better overload their mortars and they end up with a big fucking mess, expending more energy and extracting less flavor.

I really like Asian granite mortar and pestles. I don't love the French ceramic ones, because I've had so many break on me over the years. A good mortar and pestle, that's made of natural material, is a lot like a cast-iron pan—it picks up the flavors of your cooking and imparts those unique flavors into your food. In general, Asian ones seem stronger and those are the kind we use at Toro. I started using them when I was in the Bay Area, since there are so many Asian markets there. Marble is awesome if you can find one that's not too expensive. I have an old army-pharmacy marble one that we use all the time for spices. Marble or stone is great for spices because it allows you to really pound the shit out of the spices. Don't get a mortar and pestle that's so large it's unmanageable. Try it out and make sure that you can work it comfortably.

Cuisinart

Screw Cuisinart's digital dials. Go for a Cuisinart food processor with the two flat buttons on it: ON/OFF and PULSE. If you get an eight-quart Cuisinart it will last you forever because everything is replaceable on it and you can't burn it out. At Toro we have a twenty-year-old commercial kitchen Cuisinart that still runs great. Another nice Cuisinart food processor design element: there's automatic shutoff so it won't overheat. You can't kill a Cuisinart. It's the zombie of food processors.

A good blender

Every household should have a good blender and I'm a strong believer in Vitamix, despite the sticker shock. They cost between $300 to $500 but they're lifetime blenders. Vitamix gives you ultimate speed adjustment

OTHER KITCHEN EQUIPMENT THAT I REALLY LIKE:

Microplane graters: We do a lot of lemon zesting and cheese grating with these graters because they give you such a fine grate. The cheese for our radicchio salad gets Microplaned because we want it to be so fine that it disintegrates into the vinaigrette.

Box graters: I use them for everything from grating beets for borscht to grating frozen butter for biscuits (that's the trick to flaky biscuits). Every home cook should have one.

Chinois: Liquid is the only thing that will pass through a fine, conical chinois strainer. We use ours for everything from sauces to soups.

Joyce Chen kitchen scissors: We primarily devein shrimp with ours, and we go through a lot of shrimp. These scissors are also great for trussing meat and working with twine in the kitchen.

Japanese mandolines: If you have something that you want sliced consistently thin, you can't beat a mandoline. We use ours for slicing lemons for our fried anchovies and slicing fennel for the seared scallops.

and reliability. In ours, we blend drinks, make baby food, and purée chilies. A Vitamix is so powerful it can even mill grains; you can make flour in them. Before I bought a Vitamix, I probably owned at least a dozen blenders. Considering that they were all fifty, sixty bucks apiece I could have had a Vitamix and a half. They're worth every penny.

Wood cutting boards

A good wood cutting board is another must have. You can use plastic if you want but I prefer the give, feel, and workability of wood boards. You can get a lot of life out of them if you treat them right.

I regularly salt mine to keep them clean. When you salt the board it pulls the water out of it and kills any bacteria. While the board is wet I put a layer of salt on it and let it sit overnight. In the morning when I wash it off, the wood looks a few shades lighter in color. I scrub the board down really well and then take a bench scraper and scrape off any notches. After that, I put on a light layer of mineral oil or olive oil to put the oil back in the wood. That's it.

Peelers (plural)

Sometimes peelers can break your heart because you find one that you really like and then you go out and buy the same peeler a little while later and the model is different and you don't like it anymore. You probably won't even be able to see the difference, but the blade will be slightly off and it's too fine or too thick. I've had the peeler that I have now for seven years. My advice is to buy as many of the kind that you love as you can afford when you find it and stash them.

Countertop deep fryer

If you don't have a deep fryer, making our croquettes, fritters, fried anchovies, and potatoes bravas isn't going to be as easy as it could be. Every kitchen should have one. They extend your repertoire substantially, everybody loves fried food, and they're pretty cheap.

At the restaurant, we change our fry oil every day. We do everything in one fryer and we fry a lot. But, as a home cook, you'd be surprised how many times you can use the same oil for different foods. At home, you can fry anchovies, bravas, and churros all in the same oil and be golden as long as you aren't doing several batches of each.

Some words of wisdom for deep frying: don't salt before you fry. Salt breaks down oil quickly, so you should always salt after frying. Don't overheat your fryer because once it smokes, it's over; you've killed it. At the smoking point, you've broken the molecular structure of the oil and whatever you put in the basket from there on out won't fry correctly. Be patient; until you get the oil up to temperature anything you put into it will soak up the oil and get bloated with it.

Most importantly, don't overfill your fryer. At Simpatica we had this thing called "Ten Sandwiches" every Sunday, and one thing on that menu was this half-moon sandwich that was basically a spin on deep-fried gnocchi. It was just me and Troy in the kitchen and we were slammed, way too busy, burnt out and tired. I overloaded the fryer with too much gnocchi and a couple minutes later I looked over and the oil temperature was down to 150 degrees. All my gnocchi had turned to mush on the bottom of the fryer like a steamy load of shit. Don't do that.

Portland is home now, but I still do a lot of traveling. I've always had a certain degree of restlessness, maybe left over from my upbringing—from all those moves because of Gene's job. I've always wanted to see new things, and still do. I'm constantly looking for the next trip, the next experience. I think traveling wherever you can afford to go is always worth it, even if it's just the next town over.

The recipes in this cookbook are reflections of places I've been and people I've met. They also reflect a moment in time. Toro Bravo is all about pushing forward, and always trying to do more and more. My hope is that, a few years from now, the restaurant's menu will be very different from what this cookbook is. Not 100 percent—there are a lot of basics here—but my hope is that we'll continue to grow and change and bring in new recipes. Every trip brings more dishes and new inspiration. And there are a lot of trips planned.

RECItES

- GARLIC IS ALWAYS LARGE CLOVES
- SALT IS ALWAYS KOSHER
- VEGETABLES ARE ALWAYS FRESH
- EGGS ALWAYS LARGE GRADE A
- OLIVE OIL IS ALWAYS EXTRA VIRGIN
- PARSLEY IS ALWAYS FLAT LEAF
- CANNED TOMATOES ARE ALWAYS WHOLE SAN MARZANO
- BUTTER IS ALWAYS SALTED
- MILK IS ALWAYS WHOLE (NEVER SKIM)
- "OIL BLEND" MEANS 20 PERCENT OLIVE OIL AND 80 PERCENT SAFFLOWER OIL

Roasted Spanish Nuts
2 PINTS

In the beginning, our complimentary table snack was fried chickpeas: chickpeas we soaked, cooked, and fried, then tossed in seasoning. They were great. Problem was, they'd get soggy after about half an hour, so to counter that we'd dry them in a dehydrator, which made them hard. Corn-nut hard. Once we had a lady come in to the restaurant who'd just had oral surgery. We warned her not to eat the fried chickpeas, but she did anyway, and chipped a tooth. She was adamant that the restaurant fix that chipped tooth and I was adamant we didn't. (I won.)

Another time, while I was on vacation, a guy with throat cancer came in. He was undergoing radiation therapy, and the radiation made his teeth brittle, so he chipped a tooth on a chickpea too. Jason, our front-of-house manager at the time, is a nervous personality—he wasn't going to fight this guy like I'd fought the woman—so he told the guy we'd take care of it and pay for it all. In the end, that cost me $1,500. I took fried chickpeas off the menu the next day. I thought, *Fuck it. I'm not going to spend $1,500 a month to give people free chickpeas.* We started doing these Spanish nuts and pumpkin seeds instead. They're just as good, but won't break your teeth.

1 pint raw Spanish peanuts

1 pint raw pumpkin seeds

4 teaspoons olive oil

4 teaspoons Bravas salt (page 137)

1. Preheat oven to 400 degrees.

2. Put the peanuts in one large, ovenproof pan and the pumpkin seeds in another. Toss with the olive oil and salt equally divided.

3. Bake in the middle of the oven—ideally on the same rack—for 5 minutes. Remove both pans, toss or stir the nuts, and return to the oven. Repeat this tossing or stirring every 5 minutes for 15 minutes. At that point, you should begin to hear the nuts popping. Don't panic. Popping is good.

4. At this point, check on the nuts. Continue tossing or stirring them every 3 minutes or so until they are golden and nicely toasted. It should take about 20 minutes for the peanuts to roast, and about 22 minutes for the pumpkin seeds.

5. Take the pans out of the oven and combine the nuts. About 5 minutes after they've come out of the oven, give the nuts a toss in the pan to break them up and cool them down. Taste and adjust the seasoning to your liking. Once completely cooled to room temperature, they're ready to eat. Serve or tightly contain for up to 2 weeks.

Almonds Poached in Olive Oil
3–3 ½ CUPS

It's a very traditional Spanish thing to poach almonds in olive oil. By poaching them you slowly remove their water and get them nice and crispy. Our poached almonds are the base of our Romesco (page 281) and Salbitxada (page 282), and go into our Bacon-Wrapped Dates (page 98), and Cilantro Pesto (page 151). If you don't have time to make them, you can substitute roasted marcona almonds for any recipe that calls for poached almonds.

1 pound blanched whole almonds
3 cups oil blend (page 93)
Salt

1. In a medium saucepan combine the almonds and oil blend. Place over medium-low heat and cook for 1 hour, stirring occasionally. After 15 to 20 minutes you should still be able to stick a finger into the oil and not burn it. (Sorry if you do.) You want a nice, slow poach. That's how you'll get all the water out of the almonds.

2. After about 30 minutes you'll start to see slight bubbles forming on top of the oil as the almonds release moisture. After 45 minutes, the top should be covered in bubbles. After an hour, or once the almonds have turned a nice light brown, remove them from the heat, strain them onto a sheet pan, salt them, and let them cool completely. The almonds don't acquire that nice crunch until they've completely cooled.

NOTE: *Use the slightly nutty left-over oil for whatever you want—it's excellent in salad dressings.*

3. Once the almonds are cooled, they're ready to eat. Eat them on their own or on a cheese board, or use them in all sorts of recipes in this book. What isn't eaten right away can be stored in an airtight container for up to a week.

Bacon-Wrapped Dates
12 DATES

The first time I had bacon-wrapped dates was in Barcelona, where they were stuffed with cheese. At Toro, we wrap dates in bacon, iron the bacon jackets on, and serve them in a honey sauce that makes a sort of sandwich—so that you get sweetness on both sides of the bacon, along with layers of flavor: acidity from the lemon, and compelling smokiness from the pimentón.

We thought it would be clever to put the pit back in, in a sense. There's a salted almond in the middle of each date that's the same shape and size as the pit. It's a nice surprise. Every now and again people think that the almond is the pit and they'll leave it on the plate, but most of the time they understand what's up. There've been maybe three times in the history of the restaurant that a cook has accidentally left the pit in. Each time that's happened I've gone apeshit and made the guilty cook dissect every single date he or she has prepped.

I think we might sell more dates than any restaurant on the West Coast. It's crazy what we go through. When we first opened no supplier could keep up with us, so we kept switching sources and the quality fluctuated. It's taken several years, but we finally have a farm that keeps us supplied with delicious, beautiful, well-packed Medjool dates. When shopping for dates, you're looking for ones that are soft to the touch. When you split them open to get the pit out they shouldn't crack and they should be pliable and open easily. You don't want dry dates—they're hard and mealy. You also don't want them packed too moistly because mold can then become an issue.

I like to buy my dates with the pits still in them. As soon as you open a date up and remove its pit, the clock starts ticking. Opening the date means allowing air to get at the flesh; the date immediately begins to dry.

NOTE: *Good-quality dates are excellent fuel straight up when you're cooking on the line, especially at that part of the night when you feel your blood sugar dropping. Dates go straight to the blood and spike you up quickly.*

12 Medjool dates

12 Poached Almonds (page 97)

¼ cup local wild honey

½ tablespoon pimentón

1 tablespoon lemon juice

1 tablespoon hot water

6 slices Nueske's bacon or another double Applewood-smoked bacon, thinly sliced*

*We don't use our house bacon for this because we prefer the flavor and dryness of Nueske's for the dates. Since we slice the bacon very thin we want a big Applewood-smoked flavor that holds up to the sticky sweet flavor of the date. Nueske's is hot smoked and has a huge smoke flavor. There's a big difference between meats smoked in big smokehouses versus little restaurant smokers. Our bacon is a little fresher and has more water content in it. Other differences between our bacons: we use hickory and they use Applewood and their brine is straight-up salt and sugar whereas ours is more herbaceous and spicy. Thinly slice your own bacon for this or go to your butcher and have them do it for you right off a slab. Pre-sliced and packaged bacon is going to be too thick.

1. Pit the dates and stuff each one with a poached almond.

2. Whisk the honey, pimentón, lemon juice, and hot water together to incorporate and then keep this sauce warm.

3. Wrap each date with a half slice of bacon cut on a bias. You want enough bacon so that it slightly overlaps about a quarter inch but not so much that it will be flabby and won't sear up well.

A typical slice of bacon is long enough to cover 2 dates. If the bacon isn't cut 50/50 on the bias, you won't have enough coverage for the 2 dates. As soon as the bacon hits the griddle it shrinks a little bit and comes undone; that's why the right amount of overlap is crucial.

4. Cook the bacon-wrapped dates over medium-high heat in a large cast-iron or nonstick pan, starting with the flap sides down to seal the bacon. Be careful not to crowd them. Cook them until the bacon is crisp and well browned all the way around.

We sear our bacon-wrapped dates until they're dark on all sides but shy of burnt. Wrap 1 date in bacon for a test run, cook it, and see how it turns out. It might take a few tries before you get the cut, overlap, and thinness of your bacon just right. By cooking a trial date you'll also get to see how much your bacon shrinks as it cooks.

5. Drizzle the dates with the honey sauce. Eat.

Sheep Cheese Balls with Rose Petal Harissa

24 BALLS

I'm not going to bullshit you here. This recipe is a pain in the ass. The ass-hurt part comes in hand-rolling out the fresh cheese, because it really wants to stick to your hands. You need your gloves as dry and cool as possible to reduce the sticking, which means you're going to be going through a lot of latex gloves. It's worth it.

Harissa is a spicy, aged chili paste. I've tried all kinds, and rose petal harissa is one of my favorites: it's fresh tasting, not too hot, and the rose petals give it a nice extra dimension, with the floral flavor complementing the chilies. We get our rose petal harissa from the Fresh Olive Company in London and we have for years. As a substitute I recommend tubed harissa from Tunisia.

The mint offers a fresh contrast to the aged harissa, and so does miticrema, a fresh sheep cheese from the Murcia region of Spain. There are plenty of other fromage blancs that are delicious, but we think that this is the best readily available Spanish one in the states. You can substitute any soft fresh cheese, such as chevre or fromage blanc. But if you can find miticrema, use it. (NOTE: *In the spring, sheep generally have more water in their milk, so the cheese is softer as a result. That's the season when these are a real pain in the ass. At that point we'll usually use the top of the barrel for the balls and the wetter bottom for other applications.*)

½ pound miticrema (or fromage blanc or good quality fresh goat or sheep cheese)

¼ lemon, juiced

½ lemon, zested

1 tablespoon fresh mint, chiffonaded

¼ cup olive oil

½ tablespoon rose petal harissa

1 baguette

1. With clean and/or gloved hands roll the chilled cheese into ¾-inch balls in the dish that you plan to serve them in. Cover them and refrigerate.

   One trick is to keep a little bowl of ice water next to you while you're rolling the balls. Every once in a while, cup a little ice water into your palms to keep the cheese from sticking. And keep the sheep cheese in a bowl inside another bowl of ice water too, so that the cheese isn't immersed in the ice water but is cooled by it. Shaping the balls is easier when the cheese is cooler and firmer.

2. In a small bowl combine the juiced and zested lemon, mint, olive oil, and harissa.

3. Drizzle this marinade over the cheese balls, cover, and refrigerate overnight or until the balls are firm. Once firm, toss them in the marinade so that they are fully coated. Use your hands, and be careful to keep them intact.

4. Serve immediately with baguette slices, or refrigerate (pull the balls out 30 minutes before you want to serve them). They keep tightly contained and refrigerated in the marinade for 7 to 10 days.

Tomato Bread; The BLT; Charred Bread with Nettles and Fromage Blanc; Chanterelles in Sherry Cream

ALL SERVE 2–4

Even before opening Toro Bravo, I knew that tomato bread was going on the menu. It's a quintessential Spanish dish: toasted bread that's rubbed with a cut tomato, sometimes garlic, and finished with olive oil and salt. For as simple as it is, though, the tomato bread in Spain isn't always good. Sometimes it sucks. I knew that we could do better with properly grilled bread and good, in-season tomatoes.

When tomatoes aren't in season there's no point in using shitty ones. In the mid-spring and early summer, we use wild stinging nettles instead. With that first little bit of rain in the early fall we'll usually get chanterelles in the Northwest. One year chanterelles had a really bad season because of the snow, but there were hedgehogs in southern Oregon so we switched to those. Point is: it's impossible to go wrong when you start with good bread and the best in-season ingredients.

A year of charred breads looks like this: we do tomato bread, go to chanterelles, then hedgehogs, then right into nettles. After we ramped up our bacon production, we added an open-faced BLT. We get a bread called Campagnolo—a peasant sourdough–type loaf—from Grand Central Bakery here in Portland. We drizzle it with olive oil, season it, and grill it until it has a really nice char. I think that perfect grill marks are counterintuitive when it comes to flavor. I like as much char as possible all over. It's best when you have to scrape a little black off.

These charred breads are all also best if the bread is a day old. Old bread just grills better. If you have to use fresh bread for this, a trick is to throw it in the freezer for half an hour, take it out, and let it sit uncovered so that it gets slightly stale.

Tomato Bread

2 thick slices of peasant sourdough bread (we use Grand Central Bakery's Campagnolo), cut to 1-inch thickness

1 tablespoon olive oil

½ teaspoon salt

¼ teaspoon pepper

1 clove garlic

1 medium-sized heirloom tomato, very ripe and soft

½ teaspoon fleur de sel

1 tablespoon olive oil to finish

1. Drizzle both slices of bread with the olive oil on both sides, and season with salt and pepper.

2. Grill the bread until it is nicely charred. You can broil it, but you won't get the same flavor. You really want it to blacken.

3. Once the bread is nicely charred, take the clove of garlic and rub it into the crust and all sides of the bread. Use a lot of pressure. You want to rub the garlic in so hard that it falls apart.

4. Slice the tomato in half top to bottom. If it isn't falling-apart soft, score the inside cut side about ¼-inch deep a few times. Take the tomato in your hand, cut side down, and rub it all over both sides of 1 slice of bread, making sure to really get it in there. Smash and squeeze the tomato into the bread. Once the tomato meat has become one with the bread, discard the tomato skin. Do the same with the other slice of bread and half tomato.

6. Finish with fleur de sel and a dousing of about 1 tablespoon of olive oil. Cut each slice into quarters and serve.

The BLT

The BLT should be all about the tomato and just enough bacon—not too much. I also believe in a lot of mayonnaise and that it should be spread sloppily.

4 slices Bacon (page 186; we use our bacon and think it's best for this, but use any good bacon, sliced medium thick)

2 slices of good sourdough bread (we use Grand Central Bakery's Como), cut to ⅔-inch thickness

1 tablespoon olive oil

½ teaspoon salt

¼ teaspoon pepper

1 large heirloom tomato, very ripe

½ teaspoon fleur de sel

¼ teaspoon pepper

2 tablespoons mayonnaise (homemade or store-bought, like Hellman's)

1 handful mesclun greens

1. Put a medium cast-iron pan over low-medium heat and cook 4 slices of bacon until they are crispy to your liking. I like to start bacon at low-medium heat for a few minutes to render the fat and then go up to a medium-high to finish it, flipping it along the way. Remove the bacon from the pan and set it aside.

2. Drizzle both slices of bread with the olive oil on each side, and season with salt and pepper.

3. Grill the bread until it is really nicely charred. You can broil it, but you won't get the same flavor. You really want it to blacken.

4. Slice the tomato into 6 to 8 slices. Spread them out on your cutting board and season them on one side with ½ teaspoon of fleur de sel and a ¼ teaspoon of pepper.

5. Sloppily spread 1 tablespoon of mayonnaise onto each slice of bread, then top each piece with half of the lettuce, 3 or 4 slices of the seasoned tomato, and finally the bacon on top. Serve it open-faced.

Nettles and Fromage Blanc

2 slices of good sourdough bread (we use Grand Central Bakery's Como), cut to 1-inch thickness

3 tablespoons olive oil, divided

½ teaspoon salt

¼ teaspoon pepper

3 cloves garlic, divided

1 tablespoon butter

4 to 5 ounces nettles, cleaned and trimmed

¼ lemon, juiced

2 heaping tablespoons fromage blanc (we use miticrema)

1. Drizzle both slices of bread with olive oil on each side, about 1 tablespoon, and season with salt and pepper.

2. Grill the bread until it is really nicely charred. You can broil it, but you won't get the same flavor. You really want it to blacken.

3. Once nicely charred, take 1 clove of garlic and rub it with a lot of pressure into the crust and all sides of the bread. You want to rub it in so hard that the garlic falls apart.

4. Put a large sauté pan over medium-high heat and add 1 tablespoon of olive oil and the butter and the remaining 2 cloves of garlic. Add the nettles and sauté until they're just wilted, about 30 seconds to 1 minute. Add the lemon juice.

5. Spread each slice of grilled and garlic-rubbed bread with 1 heaping tablespoon of fromage blanc. Top with the nettle sauté and finish with a drizzle of a tablespoon of olive oil. Halve or quarter the bread and serve.

Chanterelles in Sherry Cream

2 slices good sourdough bread (we use Grand Central Bakery's Como), cut to 1-inch thickness

3 tablespoons softened butter, divided

4 cloves garlic (1 left whole, 3 sliced thinly)

8 to 10 medium chanterelles, cleaned

1 tablespoon olive oil

½ to 1 teaspoon salt

¼ teaspoon pepper

2 tablespoons cream sherry

2 teaspoons heavy cream

1 tablespoon parsley leaves, chiffonaded

¼ lemon, juiced

1. Slather both sides of each slice of bread, using 1 tablespoon of softened butter per slice. Be sure to get some butter onto the crust too.

2. Put a large cast-iron pan on high heat. Once it's hot, put the bread down to griddle it. Cook each slice on both sides until nicely charred, like a good grilled cheese. If it doesn't look like you're getting enough color, use a plate or a pan with dictionaries piled on it or anything with weight to push the bread down into the pan.

3. Once the bread is nicely charred, rub both pieces with the whole clove of garlic.

4. Clean and slice the chanterelles. We brush our mushrooms to get the dirt off so that we don't waterlog them.

5. In another large sauté pan over medium-high heat, add 1 tablespoon of olive oil and the remaining 1 tablespoon of butter and leave for about 1 minute until the butter is almost browning. Add the thinly sliced garlic and cook for about 30 seconds to 1 minute until the garlic is golden and slightly toasty.

6. Add the chanterelles and the salt and pepper and cook, tonging them around in the pan for about 30 seconds to 1 minute. Turn the heat down to medium.

7. Add the cream sherry and heavy cream and cook for 1 or 2 minutes. You don't want this to be too reduced, but you do want to cook the sherry out. Add the parsley and lemon juice, and remove from heat.

8. Slice the charred, garlicky bread in half on a bias and stack akimbo. Top with the mushrooms, spooning the sauce over so that it soaks into the bread. You want the bread to be wet. Serve, and make sure whomever you're serving eats immediately.

Spring Onions with Salbitxada

SERVES 6–8

If you visit Spain's Catalonia region in the spring, you'll come across all kinds of little charcoal grills in the streets smoking with calçots—a mild spring onion that's sort of a cross between a green onion and a leek. The calçots are charred, topped with Salbitxada (page 282), and wrapped in newspaper. You open the paper parcel, in which the calçots have been cooking, peel off the charred layers of onion, toss them aside, and eat the steamed insides while standing or walking. In Portland, we're only able to get calçots for a very brief moment in the spring. After the calçots are gone, we use spring onions and baby leeks; in the fall, we braise mature leeks. And because American diners maybe aren't ready for burnt onions in newspaper, what we do, instead, is roast spring onions lightly in the oven, finish them on the grill, and serve them topped with salbitxada.

4 medium spring onions (Size-wise, a spring onion falls between a scallion and a leek. If you can't find spring onions at your farmers' market, substitute baby leeks, mature leeks, or scallions. If using scallions, don't halve them in step 2.)

1 tablespoon olive oil

Salt and pepper

¼ cup water

¼ cup salbitxada (page 282)

1. Preheat the oven to 350 degrees and start your grill.

2. Trim the roots off of the spring onions and leave just a little bit of green on them so that they are 6 to 8 inches long. Wash them.

3. Cut them in half lengthwise and place them in a baking pan.

4. Season the onions with the oil and big pinches of salt and pepper, and toss to coat. Pour the water in.

5. Bake them covered until they are soft, for about 20 to 30 minutes.

6. Remove the onions from the oven and allow them to cool.

7. Once the grill is hot and the onions have cooled, grill them until they are good and charry, for 5 to 10 minutes. Sprinkle more salt and pepper on them.

8. Serve the grilled onions immediately, topped with a healthy amount of salbitxada on top.

Padron Peppers
SERVES 4–6

The first time I ever had padrons was at Toro Restaurant in Boston. It was the middle of summer—at the height of pepper season—and they were incredible: the green flavor, the slight hint of heat, the way the peppers' wrinkles picked up the salt and olive oil. On my first visit to Barcelona I had padrons in just about every restaurant, because that's what I was often after: a glass of Txakoli or dry Basque cider and a plate of salty sautéed padrons.

Every now and again you get a spicy padron in the bunch, but in Portland we're too far north to get many spicy ones. In general, the hotter the weather the spicier the peppers. A habanero grown in Portland will rarely be as spicy as one grown in Mexico. At the end of the growing season here—especially a particularly hot one—padrons can get spicy and their skin can get chewy.

We do our padrons in the fryer at Toro Bravo, but at home I sauté them in olive oil in a ripping hot pan. If you cook them for a dinner party do them like pancakes—in batches—so everyone gets them when they're good and hot.

⅓ cup olive oil

1 pint padron peppers, with the stems on

½ to ¾ teaspoon sea salt for seasoning (You don't want to over salt the food that comes at the start of a Spanish meal. There's always a lot more salty food to come.)

1. Put the oil in a large sauté pan (don't crowd the padrons or they won't cook properly) over medium-high heat, as hot as you can go without smoking, and then put the padrons in the pan. You want them to crack, pop, and blister when they hit the pan. Sprinkle them with salt.

2. Cook them quickly, for about 1 minute, and then strain them with a sieve to get rid of some of the oil. Serve hot.

107

Octopus à la Plancha
SERVES 6–8

The first time I tried octopus, as a kid in Florida, I didn't love it. It was chewy and didn't taste very good. Now I know it doesn't have to be that way. As an adult, I love the way octopus tastes grilled. Grilling chars the octopus and gives it multiple textures. When most people think octopus they think chewy, but ours is far from chewy. It's my belief that if you don't like something, you probably haven't had it cooked the right way—and if you have a hard time cooking something, you probably aren't cooking it the right way. Finding the right quality and size octopus is half the battle when you're cooking octopus. In general, smaller octopuses are easier to cook than larger ones, which require more stages of cooking.

When we visited Seville in 2011, so many people we talked to recommended the restaurant Becerrita that we couldn't ignore the suggestion. Plus, it was right by our hotel. Becerrita was serving octopus in a bunch of different ways, and we tried them all. We had four or five different octopus dishes that time, and this was our favorite: fork tender and plancha'd on a little slice of boiled potato (at the restaurant, we confit ours) topped with Aioli (page 289). They put diced chili on theirs; we use Piperade (page 287). Ours is a very classic combination. The potatoes pick up the flavor of the really good-quality olive oil, and the Aioli and Piperade are classic accompaniments to octopus.

3 small yellow potatoes, sliced into ¼-inch thick circles (you want 12 or 13 rounds)

Salt and pepper

2 cloves garlic, chopped

1 oil-cured Calabrian chili, thinly sliced

¼ cup + 1 tablespoon olive oil

1 cup cooked octopus tentacle, skinned and sliced on a bias into 2-inch pieces and grilled (Spicy Octopus and Prawn Stew, page 198)

¼ cup to ½ cup Aioli (page 289)

¼ to ½ cup Piperade (page 287)

1. Preheat the oven to 400 degrees.

2. Using your hands, toss the sliced potatoes with a big pinch of salt, pepper, garlic, chili, and ¼ cup olive oil so that they're nicely coated with oil. Arrange the slices flat and not too crowded on a pan. Cover and bake for 30 minutes or until they're soft but not falling apart.

3. Put a large cast-iron pan over medium-high heat with 1 tablespoon of olive oil. Put the potatoes in a single layer on one side of the pan, and the octopus to the other. Salt everything with about a half teaspoon of salt. Flip the potatoes regularly until they're lightly browned on both sides, about 2–3 minutes. Remove the potatoes and octopus and set aside.

4. Return the heat to medium-high and add the piperade to the pan and cook for 20 or 30 seconds until it is warmed through.

5. Assemble the pieces. Place the potato rounds on whatever dish or dishes you will be serving them on. Using a demitasse ("debutante") spoon, put a generous spoonful of Aioli on top of each piece.

6. Place a piece of the grilled octopus on top of the Aioli on each potato round. Finish with a heaping demitasse spoonful of Piperade. Serve.

Butter Lettuce Salad
5–6 SALADS

Mr. Kasey Mills put this kick-ass salad on the menu in our third year and we all love it. Who doesn't love green goddess dressing, avocados, bacon, and radishes?

This recipe owes some love to the Pig Nazi too: Mr. Paul Atkinson of Laughing Stock Farm in Eugene. You can't call Paul and order a pig. He calls you and tells you you're *getting* a pig. He's come in and out of my life through the years—I've been buying pigs and squashes from Laughing Stock since my days at Zenon. Paul's dad was a farmer too and there's actually an heirloom squash named after him, the Atkinson squash—but at the time this salad was developed we were getting whole pigs from Laughing Stock and making tesa (an Italian bacon that's similar to pancetta) with the bellies. It went so well with this salad.

We treat this salad differently depending on the season, but it always gets Kasey's green tarragon-and-avocado dressing, finely grated manchego, and toasted bread crumbs. Sturdier salad greens work well for this, including heirloom romaines. We like butter lettuce best. When we get our first radishes at the beginning of the spring, we usually get our first butter lettuce too, and that's when we rock this salad with the radishes, lardons, red onion, manchego, and bread crumbs.

1. Tear up your butter lettuce or romaine. Rinse and spin dry. Spread about ¼ cup of the dressing around the bottom of the bowl you'll be tossing the salad in. Use enough to coat the leaves. Throw in whatever seasonal ingredients you like, toss to distribute the dressing, and finish by topping the salad with finely grated manchego and bread crumbs.

2 heads butter lettuce or 1 head romaine

¼ cup dressing (next page)

Manchego, finely grated

Bread crumbs (next page)

SEASONAL SETS

Spring

Radishes

Lardons

Red onion

Summer

Sliced raw squash

Pickled beets (page 276)

Red onion

Pumpkin seeds

Fall/Winter

Honeycrisp apples

Candied walnuts

Red onion

Dressing | Makes 2 cups

(If you make a smaller batch than this, you might have problems with it not emulsifying, so make the whole batch. You'll only need ¼ cup to ⅔ cup for 5 or 6 salads, but you can also use this dressing as a dip for crudité and on sandwiches. It keeps for 4 or 5 days refrigerated.)

2 hardboiled egg yolks

1 raw egg yolk

½ avocado

Pinch cayenne

2 tablespoons champagne vinegar

2 tablespoons water

½ lemon, juiced

1 teaspoon tarragon, minced

1 teaspoon chives, minced

Salt and pepper

1½ cup oil blend (page 93)

1. Put all the ingredients except for the oil into your food processor or blender. Blend for 20 to 30 seconds until everything comes together.

2. Slowly drizzle in the oil. It should take about 1 minute to add all of it and properly emulsify the dressing.

Bread Crumbs | 1 pint

We make our own bread crumbs and recommend that you do too. They pick up a lot of moisture and flavor so they're best used the day that you make them.

½ baguette

2 tablespoons olive oil

½ teaspoon salt

¼ teaspoon pepper

1 teaspoon ground espelette pepper

1. Preheat the oven to 375 degrees.

2. Cut the baguette into 1-by-1-inch cubes and toss them with the olive oil, salt, and pepper. Transfer the cubes to a baking sheet.

3. Bake for about 30 minutes until the bread is no longer spongy when pressed.

4. Let cool completely and then pulse in a food processor with the espelette pepper until fully crumbed.

Gazpacho
1–1½ QUARTS

As with peanut butter, there are two gazpacho camps: fans of smooth, blended gazpachos and people who like chunky, food-milled ones. It all comes down to what you like. Most Americans, I think, tend to prefer the smoother ones. We've combined the best of both worlds: a silky smooth gazpacho topped with a chunky garnish with more of that raw, fresh flavor.

We make our gazpacho daily, because it's best right when it's made, but don't make it until we have the ripest tomatoes, cucumbers, and peppers in their peak season. The best gazpacho in Spain is served close to room temperature. That's how I prefer it, too.

1. In a large bowl, tear the bread into chunks. Soak it in 1 cup of water, champagne vinegar, and sherry vinegar for 10 to 15 minutes, until the bread is completely soft.

2. Once the bread is soft, combine the garlic, olive oil, sugar, salt and pepper, cucumber, onion, red bell pepper, and tomatoes in a food processor or blender, then blend until it is silky smooth. If you can't get it to silky smoothness, do your best, then pass it through a sieve.

3. Pour the gazpacho back into a large bowl, taste, and adjust the salt and pepper to your liking.

4. Take the finely diced half cucumber, finely diced heirloom tomatoes, and fried capers, and garnish each bowl with a little of each. Drizzle each bowl with olive oil before serving.

7 ounces (about ½ a loaf) Como bread, crust removed (or any nice, chewy-but-light, good-quality white sourdough)

¼ cup champagne vinegar

¼ cup sherry vinegar

4 cloves garlic, sliced

¼ cup olive oil

1 tablespoon sugar

Salt and pepper

1 cucumber, peeled, roughly chopped (if they are very large and seedy, remove the seeds)

1 medium yellow onion, roughly chopped

1 red bell pepper, roughly chopped

3 large heirloom tomatoes, flesh only, roughly chopped

½ cucumber, peeled, finely diced

2 tomatoes, flesh only and no seeds, finely diced

¼ cup capers, fried (we deep fry salt-cured capers but any capers will do; panfrying works too)

Drizzle olive oil

Groundwork Greens

SERVES 4–6

From day one we wanted one basic salad, with one dressing that we could change up seasonally. That's our Groundwork Greens. All year round, we use different greens from one farm: Groundwork Organics in Junction City. We wanted delicious seasonal salad greens, rather than greenhouse baby greens that taste like water year-round. We wanted to taste the seasons. As Groundwork's greens change throughout the seasons—from tender greens in the spring to heartier greens in the summer and big, thick, leafy greens in the fall and winter—so does the salad.

The first Groundwork Greens salad that we did was this one: a nice mesclun mix with grilled asparagus, chopped hazelnuts, and chopped eggs. It's still my favorite. There's always something great about getting to that point of the year when asparagus is in season: it means that summer's coming soon and many other vegetables aren't far behind.

Other renditions of this salad include berries, red onion, and Cana de Oveja (soft-ripened sheep cheese); blue cheese and grapefruit in the winter; and pickled beets and hazelnuts at the end of summer. In the winter we'll use heartier greens—baby kales and chard. In the spring the salad gets flavor bursts of sorrel, miner's lettuce, and heartier, spicy cresses. And right before the heat of summer we'll use leafier greens like red oak lettuce. Go to the farmers' market or natural grocery store and look for greens that change through the season. At home, I often take a whole head of butter or green or red leaf lettuce, and mix that with a chicory like frisée or radicchio. You're aiming for a good sweet-to-bitter ratio.

Back in the Bay Area, I used to visit a little breakfast-and-lunch spot in Berkeley called La Note. All their salads came in big glass bowls with serving utensils to share, and I remember thinking, *Why don't more places serve salad that way?* I'd go in there with the intention of ordering pancakes, but then a nearby table would order the salad; I'd see it and I couldn't *not* get it. It's like that in the South, too. Even if the dishes are on individual plates, the salad is always in a big bowl and served family-style. It's nostalgic for me. When we opened Toro we hunted down glass bowls like La Note's, and that's how we've always served our salads.

Dressing

3 tablespoons cabernet sauvignon vinegar*

Salt and pepper

1 teaspoon mustard powder

2 teaspoons honey

1 clove garlic, minced

¾ cup olive oil

Salad

2 eggs

15 spears asparagus

1 tablespoon olive oil

Salt and pepper

½ lemon

5 ounces mesclun greens

⅓ cup toasted hazelnuts, chopped

*Kimberley Wine Vinegars are my favorite vinegars, and Kimberly's cabernet sauvignon vinegar is really, really good. When Kimberley was testing out these vinegars I was cooking at LuLu, and got to help out with a lot of tastings and development. There is a tang to her vinegars that's really special. You don't get it with other vinegars. That said, Unio from Spain makes good red wine vinegars. As a rule of thumb, try to get a red wine vinegar that lists the specific grape. That generally means higher quality. Also make sure that there's no salt in the list of ingredients.

Dressing

1. In a large metal bowl, combine the vinegar, salt, pepper, mustard powder, honey, and minced garlic, and whisk to blend.

2. While whisking, slowly drizzle in the olive oil until it's all incorporated.

Salad

1. Start your grill.

2. Bring a medium saucepan ¾ filled with water to a simmer and put the eggs in it to lightly boil for 6 minutes. Transfer them to ice water, then peel and dice.

3. Snap the asparagus at the spot where it stops being woody and starts being soft, and discard the woody bottoms.

4. Peel the skin from the lower part of the asparagus. You want to peel about 1½ inches up the bottom of your asparagus. This step is worth it for the texture, so please don't skip it.

5. Toss the asparagus with the olive oil and season it with salt and pepper. Grill for 3 to 5 minutes. Before setting the asparagus aside, squeeze the ½ lemon's juice over it.

6. Toss the mesclun greens, toasted and chopped hazelnuts, and dressing in your medium-sized serving bowl.

7. Top the salad with the diced hardboiled eggs and the asparagus and serve.

Radicchio Salad

SERVES 4–8

When I was in the Bay Area and working with David Rosales—who was a part of the sous chefs club with me—we were getting really beautiful heads of chicories in from Tierra Madre Farm in the Santa Cruz Mountains. We made a salad with them with a dressing with this ratio of ingredients using red wine vinegar, which I eventually swapped out for the subtler sherry vinegar used here.

The sweetness of this dressing really balances the bitterness of the radicchio. Radicchio is a waxy green, so a lot of the time dressings don't want to stick to it. A secret to all of our salads, including this one, is that we microplane manchego and add it to every salad right before serving. The grated cheese here solves that problem of the dressing not sticking. It's just like flouring something to make the batter stick.

Another secret to our radicchio salad, which is one of Toro's most popular items, is the same secret of David's salad: red onions macerated in vinegar for a couple hours and then strained out. It's one of those layers of flavor that can really stump you. You think, *Where the fuck is that coming from?* Because you don't see the onions but you definitely taste them in the vinegar.

I like the texture of the crostini here with this salad, and the butteriness of our tapenade because of the olives that we use. It goes really well with the sharp radicchio.

2 to 3 heads of radicchio (4 quarts)

¼ cup good-quality balsamic vinegar

¼ cup good-quality sherry vinegar

1 red onion, chopped

1 tablespoon honey

¾ cup + 1 tablespoon olive oil

1½ cup manchego, finely grated and divided

Salt and pepper

1 baguette (for crostini)

½ cup Tapenade (page 285)

1. Remove the cores from the radicchio and discard. Chop it into 1-inch pieces. Take 1 gallon of water in a large bowl and add enough ice to make the water icy cold. Once cold, strain out the ice and add the radicchio to the water. Let it sit for 15 minutes to remove some of its bitterness, strain, and then spin in a salad spinner until dry. Fluff the dried radicchio. (NOTE: *If you don't strain the ice out before adding the radicchio you'll be pulling out ice pieces for half an hour so that you don't have wet radicchio.*)

2. In a large bowl add the balsamic vinegar, sherry vinegar, and chopped red onion. Break the onion up into pieces so that all of that oniony flavor gets into the vinegar. Let it sit for 1 hour and then strain out the onions and discard them.

3. Add the honey and olive oil to the strained vinegars and whisk.

4. Using your hands, toss the radicchio with the dressing until evenly coated. Add 1 cup of finely grated manchego, salt, and toss again.

5. Slice the baguette on an extreme bias into ¼-inch thick pieces, one piece per person. Drizzle each baguette slice with olive oil and season it with salt and pepper, then grill or broil the slices until slightly charred. Top each with 1 to 2 tablespoons of tapenade.

6. Serve the salad in 2 chilled bowls. Top each salad with another ¼ cup finely grated manchego, and the grilled crostinis with tapenade on top of that.

Potato Salad

SERVES 4–6

At Toro Bravo, we use a lot of different potatoes. We fry Kennebecs, boil russets, and confit fingerlings. This warm potato salad uses Yukon Golds. One of my opening cooks, Ryan Bleibtrey, came up with this. Ryan sliced his potatoes really thin, cooked them on sheet pans, seared them to get color, deglazed them with a great vinegar, and made a braise with chorizo and onions. It turned out awesome, held up really well, and warmed back up great. This potato salad has evolved over the years, but it's still all about searing the potatoes well and getting them as caramel-y as possible. These days the Yukons go into our salamander broiler on a sheet pan even after they've been seared in the pan, so they brown a little more on the top. Through the years this recipe has gotten better and better with every cook who's put his or her touch on it.

6 small-to-medium Yukon Gold potatoes, sliced ¼-inch thin

4 tablespoons olive oil, divided

1 teaspoon salt

1 teaspoon pepper

3 ounces Chorizo (page 162 or use store-bought)

1 small yellow onion

5 cloves garlic, slivered

3½ tablespoons sauvignon blanc vinegar, divided

¼ cup parsley leaves

1. Preheat the oven to 450 degrees and place your sheet pan in the oven to warm. (NOTE: *Later you will pour vinegar onto this pan to release the potatoes, so be sure to use a pan with some sort of lip.*)

2. Put your sliced potatoes in a medium bowl along with 2 tablespoons of olive oil and salt and pepper, and toss to mix.

3. Pull the warmed sheet pan out of the oven and spread the sliced and seasoned potatoes as evenly as possible over it.

4. Put the pan back into the oven and bake the potatoes for 15 minutes on one side. Flip the potatoes and bake for 8 minutes on the other side.

5. Small dice the chorizo and slice the onion in half. Julienne each half.

6. Put the remaining 2 tablespoons of olive oil in a medium sauté pan over medium-high heat. Add the chorizo and sauté it for 30 seconds.

7. Add the onion and garlic and lower the heat to medium and sauté everything for about 5 minutes, until the onion is just starting to turn translucent.

8. Add 1½ tablespoons of sauvignon blanc vinegar to the sauté and stir for 30 seconds before removing from heat.

9. After the potatoes have baked on both sides, broil them for 3 or 4 minutes until they are nicely crisped on top.

10. Drizzle the remaining 2 tablespoons sauvignon blanc vinegar over the potatoes on the sheet pan, then use the backside of a spatula to scrape the potatoes off.

11. Put the potatoes into a medium-sized bowl with the sautéed chorizo, onions, garlic, and parsley. Toss.

12. Taste, adjust seasoning and vinegar to your liking, and serve.

Fennel Salad
SERVES 4–6

There isn't a night that goes by that I'm expediting and don't grab a fork-ful of this salad. I love it. It's so simple and good and good for you. At Toro, we only serve this salad with our scallops and romesco, but it goes well with plenty of other seafood too. The fennel's freshness and bright, crunchy texture is a nice contrast to the rich, fatty, soft scallops. Every once in a while a ticket will come in that says "scallops, no scallops" which means fennel salad with romesco. I totally get it.

   This salad never sits around beyond several hours. We make it every day because we want it fresh and crisp, and you should too. You'll want to use a mandoline to get the fennel slices to the same thinness. My best advice for using a mandoline here—with the fennel and with everything else—is to make sure that the blade on it is sharp. It's essentially a knife, and every knife needs to be sharpened. Don't ever put your mandoline in the dishwasher—or your knives, for that matter—because they'll get knocked around and dulled much more quickly.

2 heads fennel

2 tablespoons olive oil

2 lemons, juiced

Salt and pepper

1. Clean and trim the fennel heads.

2. Shave the fennel at a thin setting on a mandoline, or slice very thinly with a knife. In a large bowl, mix the shaved fennel, olive oil, lemon juice, and salt and pepper until incorporated.

3. Let the salad sit for at least 20 minutes or up to an hour at room temperature and serve. Letting it sit for a bit allows the flavors to meld together, and also allows the salt to break down the fennel a bit and wilt it slightly.

Avocado Salad
SERVES 4–6

Garlic, cumin, and coriander is a Moorish trio that has an almost South American flair to it. We were just playing around in the kitchen one day when I came up with this one. I'd gotten some avocados and was eating some drunken pork (page 220) along with them when I realized that combining the two would make a great summer dish. Now our avocado salad comes tucked under our drunken pork, because they're amazing together. We make this salad fresh every day with very ripe avocados. Don't refrigerate it. Ideally, you should serve it within the hour after you've made it. If you wait any longer than two hours, you risk the avocados looking like shit.

2 cloves garlic

1 teaspoon whole coriander

1 teaspoon whole cumin

3 ripe avocados, chopped

¼ cup red onion, minced

½ cup roasted red peppers, skinned and minced

½ lime, juiced

Salt

1. Peel the garlic cloves and put them in a small sauté pan over medium-high heat.

2. Cook the garlic cloves largely unattended until they have browned in spots and begin to bubble on both sides, about 5 minutes.

3. Once the garlic has browned slightly, add the whole coriander and cumin seeds to the pan, shaking the pan regularly until the seeds are browned and very fragrant. If the spices begin to smoke, remove the pan from the heat.

4. Place the browned spices and garlic into a mortar and pestle and smash each garlic clove a couple times before grinding the seeds and garlic in a circular motion. Keep at it until the garlic and spices have turned into a paste.

5. In a large bowl combine the chopped avocado, red onion, red peppers, lime juice, salt, and spice-and-garlic paste from the mortar and pestle. Stir until everything is incorporated. Serve right away, and eat quickly.

Salt Cod Fritters
ABOUT 3 DOZEN, 1 QUART OF BATTER

For how simple salt cod fritters are—they're basically deep-fried fish balls—Toro's are a fucking nightmare. I wouldn't wish this process on anyone beyond our restaurant family. If you choose to disregard this warning, and tackle them anyway, I'm guessing you'll be blown away. But don't say I didn't warn you. No cook ever orders these when they come in to eat at Toro, because they know how much work they are to make. Anyone who's ever ordered and eaten these fritters, though, is inevitably amazed by how good they are.

When I first started making salt cod fritters—about ten years ago—I had a period of really geeking out on them. I read, thought about, and cooked salt cod fritters pretty much every waking moment, because I was never happy with how they turned out. I'd been using over-salted, shitty Nova Scotia cod until I had my first *a-ha* realization: I live in the land of cod. I should be buying better cod and salting it myself. The other thing was, because salt cod fritters are Spanish-peasant food, most recipes call for boiling the cod in water (rather than milk, which is expensive). Water works, of course, but results in a fritter that isn't as delicious as it could be. Second realization: if you aren't a peasant, boiling the cod in milk is a good idea, and adds a lot of depth.

We source fresh cod for our fritters and salt it ourselves. Before you make the fritters, you need to salt the cod for a week and then soak it in water for three or four days to get that salt out. Have I lost you yet? The wait is worth it, I swear. If you're pressed for time, feel free to use store-bought salt cod for these. They just won't be as good.

NOTE: *We also make salt cod patties out of these—really thin ones—and then fry them for awesome staff meal sandwiches. It's like a Filet-O-Fish—only better.*

1¼ pounds fresh cod (or 1 pound store-bought salt cod)

Salt

1 tablespoon olive oil

3 cloves garlic, thinly slivered

¾ pound russet potato, peeled and chopped

1 quart milk, divided

¾ cup all-purpose flour

⅛ teaspoon baking powder

2 eggs, separated

2 tablespoons parsley, chopped

Rice oil for frying (the exact amount will depend on how big and deep your pan is; peanut or canola will work too)

1 cup Aioli (page 289)

Salt Cod

1. Salt your cod at least 3 days in advance (a week is ideal). Use a nonreactive earthenware, ceramic, or glass dish that is wide enough for you to place all of the cod in so that each piece is about ½ inch or so apart. Put a ½-inch layer of kosher salt or sea salt on the bottom of the dish, put your skinned and boned cod down onto the salt, and cover it completely with salt on top so that none of the fish is showing. You can also stack the salt cod with layers of salt, submerging it after each layer. Keep in mind, though, that you never want any of the pieces of cod to touch, because you want all surfaces to be coated in salt in order to cure properly.

2. Once the cod is completely submerged in salt, wrap it tightly (otherwise everything in your fridge will smell like fish) and refrigerate for 3 to 7 days. Check on it every 2 days. You're checking on water content—you want your cod to become extremely firm. If any fish is peeking out at any point, add more salt. You never want the fillets to touch. Shove salt between them if they do.

3. After the salt cod has finished curing, brush all the salt off each fillet. Take some fresh salt and lightly salt each piece. Then stack and wrap the salt cod in butcher paper. Salt cod will last tightly wrapped and refrigerated for up to 1 month.

4. Before you use the salt cod, soak it in water for 3 days in the refrigerator, dumping the water out and adding new water every day until the third day, when you'll remove the salt cod and use it to make the fritters.

Salt Cod Fritters

1. In a small saucepan over medium-high heat, add the olive oil and all of the garlic and sauté for about 30 seconds. Add the potato and half of the milk and bring to a simmer. Simmer for 15 to 20 minutes or until the potato is tender, then drain off the milk and olive oil and discard and set aside the potatoes.

2. Put the rinsed and drained salt cod and the remaining half of the milk in a medium sauté pan over high heat and bring to a simmer. Simmer uncovered for 10 to 15 minutes. Remove the cod from the pan and set aside. Discard the milk.

3. Mix the flour and baking powder in a small bowl.

4. Mix the strained salt cod with the sautéed potato and garlic mix. Put the cod and potato mix, egg yolks, and flour and baking powder mix together in a food processor and blend until smooth.

5. Whisk the egg whites for 3 to 5 minutes until they form peaks. Add them to the food processor along with the parsley and pulse for 10 to 15 seconds just to incorporate.

6. Spread the fritter mix into a wide pan, cover the surface with plastic wrap, and refrigerate it for at least 30 minutes before frying. Salt cod fritters quenelle best when the batter is cold.

7. Fill a large cast-iron pan half deep with your frying oil of choice (rice, peanut, or canola), and heat it to 350 degrees.

8. Once at temperature, use 2 large spoons to scrape the fritters into the oil. You want them to be quenelled with about 1 tablespoon of batter per fritter. Do not overcrowd them; try to fry about 10 to 15 fritters at a time. As the fritters cook and turn golden, remove and strain them. Fry time should be about 2 or 3 minutes total.

9. Put a heaping serving of Aioli on a plate and surround it with the salt cod fritters. Serve immediately.

Tortilla Espanola
1 TORTILLA, SERVES 8–12

Tortillas are everywhere in Spain. They're a typical breakfast dish and around-the-clock filler in bars, restaurants, and tapas spots. I never went crazy for them until we added stinging nettles to ours. Stinging nettles are really big in Oregon. If you live in this area of the country and cook at all, nettles are something you can't help but be familiar with; they're growing wild everywhere. There's nothing like the flavor of nettles: it's like a double-green spinach with more chlorophyll and flavor. They're also really good for you as a blood and liver cleanser. If you try your hand at all of our cocktails, you'll need that. In the spring and summer we go through about forty pounds of nettles a week for our tortillas. They're foraged outside of Washougal, Washington by a bunch of kids. We wear big yellow gloves when prepping them to keep the sting off.

Everyone has an idea of what a Spanish tortilla should be: flat, thick, hot, cold. I have to give a shout-out to Emily Cafazzo of Beast, because she spent time in Spain and gave us a lot of energy and momentum for our version. Basically we confit yellow potatoes in olive oil, add them to the egg and sour cream custard, let that set up, bake, and broil. In Spain, tortillas are usually served with just Aioli, but we like to serve ours with Romesco too.

6 medium-sized yellow potatoes

6 ounces stinging nettles (you can also use the same amount of chard or kale or any other cooking green as a substitute)

1 cup + 1 tablespoon olive oil

8 cloves of garlic, thinly slivered, divided

1 yellow onion, halved, peeled, and finely diced

Salt and pepper

2 tablespoons butter, divided

12 eggs

½ cup sour cream

½ cup Aioli (page 289)

½ cup Romesco (page 281)

1. Peel the potatoes and chop them into ½-inch cubes.

2. With gloved hands, pick the nettles off of the stems, wash them, and set them aside.

3. Put a large sauté pan over medium-high heat and add 1 cup of olive oil. Cook the 4 cloves of slivered garlic and finely diced onion until clear, about 1 minute, while shaking the pan every 20 seconds or so.

4. Add the chopped potatoes and big pinches of salt and pepper to the pan, and cook for 10 to 12 minutes, or until the potatoes are soft but still have a slight bite to them. Shake and stir the pan constantly so that the potatoes don't stick to the pan. Remove from the heat.

5. Put another large sauté pan over medium-high heat and add 1 tablespoon of butter. Once the

butter is nice and bubbly, add the remaining 4 cloves of slivered garlic and cook for about 1 minute until soft and slightly golden. Add the nettles and season with salt and pepper. Cook for about 30 seconds until the nettles have just wilted and remove the pan from heat.

6. Preheat the oven to 400 degrees.

7. Crack the eggs into a large bowl, add the sour cream, salt, and pepper, and whisk until it's a uniform pale yellow, about 1 minute. Spoon the cooked potatoes (leaving behind most of the oil, 1 to 2 tablespoons of it) and nettles into the bowl, stir, and let it sit for 10 minutes. Give it a taste and adjust the salt and pepper to your liking.

8. In a large ovenproof sauté pan, heat 1 tablespoon of butter and 1 tablespoon of olive oil over medium-high heat, about 1 minute—until the butter is almost at browning point. Add the tortilla batter to the pan. Work a spatula around the edges of the pan as the tortilla cooks and lightly push the tortilla in, keeping it from sticking to the pan, as it begins to set up. After 1 or 2 minutes it should be nicely set and have a good browned shell around the edges and on the bottom.

9. Remove the pan from the stovetop and put it into the preheated oven to bake for 20 to 25 minutes. After about 15 minutes pull the tortilla out and use a spatula to push the sides in a bit so that it doesn't stick to the pan. The center should still be slightly custardy.

10. After 20 to 25 minutes remove

the tortilla from the oven. Let it rest for 15 minutes before slicing and serving it topped with Aioli and Romesco. You can also serve it as is, without sauces. (NOTE: *Always serve and eat your tortilla the day of at room temperature or slightly above. We store ours on a shelf beside the oven so it always stays slightly above room temperature.*)

Fried Anchovies, Fennel, and Lemon

SERVES 4–6

I first fell in love with little fried fishes when I was twenty-three and helping to open a casino restaurant in Ghana. There was this Italian restaurant nearby that served fried baby barracudas: tiny fish about the same size as anchovies, but with these little sword noses that were the best part because they got really crispy and delicious when fried. The restaurant served those baby barracudas piled high on a plate with aioli.

One of the first things that I ate my first time in Barcelona was Cal Pep's plate of all sorts of little fishes and octopus, fried golden. Years earlier, at Restaurant LuLu in the Bay Area, we did a fried vegetable dish with fennel and lemon. It was awesome. I had those two dishes in mind when I came up with Toro's fried anchovies.

Most places in Spain don't clean anchovies—they serve them with the heads and guts intact. I worried that Americans would be put off by all the guts, so we go ahead and remove them. It's a time-consuming endeavor, and completely clogged Toro's septic system at one point early on in our basement prep kitchen. Words to the wise: never let fish guts, no matter how small, go down your drain. They don't decompose; they just turn into this crazy goop. Anchovy guts can really stop up your sink if you don't do this over a sieve. Never let them go down your drain, unless you hate your plumber and want your plumber to hate you back.

½ head fennel, trimmed

½ small lemon

8 ounces anchovies, cleaned and trimmed

2 cups all-purpose flour, divided

½ cup Romesco (page 281)

Salt

1 lemon, cut into wedges

½ gallon rice oil for frying (peanut or canola will work too)

1. Thinly slice the fennel and lemon on a mandoline. Put them in a medium bowl, cover in cold water, and soak for 1 minute. Strain the water and repeat. These 2 soaks get a little of the bitterness out of both.

2. Get your fry oil up to 360 degrees. If you don't have a countertop fryer, you can do this very carefully in a large, deep cast-iron pan or pot. The latter is better.

3. Clean the anchovies by hand under running water into a sieve. Poke your thumb into the base of the anchovy at its belly, right where the tail ends, and move your finger up through the belly of the fish toward the head, getting all of the guts out as you do all the way into the head. Rip off the jaw and remove the sharp part of the mouth and clean out the head. You want the anchovy entirely hollowed and rinsed.

4. Once all of your anchovies have been cleaned, toss them in a bowl with 1 cup of flour until they're well coated. Toss the fennel and lemon with the remaining cup of flour in another bowl until well coated.

5. Put the anchovies into the preheated fryer for about 1 minute and then add the sliced lemon and fennel and fry for another 1½ minutes. You want your anchovies to be crisp but not overcooked.

6. Strain the anchovies, fennel, and lemon into a bowl, toss them with salt, and allow them to sit for 1 minute before serving them on top of or alongside Romesco, with fresh lemon wedges.

131

Chili Shrimp à la Plancha
SERVES 8–10

This is a quintessential Spanish dish, but it's also very much inspired by the time I spent growing up in North Carolina in the '80s. When I was ten to twelve years old, living in Murrells Inlet in Myrtle Beach, our house was right near the beach. My younger brother and I would often take our volleyball net down to the cove and walk it out into waist-deep water to trawl by foot and catch whatever was swimming—usually flounder and shrimp. After half an hour to an hour we'd pull the net in onto the beach, check out what we caught, and take whatever it was home to cook. North Carolina's shrimp are some of the best I've ever had. I happen to think that all American shrimp is great. We use Gulf prawns at Toro.

In Spain, all the shrimp—well, langoustines, which are larger and more lobster-like—are served with the shell and head on. We serve ours with the shells on, but remove the heads because most Americans aren't into them. I happen to love the heads—they're the most flavorful part—and you should keep them on if you do too. One of my favorite movie scenes is the dinner in *Apocalypse Now* when General Corman is telling Captain Willard, played by Martin Sheen, what his mission is. A big platter of shrimp comes by and Corman basically says to Willard, "I know you're a brave guy, but if you eat these shrimps with the heads on, we'll really know just how crazy you are."

Here are three very good reasons to at least leave the shells on when cooking shrimp: it amps up the flavor, makes the shrimp moist and soft, and gets you to use your fingers when you eat them. So much of that sweet shrimpy flavor is in and on the shell.

You can substitute a different type of oil-cured chili here—piri-piri works—but if you're going to really get down with this cookbook, then you should buy a jar of oil-cured Calabrian chilies. They're a big deal in our kitchen.

Chili Paste

5 whole heads garlic, cut in half widthwise (you will only use the tops)

¼ cup water

10 oil-cured Calabrian chilies

1 tablespoon red wine vinegar

¼ cup oil blend (page 93)

Shrimp

2 pounds medium (under 15 count) wild Gulf shrimp

Salt

1 lemon, cut into wedges

Marinade

5 oil-cured Calabrian chilies

1 lemon, zested

½ lemon, juiced

5 garlic cloves, slivered

½ cup olive oil

For the Chili Paste

1. Preheat the oven to 400 degrees.

2. Take just the tops of the garlic heads and put them in a pan with the water. Roast for about an hour, tightly covered, until the garlic is soft and you can squeeze the cloves out. Remove the garlic from the oven and let it cool.

3. Squeeze the cooled garlic into a food processor, add the oil-cured Calabrian chilies, vinegar, and oil, and purée to a paste.

For the Shrimp and Marinade

1. Clean the shrimp but leave them in their shells. Use scissors to cut down the back and devein them.

2. Mix all of the marinade ingredients together and marinate the deveined shrimp in that for about a half day, covered and refrigerated.

3. Put a large cast-iron pan on medium-high heat. Once it's hot, put your shrimp in the pan. You want each shrimp to completely touch the pan, so do them in two batches if you need to.

4. Once the shrimp are getting a little color and are slightly browned, flip them and put ½ to 1 teaspoon of the shrimp paste on each shrimp. Let that side of the shrimps cook until they start to brown, and then begin tossing them all together so that the chili paste coats all the shrimp and the shrimp sears a little.

5. You can add salt at this point, depending how salty you like your shrimp. After about 4 or 5 minutes of sautéing, when the shrimp are no longer translucent where you've deveined them, they're done cooking. Serve the shrimp with lemon wedges and wet towels to clean your hands and face when you're done.

133

Boquerones with Toasted Bread and Piperade

SERVES 6–12, 6 LARGE PIECES

Boquerones, which are Spanish white anchovies pickled in wine vinegar and sometimes oil, are served throughout Barcelona at most tapas bars, straight up with olive oil and bread. Americans generally don't have as much of a love for tiny, fishy things as the Spaniards do, so I wanted to make something for folks who normally have tiny-fish hang-ups. I think of boquerones as the gateway anchovy: they're less harsh and cleaner than salted anchovies, and the vinegar takes a lot of the fishiness out of them.

I've loved anchovies since I was little, but I first got into boquerones when we made them at Citron. When I was at Simpatica and the anchovy runs would come up through Oregon, we'd make house-made boquerones out of them. They were tart and flavorful and addictive. Our boquerones aren't a huge seller, but that just means more for people like me, who love these tart little fishes and have to order them every time they come in.

½ baguette, sliced on a bias into 6 large slices about ½-inch thick

1+ tablespoon olive oil

Salt and pepper

1 cup Piperade (page 287)

12 to 18 boquerones fillets*

*Generally, you're not going to have many options here, since boquerones are expensive and hard to find. I recommend going with Spanish boquerones, which are usually sold in a round white tin. You can order them online.

1. Drizzle the baguette slices on both sides with the olive oil and season them with the salt and pepper, also on both sides. Grill or broil the baguette until crispy and nicely charred, turning regularly. This should take 3 to 5 minutes.

2. In a medium sauté pan over medium-high heat, add the piperade and cook for about 30 to 45 seconds, until warmed through.

3. Remove the baguette slices from the heat and top each with a heaping spoonful of warmed piperade.

4. If you love boquerones like I do, place 3 fillets across the top of each baguette piece on a bias. (Use more or less depending on your taste.) Drizzle each portion with olive oil, sprinkle with salt and a little pinch of freshly ground pepper, and serve.

Potatoes Bravas

SERVES 6

Bravas are everywhere in Spain and they're all so different. Sometimes you get potatoes bravas pan-fried, sometimes deep fried, sometimes tossed in salt and sometimes not. When we first opened, we fried and salted our bravas and served them with the sauce on the side. They were okay, but nothing to write home about. Once we started tossing them with the sauce, we knew we'd nailed it, texturally: you get the crisp, fried potato edges fully coated in sauce, making for a perfect bite every time.

Bravas Salt
1. Toss all of your Bravas salt ingredients in a small bowl until well mixed.

Bravas Sauce
1. In a large sauté pan over medium heat, sauté the onion and garlic in olive oil until the onions are translucent. Stir in the rest of the ingredients and slowly simmer for about 1½ hours.

2. Remove the sauce from the heat, purée it, adjust the salt and pepper to taste, and let it cool.

Potatoes
1. Heat your oil to 300 degrees. In a deep fryer or large, deep cast-iron pot over medium-high heat, submerge the potatoes in rice oil for about 5 minutes. If you're using a larger deep fryer or larger pot then you can cook them all at once, but do them in smaller batches if not. You don't want to overfill and have the potatoes not cook properly. Never salt before frying; salt breaks down the molecular structure of the oil and your food won't fry properly.

2. Strain the potatoes and cool them.

3. Once cooled use the same oil (unless you are using canola; then replace with new oil) and fry them at about 370 degrees for 3 to 5 minutes until they're golden and crisp.

4. Strain the potatoes and toss them in the Bravas salt first and then in the Bravas sauce. Serve hot on a platter topped with Aioli.

4 Kennebec potatoes peeled, cut into 1½-inch cubes, and rinsed under cold water until the water runs clear (russets are fine too, and those are what we first used for our bravas, but the Kennebecs are sweeter and fry better)

½ gallon rice oil for frying (peanut or canola will work too)

¼ cup **Bravas Salt**

 ¼ cup salt

 1 tablespoon sugar

 Pinch cayenne

 1 tablespoon pepper

 2 tablespoons Spanish smoked sweet paprika (Pimentón de la Vera)

 2 tablespoons paprika

2 cups Bravas Sauce

 ½ yellow onion, thinly julienned

 1 clove garlic, minced

 3 tablespoons olive oil

 2 nyora chilies

 2 cups canned tomatoes

 ¼ cup sugar

 ⅓ cup white wine vinegar

 Splash white wine

 2 tablespoons parsley, finely chopped

 Salt and pepper

½ cup Aioli (page 289)

Seared Cauliflower with Salsa Verde
SERVES 6–8

If you have a pan, some oil, salt, pepper, and water, you can make cauliflower taste a hundred different ways. That's what technique is. With this recipe the pan has to be just so hot, the cauliflower has to be blanched just right, and you've got to have just the right amount of salt. See how delicious you can make this.

I think that cold-shocking vegetables is bullshit. One day, while I was at Caffe Centro, Jean-Pierre Moullé asked me why I cold-shocked my vegetables. I told him that's what I'd been taught. And he said, *Think about it: you're putting these beautiful vegetables in water twice, and by doing so you're taking flavor out each time.* He said, *If you treat your vegetables right and blanch them correctly, the color won't go away.* He's right. I've never cold-shocked my vegetables since then (other than fava beans, to get the skins off). And I've never had anyone complain about my vegetables not having color at Toro Bravo.

A lot of chefs try to stop vegetables from cooking by ice-water shocking them immediately after blanching. At Toro, we blanch knowing that we'll have cook time carry over once the vegetables come out of the boiling water. We put our blanched vegetables on sheet pans to cool and air dry. In my opinion, the best vegetables always have char and sear. If you blanch and then shock your vegetables you're essentially adding water to them, which doesn't allow them to char properly. By letting the vegetables steam off on the sheet pan, you allow them to lose a significant amount of water, resulting in a much better sear. I don't get into ice water baths and neither do my vegetables.

5 sprigs rosemary

2 heads garlic, just the tops, with skin still on

2 heads cauliflower, florets chopped into bite-sized pieces

2 tablespoons butter

1 tablespoon + 1 tablespoon olive oil toward the end of searing, if needed

Salt and pepper

⅓ cup pitted olives, roughly chopped

¼ cup Salsa Verde (page 290)

1. Bring 1 gallon of water to a boil with ⅓ cup of salt (you want a saltwater consistency and taste; it's what you should be going for whenever you blanch vegetables, whatever they are), the rosemary, garlic tops, and the cauliflower.

2. Once the pot is back to a boil, cook the cauliflower for 1 minute and then strain it and lay over a sheet pan to dry. Discard the garlic or use it for stock or another purpose.

3. In a large sauté pan, melt the butter and 1 tablespoon of olive oil over medium-high heat. Get it really hot (but not browning), then add the blanched cauliflower. Season with more salt and pepper once in the pan. Some rosemary can make it in, but you don't want too much.

4. Flip the cauliflower after 3 to 4 minutes, once it has a nice sear on it. If the pan is getting dry, add another tablespoon of olive oil. Add the pitted olives and cook another 2 or 3 minutes. Strain the olives and cauliflower and serve topped with the salsa verde.

Sautéed Spinach with Pine Nuts and Golden Raisins

SERVES 4–6

People go nuts over our spinach, and I think it has a lot to do with all its layers of flavor. I've always known I wanted spinach on Toro Bravo's menu. Spinach was one of my favorite vegetables, growing up. I even liked crappy canned spinach because I had a Popeye obsession. Spinach, raisins, and pine nuts is a traditional dish you find in Spain's Catalan region, but in Spain it's often done using less-than-fresh spinach. We use the freshest spinach we can find, and raisins we reconstitute in Basque cider (shout-out to Ryan Bleibtrey for thinking that up) that gives the spinach that funky, yeasty thing that I love. We finish it with a drizzle of mugolio, which Alex, my sales rep from Provvista Specialty Foods, introduced me to. I'd never heard of mugolio before. It's a pinecone bud syrup that's a little pricey—$25 for a 3.6 ounce bottle—that tastes like piney maple syrup. It's the magic in this dish. You could omit it, of course, but it's not going to be the same.

¼ cup white raisins

¼ cup Basque cider (or other good, dry, local cider)

1 tablespoon olive oil

1 tablespoon butter

5 cloves garlic, thinly sliced

1 pound spinach, trimmed and rinsed

Salt and pepper

¼ cup pine nuts, toasted

⅛ lemon, juiced

2 teaspoons mugolio (You can order this online. It'll set you back $25 for one small jar. Once we've used all of the mugolio, we use the cute little jars as cream pitchers at Tasty n Sons.)

1. Put a medium sauté pan over medium-high heat and cook the raisins and cider for about 10 minutes, until the cider evaporates. Remove from heat.

2. Heat 2 large sauté pans over medium heat with half of the olive oil and butter in each. Let them bubble and just start to brown before adding the garlic in equal parts to each pan. You don't want to get any color on the garlic. Cook the garlic for about 1 minute, until you just start to smell it.

3. Add the spinach in equal parts to the pans, then add the salt and pepper. You know you're doing it right when you hear the spinach crackle from the heat when you add it. If you only use one sauté pan, make sure it is very large; otherwise your spinach will drown in its juices and get mushy.

4. Use tongs to move the spinach every 20 seconds or so until it is finished cooking—after about 2 minutes—and just slightly wilted.

5. Turn off the heat and add the toasted pine nuts, reconstituted and cooked raisins, and lemon juice and let the residual heat of the pan finish cooking the spinach.

6. Tong the spinach into a sieve to drain off the remaining water and fat. Spoon the spinach onto your serving dish and drizzle the mugolio over the top.

141

Chard with Eggs

SERVES 4

This recipe began as staff meal: we'd top beet greens and sometimes turnip greens with eggs. Greens plus a runny-yolk egg is a common combination in Spain. At Toro, we cook the perfect sunny-side-up eggs by putting them right on top of our salamander broiler to cook very gently and slowly. I know you can't do that at home, but you can do the next best thing: cook your eggs slow and low, the way they like it.

Eggs

1 teaspoon butter

2 eggs

Salt and pepper

Chard

1 teaspoon olive oil

1 teaspoon butter

½ pound chard, cleaned and stemmed

2 tablespoons water

3 garlic cloves, thinly sliced

Salt

⅛ of a lemon, juiced

1. Put a small sauté pan over low-medium heat and melt 1 teaspoon of butter in it, then crack your eggs into the pan and cook them slow and low for 3 or 4 minutes, until the whites have set. We start the eggs before we start the greens because the greens cook so fast. Salt and pepper the eggs to taste.

2. Put a large sauté pan over medium-high heat with the olive oil and butter. When it bubbles and just starts to brown, put your chard, water, garlic, and salt in.

3. After about 1 minute, once the chard is slightly wilted, remove it from the heat, and add the lemon juice. Tong the chard onto your serving dish, and finish by topping it with the eggs.

Butter-Braised Turnips with Mojo Picon

SERVES 6–8

Sheldon Laeity of Your Kitchen Garden in Canby came into the restaurant with some amazing baby turnips one day. Naturally, I bought a couple cases. At first I thought I'd just pickle them. Pickling is a solid way to prepare turnips, but also a little boring. Growing up in the Southeast I ate a lot of vegetables—zucchini and squashes—fried in butter. I figured I could do the same with baby turnips, and did.

We were already serving our Mojo Picon (page 284) on our fried squash blossoms, but the sauce wasn't getting much use in the wintertime. There was a little Mojo lying around when we got Sheldon's first crate of baby turnips, so we drizzled it over some that I'd braised in butter. It was game on right away.

Whenever possible, use baby turnips, but don't stress if you can't find them; mature turnips taste great, too. Babies get an especially nice crust when you sear them, but a downside to the baby ones is they can take on a lot of water in the winter and get mushy. If that's the case, cook them quickly and don't let them turn to mush.

¼ pound (1 stick) butter

20 baby turnips (left whole) or 6 mature turnips (peeled and chopped into 1-inch pieces), about 2 pounds

Salt and pepper

1 cup Mojo Picon (page 284)

1. Melt the butter in a large sauté pan over high heat, add the turnips, and season them in the pan with the salt and pepper. (Don't use a nonstick pan; the heat transfer won't be high enough to brown the turnips correctly.)

2. Stir occasionally and cook for about 7 minutes. When the turnips are slightly browned and soft but not mushy, transfer them to a serving dish.

3. Drizzle with Mojo Picon and serve immediately.

Harira: Lamb and Lentil Stew

SERVES 4–6

When I was working at Café Zenon, Bill Hatch was really into Moroccan food, and cooking a lot from Paula Wolfert's cookbook, *Couscous and Other Good Food From Morocco.* Harira—a traditional Berber soup usually made with lentils, chickpeas, and a bit of meat—was one of his favorite dishes.

At Zenon we served the harira with rice, which I always thought was kind of a cop-out, a boring filler. At Toro we serve it with house-made flatbread and a really nice buttermilk cheese. You can just throw some store-bought sour cream on it and it'll be delicious, but garnishing our harira with buttermilk cheese takes it to another level.

1. In a large pot over medium heat sauté shallots, parsley, and cilantro in olive oil until the shallots are clear and fragrant.

2. Add the ginger, turmeric, cinnamon, paprika, and saffron and cook for one minute, allowing the spices to bloom.

3. Increase the heat to medium-high and add the onions and lamb. Cook until the onions are translucent and the lamb is cooked through, for 5 to 10 minutes.

4. Add the chicken stock, chickpeas, and lentils to the pot and bring to a simmer. Cook this for about an hour or until the lentils are soft, making sure to stir periodically so that the lentils don't stick to the pot.

5. Once the harira is finished cooking, stir in the lemon juice and preserved lemon. Taste and adjust the salt. (This stew—like most stews—is way better on day two. Plan accordingly.) To serve, top each bowl with a dollop of sour cream or buttermilk cheese.

Buttermilk cheese

1. Set your oven to the lowest temperature it will go (usually 180 degrees). In a nonreactive saucepan, heat buttermilk and a pinch of salt to 180 degrees. Move the saucepan to the oven and leave it alone for 10 hours, until separated.

2. Using cheesecloth, strain the solids from the whey and discard the whey. Let the cheese continue to strain for 45 minutes in your refrigerator. The stuff you capture is buttermilk cheese.

¼ cup olive oil

1 medium shallot, finely chopped

2 tablespoons parsley leaves, chopped

2 tablespoons cilantro leaves, chopped

1 tablespoon fresh ginger, minced

½ tablespoon turmeric

2 teaspoons ground cinnamon

1 teaspoon paprika

1 pinch saffron

1 onion, diced

1 pound ground lamb shoulder

2 quarts Chicken Stock (page 291)

2 cups cooked or one 15-ounce can chickpeas (if canned, rinse and drain. I never use canned beans, because they aren't nearly as good as reconstituted dried ones.)

2 cups dried brown lentils

1 lemon, juiced

¼ Preserved Lemon, skin finely chopped (page 275)

Salt

Buttermilk cheese

1 pint buttermilk

Salt

Grilled Asparagus
SERVES 6–8

I once watched Jean-Pierre Moullé peel asparagus for five hours. We were at Caffe Centro, prepping an off-site dinner for 400 people. I remember thinking: that's love. I also remember thinking: I'll never *not* do that again. It's like your mom cutting the crust off your bread—there's a touch of love in doing it. I remember when I first opened my cooks were like, *Are you fucking serious? You're going to make us peel a hundred pounds of asparagus? I am* fucking serious. It's important.

   This little set is perfect for showing off the asparagus: fried preserved lemon, chilies, olives, a little browned butter, and fried jamón. In-season asparagus is best of course, but sometimes I want it when it's not. The Southern Hemisphere has a good asparagus season too.

2 pounds asparagus

2 tablespoons + 1 tablespoon olive oil

4 slices jamon, very finely julienned

Salt and pepper

2 tablespoons butter

1 Preserved Lemon, skin julienned (page 275)

3 oil-cured Calabrian chilies

½ cup Marinated Olives (page 293)

1. Start your grill.

2. Snap each asparagus spear at the spot where it stops being woody and gets soft. Discard the woody parts.

3. Bring 1 gallon of water to a boil with ⅓ cup of salt. (You want a saltwater consistency and taste. It's what you should be going for whenever you blanch vegetables, whatever they are.)

4. Peel the skin from the lower part of the remaining asparagus. You want to peel about 1½ inches of the bottom of your asparagus. This step is worth it for the texture, so please don't skip it.

5. Once the water is at a rolling boil, add the asparagus and boil for 30 seconds to 1 minute, depending on the size. Remove the asparagus to a plate and let it cool.

6. In a medium sauté pan over medium-high heat, add 2 tablespoons of olive oil and jamón and cook, stirring constantly, until nicely crisped, about 1 minute. Strain and discard the oil and set the jamón aside. (As the jamón sits it gets crispier.)

7. Dry your asparagus, season with olive oil, salt, and pepper, and toss to coat.

8. Grill the asparagus until nicely charred—3 to 4 minutes—and remove to a plate and set aside.

9. Put the butter in a medium sauté pan and let it just get to browning, then add the preserved lemon skin and give the pan a good couple shakes. Once the lemon turns a little white, and is starting to get crispy, after about 1 or 2 minutes, add the whole chilies, then the olives, and give the pan another good shake. Stir and allow the mix to bloom for about 20 seconds.

10. Add the jamón, shake, and top the asparagus with the mix. Serve immediately.

147

Sautéed Brussels Sprouts with Bacon Sherry Cream

SERVES 4–6

Jean-Pierre Moullé and I were roasting chickens to go with brussels sprouts when he told me I should try opening the brussels and flash-sautéing them, because they're delicious that way. That's how I've cooked them ever since. The bacon-and-cream combo—along with bourbon—is a classic Southern thing; I put a Spanish twist on it with the sherry.

You'll want to serve these sprouts with bigger, bolder dishes, like the Coppa steak (page 192) or Chicken and Clams Cataplana (page 238).

Sherry Cream Sauce

1. Place a medium sauté pan over medium heat. Add the olive oil, then the bacon, and sauté until nicely browned, about 5 minutes.

2. Add the diced onion to the pan and cook, stirring occasionally, until translucent, about 5 minutes.

3. Add the sherry to deglaze the pan and cook for 1 minute, until it has reduced by about half. Add the cream, salt, and pepper, bring to a simmer. Cook for 2 to 3 minutes. Remove from heat.

Brussels Sprouts

1. Using a melon baller, scoop out the core of each brussels sprout, taking care to leave as much leaf behind as possible. The core is naturally more bitter, because flavors intensify in that area, so we like to remove it. Break apart the leaves of the brussels in a large bowl.

2. Place a large sauté pan (14 inches wide) or 2 medium sauté pans over high heat. Add the butter and olive oil and cook until the butter releases most of its water and begins to brown.

3. Add all of the brussels sprout leaves in a fairly even layer in the pan. You should hear loud crackling at the beginning. Resist the urge to stir until the brussels have been in the pan for about a minute. After that initial stir, you'll still want to be pretty conservative with the stirring—stirring very occasionally so that the brussels wilt, release their water, and brown—for about 10 minutes. Add the salt and pepper.

4. Stir the sauce into the brussels in the pan and simmer for a couple minutes, until the brussels are well coated but the sauce has cooked down and is no longer wet. Season to taste and serve.

Sherry Cream Sauce

1 tablespoon olive oil

1 cup double Applewood-smoked bacon, diced (cheaper ends and pieces are great for this)

½ yellow onion, diced

2 tablespoons sherry

2 cups heavy cream

Salt and pepper

5 sage leaves, rolled and sliced thinly into a chiffonade

Brussels Sprouts

2 pounds brussels sprouts

2 tablespoons butter

1 tablespoon olive oil

Salt and pepper

Grilled Corn with Cilantro Pesto

10–20 SECTIONS OF CORN

One of my first cooking jobs was at Parker's Barbecue Restaurant in Greenville, North Carolina. They serve Eastern Carolina–style family food: things like barbecued chicken, pulled pork, Brunswick stew, corn on the cob, fried chicken, and chitlins. They cooked their corn in a pound of butter and milk in big hotel pans on the steam table, and before serving they'd roll the cobs in soft butter and then salt and pepper. I never met anyone who tried and didn't love that corn.

At Toro, we give that Parker's twist to our corn. Milk really brings out the sweetness of corn, and the milk and butter clinging to the kernels makes for a nice caramelization on the grill that you really can't get from anything else. Chefs often come in and say, *Wow, what the fuck did you do to that?* It's not complicated, and now you know our trick. Topping the grilled corn with cilantro pesto before serving it is just another way to say I love you.

NOTE: *Always try to make cilantro pesto the day that you're going to use it, because it's quick to die and no good at all after two days. I like it best when the prep cooks make the cilantro pesto at four thirty for us to serve for dinner at five. Make a full batch and whatever you don't use for the corn, serve with bread or toss with pasta like any other pesto.*

Cilantro Pesto (1½ cups)

1 bunch cilantro, stemmed and finely chopped

¼ lemon, zested

¼ cup Poached Almonds (page 97), finely chopped

2 cloves garlic, smashed and minced

1 cup manchego, finely grated

1 cup olive oil, add slowly and to taste

Salt and pepper

Corn

1 quart milk

½ pound butter

5 to 10 corn cobs, cleaned and cut into 2 or 3 2½-inch pieces*

*Yellow or white, as long as it's fresh. Ask when it was picked. If they don't have an answer for you, ask to try it—if they can cut you off a couple kernels. Corn should always be sweet, never a starch bomb. The moment that it's picked, its sugars start converting to starches. We always try to process corn as soon as it comes in. If you have more corn than you can eat right away, the milk method in this recipe is great because it immediately stops that sugar-to-starch conversion and keeps the corn's natural sweetness intact.

Cilantro pesto

1. Mix all of the ingredients except the olive oil in a medium bowl.

2. Slowly stir in the oil. Adjust salt and pepper to taste.

Corn

1. Start your grill and get it good and hot.

2. Take a metal braising pan and bring your milk and butter to a boil. Lay the corn into the pan in a single layer, rolling them around for the next couple minutes as the mixture boils. Remove from the heat.

3. Remove the corn cobs from the milk and butter, salt and pepper them, and grill until you start to hear popping and get some nice color, about 5 minutes. Remove the corn from the grill and top each piece with a tablespoon of cilantro pesto.

151

CHARC

Bill Hatch at Café Zenon was a charcuterie genius. At Zenon, it was punishment to do the charcuterie. If you showed up to work hungover, you got to stuff the boudin blanc. After a while, though, Bill realized that this wasn't a punishment for me. I loved doing it. And before long, I was making duck-liver mousse, pork-liver mousse, chicken-liver mousse, and country pâtés right alongside him.

Zenon was where I really first felt the magic of working in a kitchen, and learning charcuterie was a big reason for that: with charcuterie, you get to transform your initial product into something entirely different—something incredibly unlike its initial state. You get to use all parts of an animal. Nothing goes to waste. It's about preservation—making food last longer, and taste better. It's about tradition, too. People have been curing meat forever, and when you do it, you're part of that tradition.

Charcuterie is endlessly fascinating. It takes a lot of attention, a lot of studying, and a lot of skill, but it's really gratifying to learn.

When it comes to making your own dry-cured charcuterie, I'll be honest with you: most people shouldn't!

I've had some house-made charcuterie here in Portland that was fucking rancid. I thought, *Guys, if you don't know what the fuck you're doing, you should stop doing this!*

If you still want to, know what you're getting into: a lot of work. Do your research, get somebody to teach you, and make sure you understand what's going on, because there's a lot of science to charcuterie. Take your time and learn it so you don't endanger yourself or other people. So many people just don't know what they're doing. If you don't, you're going to wind up hurting yourself or somebody else. It's gonna give the people who *do* know what they're doing a bad rap. The state and USDA are going to come after us, or give us more and more hoops to jump through, because more amateurs are doing it and not doing it right.

Josh Scofield, who's responsible for all the restaurant's dry-cured charcuterie, has a very exact, by-the-book, scientific mind. Once, during a Toro Bravo camping trip, he got up in the morning and started making mimosas according to his recipe: two-thirds champagne and one-third orange juice. Josh jiggers his mimosas!* When he's down

there in our basement with the charcuterie, he's that way too. That's how we get a consistent—and consistently safe—product.

Technique is always important, but especially in this chapter. If you overcook the livers in our Sherry Chicken-Liver Mousse (page 174)—even a little bit—you're fucked. If you put everything in too hot, you're fucked. If you blend it and then don't pass it soon enough, you're fucked. So follow our instructions. We aren't messing with the yield too much here or dumbing anything down. We go for really classic flavors in our charcuterie—these are tried and true recipes that we hope you'll want to make at home.

Not all recipes here are broken down yield-wise as they are elsewhere. The recipes that could be scaled down without compromise—the Bacon, Coppa Steak, and Chorizo—have been reduced to smaller, more manageable yields. But you might just need to throw a party for the Sherry Chicken-Liver Mousse (page 174), or the Duck-Liver Mousse Terrine (page 178). In fact, I encourage it.

*Josh, however, denies this: "I was making French 75s. I would never jigger a mimosa. That's crazy!"

EQUIPMENT AND RESOURCES

Digital scales

A large digital kitchen scale usually has a 12-pound capacity with gram increments. A smaller, more precise digital scale costs about $10, and will get you to one one-hundredth of a gram, which is necessary for some of the cultures and dextrose in dry-cured recipes.

Grinder

A $50 KitchenAid meat-grinding attachment for your stand-up mixer works just fine at home. You won't have as many options for plate sizes with this attachment—just small and large—but it's still a good start. (These grinders also have a tendency to smear, so make sure that your meat is half frozen.) The next step up is a stand-alone grinder, which is essentially a motor with a grinder head. Those start around $300. Josh bought his stand-alone grinder from Cabela's outdoor supply; it's a good investment if you're making a lot of charcuterie at home.

Mixer

A small KitchenAid mixer will not be strong enough to make sausage and salami, but a larger KitchenAid or Breville mixer will work fine for small batches. If you don't have one of those or a bigger, industrial mixer, do your mixing by hand. It's good to learn by hand anyway, so you get a feel for it.

Blender

We have a 1-gallon Waring blender. They aren't cheap, but they're worth it, and last for years. Vitamix blenders are great for finer blending too.

Stuffer

I can't recommend the KitchenAid grinder for stuffing. For small batches it's not terrible, but be smart with it, because you're basically running the ground meat through that auger again, which means you run the risk of overworking it. A lot of smearing happens with these stuffers. You can get a home version of our 25-pound-capacity Tre Spade stuffer for a decent price. Josh got a new 5-pound stuffer for his brother online for Christmas for $80.

Cast-iron pans

Meat loves cast-iron. Cast-iron pans get nicely seasoned over the years and regulate temperature well.

Smoker

You can do a lot with the Big or Little Chief smokers. Toro did for the first few years. Getting our first commercial smoker, though, was exciting: it was way better, with cleaner and more consistent smoke and heat. The Big Chiefs are made in Hood River, Oregon, and are cheap as shit and work fine for a home cook. They're just as good as the commercial ones, actually, but can get worn out over time and develop hot spots. In the first few years we would buy five at a time, straight from the factory, and have them shipped to the restaurant. After a while we said, *This is ridiculous. Let's just do this right and invest in a smoker that'll last us longer.*

Dehydrator

We have the full-size Cabela's dehydrator and it's a workhorse. Get whatever you can afford but if you can pony up for one with a fan, I recommend doing that. It really helps with consistent drying.

Thermal immersion circulator

We sous vide all of our forced meat terrines and foie gras at Toro Bravo. But the equipment costs a pretty penny, and you can make do without it.

Casing pricker

Once sausage or salami is twisted, you always want to prick the links all over with a casing pricker, so that any internal air is released and they don't explode on you. These are generally under $10.

pH tester for dry-cured meats

Strips are the cheapest. If you'll be testing pH all the time like we do at Toro, a more spendy pH meter might be worth investing in.

Vacuum sealer

If you get into charcuterie, I can't stress enough the importance of a vacuum sealer. If you can get air out of the picture, you can make a pâté that's good six months down the road. It'll only set you back about $80 for a decent vacuum sealer. I've owned both the high-end ones and the cheapest ones, and I actually prefer the cheapest. With the high-end ones, you'll wind up using a little extra plastic with every bag that you make. That adds up, because the bags aren't cheap. With the real basic $80 ones, it's just the suction and the sealer, and you wind up with very little waste.

Asian markets

At Asian markets you'll find minimally processed, affordable larger cuts of meat. For shoulders, leg meat, tongues, livers—all of the stuff that people aren't clamoring for—you can't beat Asian markets.

Butcher & Packer

This online business based in Michigan sells most of the equipment I've just mentioned, and then some. We source a lot of charcuterie and meat-processing items from them, including ingredients and equipment. Their website is *butcher-packer.com*, and you can find a lot of what you need there.

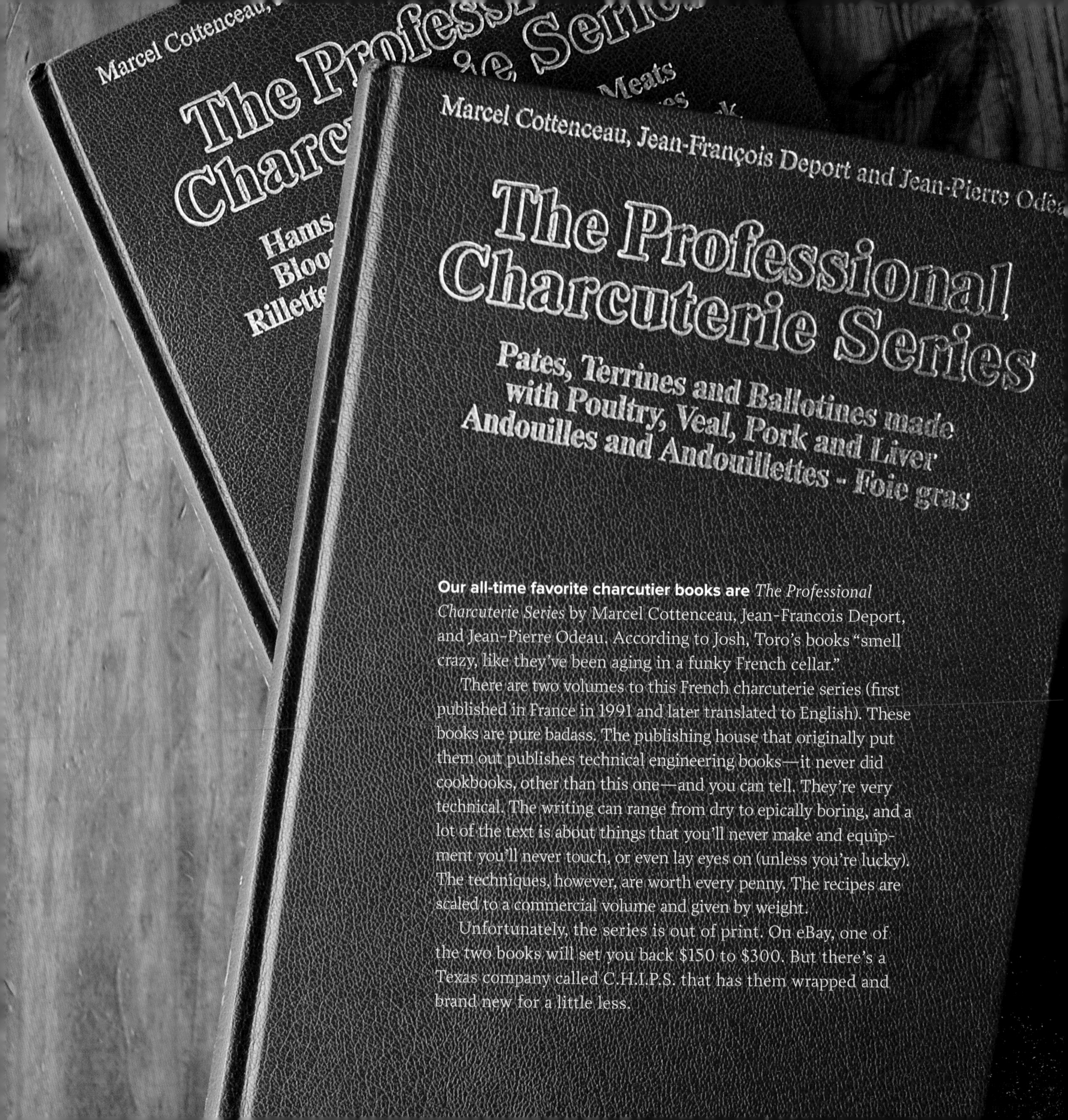

Marcel Cottenceau, Jean-François Deport and Jean-Pierre Odea

The Professional Charcuterie Series

Pates, Terrines and Ballotines made with Poultry, Veal, Pork and Liver Andouilles and Andouillettes - Foie gras

Meats

Hams
Bloo
Rillette

The Professional
Charcuterie Series

Our all-time favorite charcutier books are *The Professional Charcuterie Series* by Marcel Cottenceau, Jean-Francois Deport, and Jean-Pierre Odeau. According to Josh, Toro's books "smell crazy, like they've been aging in a funky French cellar."

There are two volumes to this French charcuterie series (first published in France in 1991 and later translated to English). These books are pure badass. The publishing house that originally put them out publishes technical engineering books—it never did cookbooks, other than this one—and you can tell. They're very technical. The writing can range from dry to epically boring, and a lot of the text is about things that you'll never make and equipment you'll never touch, or even lay eyes on (unless you're lucky). The techniques, however, are worth every penny. The recipes are scaled to a commercial volume and given by weight.

Unfortunately, the series is out of print. On eBay, one of the two books will set you back $150 to $300. But there's a Texas company called C.H.I.P.S. that has them wrapped and brand new for a little less.

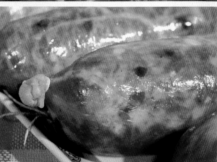

Chapter 3
Sausages and Sausage Meat

A Large Variety of Products made with Ground Meat

The family of sausages encompasses many preparations, from traditional products to the original creations of the modern charcutier. These more recent additions to the charcuterie repertoire use a wide range of ingredients.

Traditional sausages include basic ground meat mixtures and small and large sausages with various flavorings. Many regional favorites as well as sausages from outside of France have become standard preparations in many charcuteries.

This chapter presents 14 basic sausage preparations

Chapter 4
Pâtés and Terrines made with Liver

A long-term culinary tradition

This chapter presents one of the most important products of the French charcutier-caterer.

The common denominator in all these preparations is liver, the largest organ of the digestive system.

It is a complex chemical factory, serving as a filter to separate, organize, direct and store the nutrients that nourish the body.

Liver based pâtés and terrines are traditional and new; they have been made since ancient times and the modern charcutier offers classic products as well as creations featuring a variety of ingredients.

French Kisses
20 PRUNES

French Kisses are prunes covered with brandy, marinated for a few days, and stuffed with foie gras torchon pieces. We sold the shit out of them at Viande, and I knew they'd be a really great tapa.

They weren't on the menu when we first opened—I wasn't comfortable having my cooks play with foie gras while we were so busy and running around. I didn't want to kill anyone. When I finally thought we could handle it, I added the trickier things. Right around Thanksgiving of our first year I started playing with these French Kisses.

During this time I was having my gallbladder issues. I'd been in and out of the hospital, and my doctor finally said that I needed to have my gallbladder removed. I scheduled my surgery for New Year's Eve, because it would be free; I'd paid all of my deductibles for the year. That week I prepped a huge amount of French Kisses. I soaked the prunes in Cardenal Mendoza brandy and got all of the foie gras torchons ready. The day before I went in for surgery, I sat down with Kasey and said, *Whatever you do, Kasey, do not fuck up New Year's Eve. Everything's done and planned and you just have to remember to get the fucking French Kisses on the menu.*

As I was going into surgery in the morning I called Kasey to say again, one last time, *Don't forget to put the French Kisses on the menu.* So I had the surgery and they took out my gallbladder. I called Kasey first thing in the morning, since I always close the restaurant on New Year's Day, and asked him how New Year's Eve went. Kasey said it was great, twice in a row, but I could hear nervousness in his voice. I asked him, *Did you put the French Kisses on the menu?* And he said, *I forgot.* I lost my shit. I told him I was thinking about them going into surgery, that they were the first thing I thought of when I came out of anesthesia. I thought New Year's Eve was a perfect night to launch them. I think that's the most that I've ever yelled at Kasey. I even came in the next day with an open wound to yell at him some more. Motherfucking Mills. They've been on the menu ever since.

Foie Gras Torchon

⅓ pound foie gras, broken into pieces (It's much cheaper to buy foie gras in pieces than whole. You can also buy foie gras already formed into a torchon and skip all of this.)

½ to 1 tablespoon salt

½ teaspoon pepper

French Kisses

25 good-quality prunes, not dried out (If they're on the dry side, take boiling water and cover them for a minute or so and drain to rehydrate.)

Cardenal Mendoza brandy (or another nice-tasting brandy, since it won't be cooked off)

1 teaspoon sea salt, anything with a little crunch to it

Foie Gras Torchon

Thaw and devein the foie gras. Thaw the frozen foie gras in the refrigerator. Anything that's more fat than meat like foie gras thaws very quickly because it has a low water content. With gloved hands, break up the foie gras and remove any veins. The veins are pinkish and when you pull apart the pieces of foie gras, the veins kind of drag behind. Be careful, because the veins will tear if you pull them too hard, and then you'll get blood in the torchon. You don't want that.

Season and refrigerate the foie gras. Salt and pepper the foie gras, then mash it with still-gloved hands into a smooth but slightly chunky mix. I always taste at this point to make sure that it's seasoned well. If you're not comfortable doing that, see what it tastes like after it's gone through the sous vide. (It should be on the salty side; the salt will be less pronounced when it's served cold.) Cover the surface of the mashed and seasoned foie gras with plastic wrap, and refrigerate overnight.

Shape the foie gras. The next day, form the foie gras into a log shape. Do this by doubling plastic wrap over the foie and rolling it. Squeeze as much air out as you can. Roll it up and then twist off the ends.

Sous vide the fois gras. Vacuum seal the foie gras torchon and poach

it sous vide at 165 degrees for 45 minutes. You can also mimic sous vide on the stovetop. (Just Google it.)

French Kisses

Soak and hollow the prunes. Soak the prunes in the brandy to cover for at least 24 hours in the refrigerator. You can't soak them for too long. Look for where the pit was removed from the prune, then hollow it out to make room for the foie gras with your finger.

Stuff the prunes. Freeze the torchon for 10 to 15 minutes before stuffing the prunes with it. They'll come out ugly if you skip this step and the foie will kind of turn into liquid in your hands as you form them. You can also keep the torchon in a bowl on top of another bowl filled with ice to keep it cool while making these. With gloved hands, stuff each brandy-soaked prune with about 1 teaspoon of the foie gras torchon. Roll the teaspoon of torchon into a ball first, press it into the brandy-soaked prune, and tidy it up a little bit with your fingers or a towel.

Salt and serve! Sprinkle the French Kisses with sea salt and serve slightly chilled.

NOTE: *When left unwrapped, foie gras oxidizes quickly and will turn dark brown and develop an off taste. Either make these last minute or vacuum seal them days in advance.*

Chorizo
8 KILOGRAMS RAW, 5–6 KILOGRAMS DRIED

This chorizo is 100 percent Toro Bravo's, and our gold standard. Josh makes several different cured meats for the restaurant and the chorizo is his favorite to make and eat. That's a good thing, because we go through a lot of it. Josh started making Toro's chorizo at home in 2010 and moved it over to the restaurant once he had the recipe nailed, and our fermenting and curing rooms were built.

This is our house recipe, straight up, with no dumbing down. We've included percentages as well as grams, because you really don't want to mess around with the amounts of ingredients in dry-cured meats until you're experienced with them. I recommend using two digital scales which combined will cost you $40 to $70. You want one for the larger measurements and another that's more precise for the smaller measurements.

We make eight-kilogram batches of chorizo twice a month. Generally, with dry-cured charcuterie you're going to lose about 40 percent of that original weight during the curing and drying process. Of that original eight kilograms of raw chorizo, we end up with five or six kilograms of dry-cured.

Josh makes two and four kilogram batches of our chorizo at home and that works well for him. Make whatever batch size makes the most sense for the equipment you have on hand. The ingredients listed here are for our eight-kilogram Toro Bravo batch, but it's okay to break this down to any size batch you want (that's why we've included the percentages!). Your meat and fat should add up to 100 percent; you'll calculate the other ingredients based on that quantity, whatever it is. Brush up on your math!

Sanitize all your grinder and sausage-making equipment (don't forget the casing pricker!) with bleach and water to eliminate any chance of contamination. We use 1 ounce of bleach per gallon of water. Wear gloves and wipe everything down with bleach water. Let it sit for about a minute, then rinse the solution off with warm water. This is a very important step, because you aren't cooking your chorizo at any point during the curing process. You're relying on good bacteria to do the curing work. You want to give the bacteria that you add to the meat

---

90% (7,200 grams) pork shoulder (We usually use 2 pork shoulders for the 8-kilogram restaurant batch)

10% (800 grams) fatback

2.6% (208 grams) salt

.7% (56 grams) garlic

2% (160 grams) Rioja or other medium-bodied red wine (160 grams)

.25% (20 grams) cure #2

.25% (20 grams) dextrose

.75% (60 grams) espelette pepper (we use Viridian Farms Piment Basquise)

.75% (60 grams) Pimentón de la Vera Dulce (smoked sweet Spanish paprika; we use Viridian Farms Choricero Powder)

.7% (56 grams) Pimentón de la Vera Picante

.075% (6 grams) Mexican oregano

.075% (6 grams) ground cumin

.075% (6 grams) ground coriander

.02% (1.6 grams) B-LC-007 (available at *butcher-packer.com*)

.5% 40 grams + 400 milligrams + 2 teaspoons distilled water

5 grams Penicillin mold culture, mold 600 from CHR Hanson's Bactoferm line of cultures

5 meters hog casings, 45-millimeter-wide

Twine (for tying off the chorizo)

---

via your culture the best chance to win its fight against any unsavory bacteria.

Trim and clean meat. With dry-cured salami, Spanish-style chorizo included, you want to get rid of the connective tissues, glands, veins, and silver skin even more meticulously than when you are preparing meat that will be cooked. When meat cures, all of those undesirable textures intensify and get tougher to the point of often being inedible. Once you've trimmed the meat, slice it into chunks or slices that will fit into your grinder.

Fat content. With chorizo you want between 15 and 20% total fat content. Shoulders are typically lean, so we supplement them with fatback. If you have a particularly fatty shoulder, then you don't need to add fatback. With a good grinder you should be able to grind the fully frozen fatback, which is ideal because fat has a tendency to smear when you grind it. The colder the fatback, the better.

Freeze. Put as much of your equipment as possible, as well as your trimmed and cut meat and fatback, into the freezer while you prepare to make chorizo or any salami. The larger the batch size, the more important this step becomes because the longer it takes to make.

If you don't have room in your freezer for everything, make sure the meat gets partially frozen and the fatback fully frozen (put it in your freezer for 1 to 4 hours and rotate it once or twice so that it freezes evenly) and just make sure that the equipment is as cold as possible and not straight out of the dishwasher. Grinding five pounds of meat usually only takes a minute or two.

Weigh out garlic and red wine. Take 1 teaspoon of salt from the total amount of salt and pound it with the garlic into a paste, using a mortar and pestle. Bring the wine to a boil in a small saucepan and set it on fire. When the flame subsides, add the garlic paste and simmer for about a minute. Remove it from the heat and let it cool in the freezer. Raw garlic can be a source of botulism, so that's why we cook it before adding it to the chorizo mix. It's very rare, but better safe than sorry (or dead).

Weigh out dry ingredients. The cure is very important, and that's why you need digital scales for weighing it. Go down the list and weigh out each of the spices, the cure #2, dextrose, and the rest of the salt. Put each into a quart-sized container one by one.

The culture and dextrose. The bacteria that you introduce to the meat is called B-LC-007 and is produced by CHR Hanson. The B-LC-007 eats the dextrose and creates lactic acid. This process lowers the pH and makes the chorizo stable, while .25% dextrose produces the right level of acidity. Any more than this amount will make the chorizo acidic and sour. Playing around with the amount of dextrose can really affect your end product, so we recommend that you stick with what we tell you. The culture contains several different strains of bacteria and some have been added to attack listeria, one of the particularly bad bacterial genuses that can do horrible things to you. As with most cultures, you want to store whatever you don't use tightly packed in the freezer.

Start your cultures in distilled water. Put your B-LC-007 in a small dish and add 40 grams of distilled water to it. Set it aside for 20 to 30 minutes. Put 5 grams of your penicillin mold culture into another small dish and add a couple teaspoons of distilled water to it and do the same. Only use distilled water with both because there are elements in tap water, including chlorine in some, that can kill the culture and mold. After at least 4 to 6 hours (up to 10), mix the penicillin slurry into a spray bottle with 400 milligrams of additional distilled water in it. You will use this mold spray later to spray the casings of the chorizo.

Hog casings. Use about 5 meters of 45-millimeter hog casings for the chorizo. That sounds like a lot, but again, dried salami always ends up being about 60% of its fresh weight. If we made chorizo with the casings that we use for our fresh sausages, the chorizo would be the size of pepperoni sticks. Always pull a little extra casing out, because you don't want to have to stop and soak them while you're making the chorizo. Casings are always packed in a salt solution or dried salt, so you need to unspool them and flush them with lukewarm water, pushing the water through the insides to clean them of the salt. Once you've rinsed them thoroughly, leave them in the tub of lukewarm water until you're ready to stuff them. They're good to go for up to a few days or even a couple weeks in that water, so you can always do this step ahead of time. The casings are pretty stable since they've been salt cured.

Apply mineral oil to the grinder in between the blade and the plate. While you're grinding meat and fat, you always want to keep a steady stream so that the blade is okay. You'll dull it pretty fast if you leave it on with nothing moving through.

Work as fast as possible once the meat is out of the freezer. With all of our charcuterie you want to have your mise en place carefully laid out before you start grinding, mixing, and stuffing. Have all of your ingredients measured out and your equipment nice and cold and not right out of the dishwasher. With a $3/8$-inch plate, grind your fatback. Set it aside in the freezer. Then grind your shoulder.

Mix everything together. Mix by hand or mixer all of the spices, salt, and dextrose, the culture with water, and the wine and garlic mixture, along with the ground lean shoulder.

Mix it for 1 minute on low speed, then 20 to 30 seconds on medium speed, and then fold in the frozen ground fatback. Many home mixers are not strong enough for this sort of project. If that's the case with yours, just do your mixing with gloved hands. If you are mixing by hand it should take you 5 to 10 minutes, by mixer 1 to 2 minutes.

A note on myosin. When you blend meat, myosin is a protein that reacts kind of like gluten does in bread. You want to mix until you start to see these myosin strands forming. Mixing by blender or by hand will make a nice tight bind when done. Fresh sausages that have been lightly mixed, and haven't properly activated the myosin, will just crumble. (I'm sure you've had sausage that's done this.) The longer you mix the chorizo, the tighter the bind. (That said, I don't want to encourage overmixing here.) This is an important step in sausage-making, and it's good to begin by doing this by hand so that you can get a feel for it. Don't taste the resulting blend raw (unless you really want to). You can kind of get an idea of how the final product will taste by doing so but it's not too accurate. Just trust us. We've done the math for you.

Pack it into the stuffer. Now's the time to pack the meat mixture down into the corners of your stuffer. Try to eliminate as much air as possible in this stage. Wear gloves to do this or spend a lot of time washing your hands.

Insert the hopper and lower the press of the stuffer. Or get whatever stuffer attachment that you're using ready. Have your rinsed and soaking casings next to you and begin stuffing. You want the chorizo to be tight in the casing but not split. Push the limit, but be sensitive— it's a fine line between over- and under-stuffing. Keep in mind that casings are a natural product, so they're not standardized. Some are going to be thinner than others and sometimes you'll get a particularly temperamental batch. There's no way around this and it can be very frustrating. Make the sausage whatever length works best for your fermentation and drying setup.

Tie them off. When Josh makes chorizo at home, he usually makes horseshoe shapes out of them by tying one length of string to each end of one larger, 1½-foot-long sausage. This completes the circle and allows the chorizo to cure in a U-shape while hung. This is the easiest way to do it at home. At the restaurant we tie our chorizo off in a more complicated way, but the knots are all pretty easy. Look it up on the Internet, and tie them however you want. Just be sure to cut off any excess casing from the ends when you're done so that there is just ⅛ inch left after the knots.

Prick. Once the chorizo is tied, prick all over with a sanitized casing pricker and squeeze the chorizo a little while doing so in order to force out any remaining air.

pH. Test the pH at the beginning as well as at the end of fermentation by tying off a small section of chorizo in the casing and using whatever you have to pH test it. The chorizo should start fermenting at about 5.7 (pork is naturally about 6), and then 5.3 is where things start to get safe and stable. I try to get my chorizo to 5.1 before I move it from the fermenting to the curing

room—that's the level of acidity that I like flavor-wise as well as safety-wise. If you go to 4.9 or even 4.7, you're getting into more of the San Francisco Molinari salami's tart and tangy flavor profiles. If you only go to 5.3 that almost doesn't even taste fermented to me. This should happen within about 24 hours. Once these get between 5.3 and 5.1, they go into the curing room. I always throw away my test sausage at the end, since it is no longer sterile.

Fermenting and curing closets. At the restaurant we have a small fermenting closet that is right across from the larger curing closet. Do your own research on how you want to set up both at home. People use everything from closets, converted refrigerators, coolers, and attics for both. You want your fermenting closet to be 90% humid and about 70 degrees. Josh uses a big Rubbermaid tub with a seedling heat mat underneath it to get it up to 70 degrees (page 168). You need to have some air circulation in whatever you use. The chorizo will be in there about 24 hours before it goes into the curing room at 5.3 to 5.1 acidity. If the test piece of chorizo is not in that range, you can wait for up to 3 days to see if it gets more acidic. You don't want to ferment for more than 3 days.

Hang the chorizo and spray the mold. Once you've hung your chorizo in the fermenting closet (with pans to collect the drippings underneath and a good deal of space in between the sets so that none are touching), spray it generously with the penicillin water that you made. (You can also make your own mold spray by soaking pieces of casings from older dry-cured meats. We won't go into that here. Do your own research.) We usually spray the chorizo again several hours later as well. Aim at the top of the chorizo and work your way down. The mold takes hold during the fermentation stage at the right humidity (around 70% to 80%) and at about 70 degrees. You won't see the mold on the chorizo when it comes out of the fermentation closet and goes into the curing closet, because it takes about a week for it to really take hold. The longer you cure, generally, the thicker the mold; the thicker

Josh has only ever had one batch of salami that never dropped below 5.5, that got stuck. He had to throw it out. He thinks that maybe it had to do with how it was ground. The fat and meat smeared a little too much and he thinks that that kept the bacteria from moving around the sausage properly. That said, you most likely won't en-counter this or any other problems if you follow our recipes.

the casing, generally, the thicker the mold too, because it has a better foundation to stick to. The mold helps regulate drying; it's also a good inhospitable barrier against less desirable molds.

Move into the curing closet. After 24 hours in the fermentation closet, and once the chorizo is at the right acidity level, transfer it to your 55 degree, 70% to 80% humidity curing closet or space. Keep them at least 4 inches apart; none should be touching. Eyeball them every couple of days to see how they're doing. Unless something happens with the humidity level, the curing will usually move along without a hitch. Josh came in from his weekend once and the curing closet was at 55% humidity, which is a little low. He quickly adjusted the humidity and the chorizo turned out fine.

Store. Once the chorizo has finished curing, after about a month, it keeps while in that safe pH range of 5.3 or lower. At home, Josh vacuum seals his chorizo. You can wrap them in butcher paper or parchment paper if you don't have a sealer. Just know that if you store them in either paper they'll continue to dry out. You could pull them a little early and let them keep drying in paper. But there's nothing that beats vacuum sealing once your chorizo's reached the perfect level of dryness. Once your chorizo has been vacuum sealed and refrigerated, it'll last you at least 6 months.

Problems. Josh had problems with drying with some of the first salami and chorizo that he made at home. While they were curing, they weren't separated enough; they didn't have enough exposure to air and didn't dry evenly. One batch had a yeast breakout as a result and he had to get rid of it all. It's important to leave at least 4 inches between each link. Getting the percentage of salt just right was another of the big hurdles, but lucky for you we've suffered through that one so that you don't have to.

DIY MEAT CURING SETUP

JOSH: The book that got me started was *Charcuterie: The Craft of Salting, Smoking, and Curing* by Michael Ruhlman, which came out in 2005. When I was first starting out, I made basic cures like prosciutto, which you just salt overnight and hang. That's pretty much it. I did that, along with bacon and other simple cures.

When I was initially hired at Toro Bravo, it was for a prep-cook position. At that point, I'd been doing charcuterie at home for maybe four or five years. John was interested in expanding Toro's charcuterie, so I learned how to make and link sausage and started researching salami.

I focused on chorizo at first because I knew that if I nailed that, and John liked it, we'd have a million uses for it—it could go in paellas, it could go in cataplanas— and maybe that would persuade him to build a curing room at Toro Bravo.

I made chorizo at home using a plastic storage container and an old-but-working refrigerator to ferment and dry-cure my chorizo, respectively. My third or fourth batch came out pretty good and I brought some of it to John to taste. After tasting it, he said, *Let's do it. Let's build a meat-curing room.* He told me I'd have to give him some time, but that we'd make it happen. John is nothing if not a man of his word, and it did happen—about six months later.

If you're not ready to build yourself a meat-curing room, and MacGyvering yourself a smaller scale DIY meat-curing setup is more your speed, I'll tell you exactly how to do it.

Making your own dry-cured meats requires two basic things: a place for the salami to ferment and a place for the salami to cure. That initial fermentation happens in a pretty hot environment; the second stage of meat-curing needs to happen in a humid, but colder climate.

My home meat-curing refrigerator took a while to get dialed in. Setting the temperature was easy, but getting the humidity level right was trickier. You can put a humidifier in your curing fridge but if it's on all the time you'll get black mold, yeasts, and other malevolent characters from too much humidity. Another problem is that even on the lowest setting, most humidifiers will run out of water in a day or two. If you run out of water and the humidity drops below 50 percent, the casings dry out and whatever is curing becomes compromised.

So I got a humidistat, which is exactly what it sounds like: a thermostat for humidity. You plug the humidifier into your humidistat and once the air reaches a certain level of humidity the humidifier turns off.

That worked well, but I still had issues with too much humidity. I tried propping the door of the refrigerator open a bit in order to get some air in, which worked okay but was still hard to control and not ideal. Someone online suggested cutting a hole in the refrigerator and installing a computer fan. I was hoping to avoid that—once you cut a hole in a refrigerator there's really no going back—but I bit the bullet and got out the drill. I drilled a hole for the computer fan and then drilled a smaller hole on the opposite side of the refrigerator, on the upper part, which gave it some cross-ventilation.

It worked. Once I installed the computer fan, conditions were perfect. I set the fan running at a very low speed so that there was a constant flow of fresh air dehumidifying the refrigerator at the same time it was being humidified. With the computer fan, I could leave everything unattended for four or five days until the water in the humidifier ran out and I had to refill it. Prior to that I was checking on the refrigerator constantly.

The humidistat is an essential piece of equipment because without it, the humidifier is on all the time.

The other thing that I had to figure out was how and where to ferment salami. For salami to ferment it needs to be in an environment that's warm (around 70 degrees) and humid (around 90 percent).

Building a fermentation chamber was pretty easy. It required one trip to Home Depot and maybe 60 bucks worth of crap. A couple hours later I had something that worked pretty well: basically just a Rubbermaid tub with some holes drilled into it, some PVC piping running along the top of it for the salami to hang from, and a seedling heat mat, which keeps whatever you put on top of it about 10 degrees warmer than the ambient temperature. In my basement that usually translates to 70 or 75 degrees, which is perfect for fermenting salami.

The hardest thing for me when figuring out my home meat-curing setup was all the contradictory information out there. This setup is my take. It's not going to be the absolute solution for every single reader, especially since there are so many different factors. If you live in Arizona, for example, you're going to have vastly different climate challenges than we do in Oregon. That said, I think that this setup can work just about anywhere with minor adjustments. This is a good jumping-off place.

I bet some of you are thinking, *I have a really consistently cool basement or cellar, does that negate the need for having a curing refrigerator?* I've heard people say, *Oh I just hang my salamis from the rafters and they do fine.* Maybe that's true but I've never wanted to find out. It's a long and expensive test and by my logic, knowing the ideal parameters for temperature and humidity, most basements don't offer that. It might work, but I have no desire to find out the hard way. Some people will take a cold part of their basement or cellar, drape it in plastic, and then once a day or so go in with a spray bottle and spritz water to keep the humidity

level up. If you want to try something like that, by all means go for it, but I can't personally attest to whether it will work or not, and I can't guarantee the success of your salami.

Once it's fully assembled, my setup is pretty low maintenance. You need to refill the humidifier every five to ten days. You need to wipe everything down and keep it clean. And that's about it.

Once you get things running smoothly, and you get the parameters dialed in, you can figure out how to make the best use of your fermenting and curing spaces. You can get twenty-plus pounds of cured meat going all at once with this setup. I typically have a small batch of chorizo or a couple small batches of salami and then a few coppas and some bresaola going all at once. Just

be careful not to make your salamis too long. If you're making long straight salamis don't let them touch the bottom of the refrigerator or tub. Keep the strings that they hang from short.

Basically, you never want your salamis to be touching anything else. If they touch each other, they'll feed each other moisture and then you'll get weird molds and yeasts and things like that. I've lost a batch once by hanging my salami too close. The moisture had nowhere to go and the salamis ended up with bad molds. Ideally, you want 4 inches between each product. Pack your fridge to the gills just as long as everything has at least 4 inches of breathing room.

Here's what you need to make your own DIY home setup.

DRYING CHAMBER

A working refrigerator
The size and type doesn't matter as long as the fridge runs and has a working seal on the door. You can use a mini fridge but if you want to do whole-muscle cures like coppas that take several months it's nice to have a full-sized fridge.

55 degrees is the ideal temperature for drying. If you want to use the refrigerator again for its intended use, after drilling the intake/outtake holes in it, just plug in the holes and set it to 40 degrees and you'll be good to go.

Thermostat

I used industrial Velcro to attach the thermostat but you can also just screw it in. Velcro is obviously less permanent, which is why I used it. The refrigerator plugs into the thermostat, and the thermostat plugs into your power source. This additional thermostat overrides the refrigerator's thermostat.

Humidistat and humidistat

You'll plug the humidifier into the humidistat. The humidistat plug goes out the door. I set the humidistat at 75 degrees or so. When the humidity level drops below 75 degrees, the humidifier kicks on. You're aiming for between 70 and 80 percent humidity.

Extra thermometer and humidistat or all-in-one

I like to have an extra thermometer in the drying fridge for peace of mind. It's the same reason that I use two humidistats—just to make sure that everything is where it should be. At the restaurant we use a little digital temperature/humidity sensor and it's a little more expensive all-in-one but it's a quick, easy, reliable read.

Computer fan

For a standard sized refrigerator you'll want a roughly four-inch computer fan. If you use a much larger fridge, of course, you'll want a larger fan. I went to RadioShack and just picked out a fan that I thought looked about right (it's listed on their site as a "four-inch cooling fan"). Fortunately for me it was. These types of fans are built to go inside desktop computer towers so they're quiet and small.

Enercell Universal 1000mA AC Adapter

This part allows you to plug the computer fan into an outlet and adjust the fan speed. A computer fan, right out of the box, is wired to be put into a computer tower and run off the tower's electricity. This adapter just allows you to power the fan without the computer and control speed. I keep mine either on the lowest speed or the next to the lowest speed. People with professional charcuterie operations are generally aiming for one mile an hour to five miles an hour speed: a really slow draft. You don't want it to be a wind because that will lead to drying out the casings. I also got this part at RadioShack.

Cutting the holes

You need to cut out two two- to three-inch holes in the sides of the refrigerator—one for the electrical and the other one for the computer fan. What I did is pretty amateur because I'm not a super-handy person. I just bought a hole saw with a drill bit. I used a hole saw and cut four holes and then used a hacksaw to connect them.

The hole for the electrical is dual-purpose because it's also a source of fresh air. The fan is pushing old air out and the other hole allows fresh air to come in. The two holes create a cross-flow of fresh air. Ideally you want the two holes to be as far away from one another as possible. You could probably do a cleaner job than I did with the holes; you could rim them with PVC so that there's no exposed Styrofoam.

When/if you want to use your refrigerator again for its intended use you can just stuff the holes. I used a piece of Styrofoam packaging that I found around the house, and I put that in one hole flush against the fridge wall, then I just shoved a towel in the other hole.

Carabiners and dowls

I usually use carabiners for hanging my salamis because they make moving things around in the refrigerator pretty easy. One thing that I've found with this type of a setup is that you're going to get little pockets that have better airflow than others. Every week or so I'll take something out, make sure it's okay, and then put it back in a different spot. That keeps things under similar conditions. Ideally when something goes from the fermentation to the drying chamber, it's going to be better off with a little bit more humidity early on and a little bit less airflow. As it gets closer and closer to being done, it can be in a slightly drier environment with more airflow.

FERMENTATION TUB

Rubbermaid

I have an eighteen-gallon snap-top Rubbermaid tub for fermentation.

Fermentation only lasts for a day or two. The humidity level just needs to be high, at 90-something percent. That's easy to do. You just turn on a humidifier and it's good to go.

Cutting the holes

Again, I did it the amateur way and used a hole saw to cut the holes into my tub so that I could fit the PVC piping through.

Humidifier

You can use the refrigerator humidifier or if it's in use you'll need another one. You don't need a humidistat for the fermentation tub. I don't blast humidity but I turn it on really low so it's just constantly adding humidity and keeping the tub pretty swampy. You want it really humid to get that surface mold going. The culture needs a warm, moist environment to thrive.

PVC piping

This is a half-inch-wide PVC or nylon piping to hang the meat from that runs the length of the Rubbermaid. (I used wooden dowels originally but I think that they were a source of mold so I stopped using them.) And then you need inch-wide PVC or

nylon piping for the humidifier to pump into. With a really small humidifier you could even just drop the humidifier directly into the tub.

Seedling heat mat

One of these set under the Rubbermaid tub brings the internal temperature up about 10 degrees. In my basement that translates to the 70 to 75 degree range which is generally the temperature range that you want to be in during most meat ferments.

Ridgerest

You can get these foam sleeping pads at any outdoor store. I put one of these down on my basement floor, then I put the seedling heat mat on top of that and the Rubbermaid on top of the seedling heat mat. It basically gets the heat mat off of the basement floor and eliminates some of the cooling properties of the floor.

Thermometer for tub

Your fermentation tub should hover right around 72 degrees. I use a greenhouse thermometer, but any thermometer will do. You just want the temperature between 68 and 75 degrees.

Sherry Chicken-Liver Mousse
SERVES 25

This is a variation of a chicken-liver mousse that was always on the menu at Café Zenon. Theirs tended to be a little livery for my taste, so I upped the dairy in mine. I know it sounds funny—well, cheesy—to have cream cheese in something like this but that's what makes it special. A lot of people add cream to their liver mousse because it stabilizes it, but I don't like the consistency. A really good mousse should have a lot of air whipped into it and be mostly protein. When you start adding cream, you get a looser product. This recipe is a variation of an old Julia Child recipe that included cream cheese. If you've got a problem with it, take it up with Mrs. Child. RIP.

This recipe is incredibly adaptable. Over the years I've made this mousse appropriate to almost everywhere I've worked. When I was working in Italian restaurants, we'd do a Marsala wine chicken-liver mousse, in French restaurants I made it with Madeira, at Viande we did a bourbon chicken-liver mousse. If I change the spirit or wine, I switch up the spices and herbs as well. This is a very playful recipe and hopefully once you've got the techniques down, you'll make your own variations of it too.

Get really good livers for this and never use frozen ones. Be vigilant about the quality of your livers: you want them really red, and cleaned well. You don't want to see any browning, or dark or white spots on them. Our purveyors know to give us the best. We go through five to eight pounds of liver a week.

You can keep this mousse for about five days, but whatever you do, don't freeze it. If you want to make this large of a recipe at home, but you're worried about the quantity, make it around the holidays, take it to parties all week, and give out containers of it as gifts.

Making our chicken-liver mousse is a workout. Your arms will do a lot of maneuvering and lifting, and you've got to move fast. If you're lagging while making this it'll break on you and then it's fucked. I suggest making this either a day before you want to eat or serve it, or on the morning of that day.

After fifteen years of making this mousse I won't lie: I've definitely gotten a little sick of the process. I've made it thousands of times and every one of those times we ramekined it out for each person. There's a reason why I always come back to it though—it's that fucking good. Even my eight-year-old daughter loves it. When Ruby comes to Toro she always orders the Sherry Chicken-Liver Mousse. She asks for nothing with it and eats it with a spoon. I kid you not.

7½ pounds chicken livers

2 tablespoons salt

1 tablespoon pepper

2 pounds + 2 tablespoons unsalted butter

1½ pounds bacon (cheaper ends and pieces work well here)

3 yellow onions, roughly julienned

2 large or 3 small sweet and slightly tart apples (we usually use Galas or Braeburns)

20 cremini mushrooms, sliced

8 to 12 sage leaves, roughly chopped

4 rosemary leaves, roughly chopped

1 teaspoon ground cinnamon

1 tablespoon paprika

2 cups cream sherry

¾ pound cream cheese

¼ cup cold heavy cream (in case the mousse begins to break)

A few ice cubes

Prep livers. Line a large baking pan with paper towels and pat the livers dry. Once dried, season the livers with salt and pepper.

Cook bacon. Put a large saucepan and 2 tablespoons of butter over low-medium heat and add the bacon once the pan is warm. As the bacon cooks and slowly renders bring the heat up to high, cooking it for a total of 3 to 5 minutes.

Cook everything but the livers. Add the onions, apples, and mushrooms to the pan and stir, until the onions are clear and just beginning to caramelize. (At this point our photographer David would like to point out that: "It smells like Thanksgiving.") Add the herbs and spices to the pan and let them bloom for a minute or so. Deglaze the pan with the sherry so that everything is floating in the liquid, stir well,

and keep the pan on high heat until all of the sherry evaporates which should take 4 to 5 minutes. Once you hear the pan start to sizzle again you're not braising anymore; you're sautéing. Remove the pan from the heat and set it aside.

Cook the livers. Heat 2 large cast-iron pans over high heat. Add 2½ tablespoons of butter to each pan. Once the butter is melted and about to start browning—when the bubbles and sizzling have stopped—put all the livers quickly in the pan. Be careful because the livers will try to spit hot oil at you. The more you dry them the less they'll pop, although livers naturally have a lot of water in them. There are 2 reasons you want to dry your livers well: to save your ass (more particularly, your face), and to get a nice sear.

Don't touch the livers. Let them hang out in the pan for about 2 minutes. You want them to start to gray around the edges before you flip them. When you think you should flip them, wait 30 more seconds. You're aiming to cook the livers mostly on one side. Flip the livers and take them off the heat and leave them in the pan for about 30 more seconds as the residual heat continues to cook them. You want the livers to still be very pink in the center. If you overcook them your mousse will be gritty and, to be perfectly honest, it will suck.

Blend. You have to work very quickly from here on out, or your mousse will break. In a large blender combine the rest of the butter and all the remaining ingredients (except for the heavy cream and ice cubes), and blend for 4 to 5 minutes until very smooth. If your blender is too small, do this in equal-part-ingredient batches. The mousse can break if either your bacon/herb/sherry braise or the seared livers is too hot. If you see that happening and the mousse is emitting a lot of thick steam add cold heavy cream and a couple ice cubes.

Pass the mousse. Once the mousse is blended pass it through a fine sieve. Use a large ladle to help you pass the mousse: push the mousse in circular motion through the sieve and into your small, relatively shallow containers. We use 16 small flaneras and a few bowls for this sized batch. If you've done a shitty job blending the mousse the sieve will be full and the mousse hard to pass. If it's easy to pass, you know you've done a good job. Do this part quickly too. You'll see the mousse getting tighter as it cools and this is why you can't take a break between blending and passing/moving it because the fats and solids will

separate and the mousse will break. It wants to set. I haven't let a lot of people in my life make this recipe. The very first time I let an employee make it she decided to take a cigarette break between blending and passing the mousse. By the time she came back the entire batch was broken. That's one of the last times that I truly yelled at someone. I was pissed. You absolutely cannot let this liver mousse cool before you move

it through the sieve and into your serving containers.

Let it set. Once you've filled all the containers you'll see the fat rising to the top. Wrap your mousse in plastic wrap, pressing the plastic directly on the surface of the mousse. You don't want any browning from oxidization. Let the mousse cool completely. Invite all your friends over. Serve.

Duck-Liver Mousse Terrine
SERVES 25

Bill was the only one who got to make the liver terrines at Café Zenon. One day he came to me and said, *All right, I trust you now; you can do it.* He left me the recipe and didn't talk me through any of the steps. I remember being really intimidated and daunted and it took me all day and night to make. I made a mistake and used the wrong duck fat—stuff that had been used for confit rather than freshly rendered duck fat. Although Bill had been making these terrines forever and everyone loved them, my mistake resulted in a terrine that was actually better than Bill's. I remember the co-owner telling Bill, *That kid made better terrines than you!* Bill gave me some shit about not being consistent, of course, but he wasn't actually upset. This is a great recipe, and if you mess something up, it'll probably forgive you. The recipe came from *The Professional Charcuterie Series* (page 158), but we changed it at Zenon and we've changed it at Toro as well, and now it's just a telephone version of the original.

This is a much more refined terrine compared to the Sherry Chicken-Liver Mousse (page 174). It's super smooth and we set it in a mold. But as with our Sherry Chicken-Liver Mousse, you have to be absolutely committed to making our duck liver terrine the moment you start. You can't walk away. I can't stress this enough. This is a very temperamental recipe and if you screw it up there's no saving it. I guarantee that the first time you make this terrine it will take you all day, especially if you prep it the same day that you make it. It's a lot of work. We prep it the day before now so that when someone comes in they can just go at it.

Throughout this recipe you'll be layering in the salt, sugar, and spice with every step. The spices react differently depending on what's done to them. You tease out certain flavors from them when they're boiled and reduced to a syrup, cooked in milk, bloomed in a sauté, and added raw with the livers. Each step is important to the nuanced and complex final result.

We serve our duck-liver terrine with sidra mustard, some soft bread, crostini, and pickles. You can serve it with cornichons like we did at Zenon.

Epices Fines

This is a large batch of herbs and spices that can be used in all sorts of charcuterie. Make a batch and keep it contained and refrigerated for up to a month. You will use 2 teaspoons of this in these terrines in the Salt and Sugar Mix.

½ cup pepper, finely ground

¼ cup bay leaf, finely ground

¼ cup ground cloves

¼ cup ground coriander

¼ cup ground nutmeg

¼ cup paprika

¼ cup dried thyme

2 tablespoons dried oregano

2 tablespoons cinnamon

1 tablespoon juniper, ground

Salt and Sugar Mix

2 ounces kosher salt

1 ounce curing salt #1

½ ounce sugar

2 teaspoons pepper

2 teaspoons Epices Fines

2 teaspoons ground coriander

2 teaspoons paprika

Terrine

3 pounds duck livers (They should be clean and red and not too fatty. All livers have fat, but fattier livers are bigger and duller. You can feel when a liver is fatty because, just like foie gras, it gets engorged. Keep that dick joke to yourself.)

6 pounds fatback

8 cups milk

1 bottle of ruby port

1 quart Chicken Stock (page 291)

2 ounces dried morels (We use dried morels because when dried they get this big, smoky flavor. We reconstitute them with chicken stock and spices and once they're cooked and soft again, we take the stock and reduce it to a syrup. That reduced stock is a morel smoke bomb that adds so much flavor to the terrine. Morels always grow in pine and the best come up after a forest fire so they naturally pick up that smokiness. The dried ones seem to have more of that smokiness in there.)

1½ pounds rendered duck fat

1 quart sliced shallots

14 egg yolks

1 quart heavy cream

24 slices of Nueske's double Applewood-smoked bacon (for the terrine molds)

Divide the livers in half. Half will go through the grinder with the boiled fatback. Dry the other half with paper towels and season them with a tablespoon of the epices fines, a teaspoon of the salt/sugar mix, and a teaspoon of pepper.

Prep fatback. Cut the fatback into strips that will fit into your grinder, then place them in a large stockpot over high heat along with the milk, half of the bottle of ruby port, 1 tablespoon of the epices fine, and 1 tablespoon of the salt/sugar mix. Bring the pot to a simmer, lower the heat to medium-high and let it simmer. A lot of the old French recipes just boil the fat in water but I think that the milk adds a nice creaminess. You have to deal with the foam as a result; skim it off and discard it as it rises to the

surface. Once the strips of fatback have turned translucent (like cooked bacon fat), after about 10 minutes, remove the pan from the heat. Any bacteria in the fat will die after being simmered for 10 minutes. Simmering also softens the fat for the grinder.

Rehydrate morels. In a medium saucepan over medium-high heat pour the chicken stock, add the dried morels, 1 teaspoon of the epices fines, and 1 teaspoon of the salt/sugar mix. Bring to a light boil and cook the morels for 5 to 10 minutes until they're soft. Strain the morels through a fine sieve, taking care to reserve the stock. Press the morels into the sieve with the back of a spoon in order to get all of the liquid out without breaking up the mushrooms. Set the morels aside, return the stock to the heat, and reduce it at a boil to a thick syrup until it's about ¼ cup or until you can make a line in the bottom of the pan that holds. This should take about 20 minutes.

Grind. Once the fat is soft and slightly translucent strain it and discard the milk. Take the fat and half of the livers (the ones you haven't seasoned or dried) and finely grind them both in your grinder. I like to grind the fatback first and the liver afterward so that the hot

fatback doesn't cook the raw liver. Slice the morels, put them in a large bowl, and set it aside.

Cook the livers. Put 2 tablespoons of duck fat into each of the 2 large nonstick pans over high heat (4 tablespoons total). Let the pans get ripping hot and then sear off the dried and seasoned livers. (You don't want to use cast-iron here because you'll be using the same pans for the shallots and iron isn't good for them.) You want the livers to get really darkly browned on the bottom. This will take about a minute in a very hot pan. Once cooked, remove them from the heat and the pan and set them aside. If you pull them apart, they should still be pinkish on the inside.

Cook shallots with port. Put those still-hot pans back over the heat, lowering the flame to medium-high, and add the shallots. Sauté for about 1 minute before adding the rest of the epices fines and salt/sugar mix. Sauté the shallots until they gain some color, a few minutes. Add the rest of bottle of port to the pans in equal portions. (The port should flame up and then quickly die down.) Combine the contents of the 2 pans, and let the port in the mixture cook down into a syrup, a couple minutes. Add the reduced chicken/morel stock to the shallots, and stir

to incorporate. Remove the pan from the heat, and combine the contents with the cooked and raw duck livers and fatback.

Emulsify. Now you have all of your mise en place, it's time to take the big blender out. If you have a large industrial blender, you'll be able to pour about half of the liver slurry along with 10 yolks, most of the cream, and a little less than a quart of the duck fat. Start the blender. No matter what the size of your blender, combine the components in equal parts so that you get a good emulsification. That *g-gunk* sound that usually happens at 2 to 3 minutes or so is your signal that the emulsification is coming together. Once this happens, you want to continue blending for another minute or so. You want your duck-liver terrine to be very smooth. We're used to our big beast of a Waring blender making all sorts of loud noises. It often sounds like I dropped my keys in it.

Be patient. Keep in mind that this emulsification does not come together until the end. We have to emulsify this protein and fat mixture, and it has to be just the right temperature. At first it will be loose and you'll see the proteins mixing together and then you let it go a little longer and all of the sudden it sets. Unlike any other type of emulsification, this one begins broken and then all of the sudden it comes together. I've had so many sous chefs say, *Oh shit, oh shit it's not emulsifying* and I say, *Just wait*. Then, boom! All of the sudden everything tightens up and comes together. This is often the case with terrines.

Blend again. Once the first batch is blended, spatula it out into your large bowl with the sliced morels and set to emulsifying the second batch with the remaining milk, cream, duck fat, and egg yolks. No matter how big your blender is, just add the ingredients in equal parts for each batch and blend them all the same way that you blended the first batch, until the contents emulsify. Add the emulsification to the bowl and

---

The first time I ever used one of these blenders I was making mussel fumé at Café Zenon. I cooked all of these mussels off and then I was going to blend them and pass them for the soup. I had this liquid that I put in the blender with the mussels. I hit go without covering the blender and it rained boiling liquid everywhere. BLAM! I turned it off but by then it was empty and I was covered in mussel juice. Make sure the lid's really on your blender before you blend, unless you want to be covered in the equivalent of a meat milkshake.

stir to incorporate. At this point, it will look spot-on like a chocolate milkshake. If it's April Fool's Day you are in luck.

Taste. Now you've got the entire batch emulsified and mixed together with the morels, you've gotta get over yourself and try a little raw liver because you want to make sure that it's all right. Remember that whenever you serve something cold that's been hot, that saltiness significantly goes away. So, you want this to taste slightly too salty at this temperature.

Line terrine molds with bacon. We used to get these big pigs when we first started making these terrines and they had this backfat that was a few inches thick and we'd slice these beautiful slices and line our terrines with it. I've had a hard time getting that lately so now we line our 4 classic-sized terrine molds with 24 strips of bacon slightly overlapped. (See the photos on the previous page for what I mean.) Once you've lined the molds with bacon, pour the liver mix into them. Fold the bacon over the top, put parchment paper cut to size of the tops over each mold, and then wrap the tops tightly in foil. Put the terrine molds in a hotel pan and add water up to about three-quarters the height of the pan using cold water. The idea is to bring the temperature up slowly in the oven.

That's why you want to start with cold water.

Cook slow and low. When you have an emulsification like this, it's delicate. If it gets too hot in the oven, it's going to separate. We want to start it at a very, very low temperature in the beginning and then we bring the heat up little by little. We start the terrines in the oven at 275 degrees for a half hour and turn it up to 325 degrees for another 90 minutes. Place the terrines in the oven wherever they will get the best circulation—usually on a rack smack dab in the middle. Start checking the temperature of the middle of the terrine at 90 minutes. (Bill Hatch taught me to cut a puncture through the foil to get into the terrine first so you don't get any foil in it. Cut a little hole first and then go in.) You want to pull the terrines out when they get to 155 or 160 degrees internally. You will most likely need another 30 minutes at 325 degrees to get to 155 or 160 degrees.

Done! Remove the terrines once they've reached the right temperature. Cool them or put them directly into your refrigerator or walk-in. We usually weigh them down slightly with another terrine on the top. Slice and serve once completely cooled.

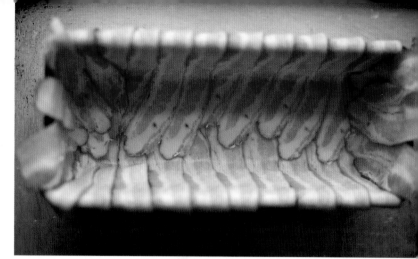

Pork Rillettes
4 QUARTS

Rillettes are sometimes served cool, sometimes at room temperature, and sometimes hot. You can bake them and serve them on bread. It all just depends on your preference. When we first opened we were trying different rillettes on for size—chicken, rabbit, and pork—when, one day, we made one of our simplest renditions. We took pork shoulder, then dried, confited, and smoked it. That was it. It was so good that that's been our confit ever since. The great thing about confits is that—because they're preserved with fat—they keep for a very long time. That was how rillettes came to be—a way to preserve certain meats in fat.

1 boneless pork shoulder, 8 pounds (that's a little on the larger side; shoulder generally ranges from 5 to 9 pounds)

¼ cup salt

¼ cup pimentón (or other smoked paprika, something sweet and not at all spicy)

¼ cup paprika

2 quarts duck fat (pork fat will work too)

1 yellow onion, finely diced

½ to 1 tube harissa (harissa spice levels can really vary)

1 cup honey

Slice the shoulder into 2-inch cubes. It is very important to keep these pieces consistent in size so that they all cook properly.

Season and cure the meat. Sprinkle the cuts of meat with the salt, dredge them in the mix of pimentón and paprika, and let the cure absorb into the unwrapped meat in the refrigerator overnight.

Smoke. The next day take the meat out of the refrigerator and smoke it for 30 minutes at 100 degrees to impart the meat with smoky flavor but not cook it at all.

Melt the duck fat. We use our duck fat for our rillettes 3 times before recycling it. It gets a little orange from the paprika. You just want the duck fat to get to melting point—but not too hot, because if so, it will fry the outside of the meat.

Cook the confit. Pour the melted duck fat over the sliced, cured, and smoked meat, cover it and put it in an oven set to 350 degrees. A dutch oven or Le Creuset is ideal for this because of the way it regulates heat. Use whatever pot you can fit the meat into in one layer in along with the melted duck fat. Put a layer of parchment over the meat and fat first and then foil if don't have a dutch oven. You want a very slow simmer for this throughout its cook time and very minimal bubbling. Check it periodically and adjust the oven temperature accordingly. Avoid a rapid boil because that will fry the meat. After an hour bring the temperature of the oven down to 250 degrees and cook it for 2 to 3 hours.

The meat is done when you can push into it with a fork or tongs and it easily falls apart. Every once in a while a cook tries to rush this step by cranking up the heat and winds up with meat that's too cooked. If there is any crust on the shoulder it won't let the fat emulsify into the meat.

Cool the confit. Remove from the oven and let cool to room temperature before putting in the refrigerator uncovered overnight (or up to a month). The whole purpose is to preserve meats in fat.

Bring back up to temperature. After a day (or up to a month) later bring the meat and fat back up to temp in the oven at 300 degrees for about 30 to 35 minutes, until the duck fat is melted and warm. Take all the meat out and set it aside. Pour 2 cups of the fat into a large sauté pan over medium-high heat and sauté the onion, harissa, and honey for 3 to 5 minutes, or until the onion is translucent.

Emulsify. Put the meat along with the onion/harissa/honey/duck fat sauté into your mixer (any mixer will do just fine for this) along with the remaining fat and seasoning and mix on low for 5 to 10 minutes or until the meat is emulsified. You want all of that duck fat to emulsify into the meat, and you want the meat to take in as much fat as it can before separating. Taste it to make sure that there is enough fat and adjust accordingly.

Portion. Cool and portion the rillettes into cazuelas or other small ovenproof dishes and bake until the rillettes are hot all the way through with a nice crust on top. We cook our rillettes to order at 450 degrees for 8 to 10 minutes.

Bacon

10 POUNDS

Making bacon isn't hard and just takes a little time and space. In the spring at Toro Bravo we ramp up bacon production to be prepared for all the Ts that are coming into season for BLTs. Four or five bellies of bacon usually last us about a week. When we make eight times this recipe and fill several sheet and hotel pans with pork jowls and bellies it looks like a giant, morbid patchwork quilt. And yes, *Silence of the Lambs* jokes are made. I'll say this though: if you're a cook on bacon prep, your hands are going to feel as soft and pretty as a little girl's when you're through.

NOTES: *We normally make pork belly and jowl bacon but once in a while, when we get lamb belly, we'll make bacon out of that with the same cure. Once you've conquered this recipe, try it with lamb belly.*

Be as accurate as possible with the pink salt (aka curing salt) here because too much can be bad for you. Pink salt (named for its pinkish-coral color) basically keeps meat from browning/graying when you cook it. It keeps the meat pinkish but doesn't do much more than that.

---

1 pork belly whole or 2 jowls (about 10 pounds)

1 cinnamon stick

2 tablespoons whole coriander

2 tablespoons juniper berries

2 cups brown sugar

1 cup salt

1 tablespoon ground pepper

1 tablespoon paprika

½ ounce curing salt (aka pink salt)

Skin the jowl. If using pork jowl, be sure to remove the skin—ideally with a long curved knife, or with your longest and sharpest knife. Remove the glands if they haven't been removed already.

Grind and mix the dry cure. Using your mortar and pestle, grind the cinnamon, coriander, and juniper berries each in separate batches until they're roughly the consistency of coarsely ground coffee. Use a towel to cover the mortar while you do this so that you don't lose the spices as you grind them. In a large bowl, mix all the ingredients except for the pork by hand, making sure to break up all of the clumps of sugar. Imagine you're a kid in a sandbox. Also, if you plan to make bacon regularly make a large batch of the salt/spice mix and keep it tightly covered in the fridge. It keeps for a few months.

Apply the dry cure. Place the jowl or belly in a pan that's about the same size and depth as the meat, ½ inch to 1 inch larger in both directions. Rub the seasoning mix over all parts of the pork and coat it. Once entirely coated with the cure place the slab in the pan fat-side-up. Top the meat with the remaining cure. If you're doing multiple bellies or jowls, distribute the remaining dry cure to the tops of all of the meat slabs evenly.

Cure. Place the pan with the meat uncovered in the refrigerator for a week. Eyeball it occasionally throughout the week to make sure that the liquid releases and does not overflow. If you've used the proper-sized pan, the liquid should come up just about to the lip of the pan after a couple days and then remain at that level for the remaining days. You want a pan that's about the size of the bacon so that the entire slab soaks in its juices during the week with the cure mixture.

Smoke. Start your smoker and get it up to 200 degrees. Remove the bacon from the cure. We cold smoke our bacon with hickory in our commercial Cookshack smoker, although we used Big Chief smokers for years. We smoke meats in the mornings through mid day on the restaurant's front stoop. The smoke time will vary from smoker to smoker but you want to get the bacon to an internal temperature of 150 degrees, which should take roughly 2 to 4 hours. Temperature gauges on smokers are very unreliable, so that final temperature is what you're most concerned with. The bacon should be brown and look nicely smoked when it's done. If it gets to the point where it is done smoking but still hasn't been cooked to that 150-degree internal temperature, finish it in the oven at 200 degrees.

Serve and store. Once the bacon has cooled, wrap it tightly in plastic wrap or vacuum seal it if possible. It will keep for several weeks refrigerated, but we usually go through ours in a week. It also freezes well.

Merguez Sausage
10 POUNDS

Any time you do fresh sausage you want everything cold: both your ingredients and your equipment. Meat needs to be between 33 to 35 degrees to emulsify correctly. We make about forty pounds of this a week and Josh usually makes it twice a week since the capacity of our mixer is about twenty pounds. Over time we've punched up the harissa and spice for our Merguez but it's still a straightforward recipe, without too many frills.

At Toro Bravo, we serve our Merguez with french fries, buttermilk cheese, and harissa; at Tasty n Sons we serve a smaller version in sheep casings for breakfast sausages that we serve with couscous, fried eggs, and harissa sauce. My favorite way to eat Merguez is the French street food way: in a soft roll filled with harissa, mayo, and topped with french fries. You can also skip casing this sausage and scramble it loose or use it in soups or stews.

1 bunch cilantro

1 bunch mint (When Moroccan mint is available we use that. Viridian Farms usually has about 20 different types of mint to choose from in the summer.)

5 tablespoons paprika

2 tablespoons whole coriander

2 tablespoons whole cumin

1 tablespoon ground cinnamon

5 tablespoons salt (you might want to add more when you test cook a piece and taste)

1 onion, finely diced

4 tablespoons garlic, minced

3 tubes of harissa (any harissa from France will work well), a little less than 2½ cups

2 to 3 lamb shoulders, 10 pounds total (20% fat is most desirable and that's what you'll get with most lamb shoulder. If your shoulders are particularly dry you'll want to add fatback, and if they are too fatty trim off some of the excess. Really young spring lamb yields a boneless shoulder that's about 3 pounds, but the average lamb shoulder is 3½ to 6 pounds.)

8 meters lamb casings, 28- to 30-millimeters wide

Prep spices, onion, garlic, and harissa. Roll up the cilantro and mint and chiffonade them, then go back over them to get them as light and thin as possible without bruising them. Use your sharpest knife for these because you don't want to over chop. Grind your dried herbs and spices with a mortar and pestle or coffee grinder until fine and measure them out along with the salt into the same container. Refrigerate the spice mix and get your lamb out. Finely dice your onion, mince your garlic, measure out your tubed harissa, and place everything in one container. Refrigerate.

Grind the lamb. You want your equipment as well as your lamb shoulder to be as cold as possible just as you do when you're making our Chorizo (page 162), so if you have room to keep both in your freezer before grinding then do that. Cut the lamb into pieces that will fit into your grinder before freezing it. If you don't have room in your freezer for everything make sure that the meat gets partially frozen (put it in your freezer for 1 to 2 hours and rotate it once or twice during so that it freezes evenly) and make sure that the equipment is as cold as possible and not straight out of the dishwasher.

Apply mineral oil to the grinder in between the blade and the plate. While you are grinding meat and fat you always want to keep a steady stream so that the blade is okay. You'll dull it pretty fast if you leave it on with nothing moving through it. We like to drape plastic wrap over the top of the grinder while grinding so that it doesn't spit out meat. We use a ¼-inch plate for the Merguez and that's the go-to size for most sausages and salamis. On KitchenAid grinder attachments you have large and small settings. Both work well, so just decide which you prefer.

Mix the ingredients. Mix all of the ingredients—except for the casings of course—on NUMBER ONE or LOW in your mixer if it is a larger commercial or industrial mixer, or by hand. Most home mixers are not strong enough for this sort of project, so if that's the case with yours then just do it by hand. By hand this should take you 5 to 10 minutes, by mixer 2 to 5. Refer to the Chorizo recipe if you want to know more about myosin, the protein that reacts similarly as gluten does in order to bind the meat (page 165).

Taste before you case. Once the sausage is well mixed take off a small portion and cook it up in a small piece or patty in a pan over medium-high heat in a little oil for a couple minutes and taste it. Adjust the seasonings accordingly.

Flush the casings. Flush your casings in water before stuffing them and then keep them in a container of lukewarm water next to the grinder.

Pack the stuffer. Pack the meat mixture down well into the corners of your stuffer. Try to eliminate as much air as possible. Wear gloves to do this or be sure that you wash your hands well before and after.

Insert the hopper and lower the press of the stuffer. Or get whatever stuffer attachment that you are using ready. Begin stuffing. You want the Merguez to be tight but to not split, and you want it a little less stuffed than the chorizo since you won't be drying it. Sometimes if you overstuff them they'll burst when cooked.

Remember that casings are a natural product so they're not standardized. Some are going to be thinner than others and sometimes you'll get a particularly temperamental batch. There's no way around this and it can be very frustrating. Make the sausage whatever length works best for your fermentation and drying setup and then twist them and tie off the ends.

Twist the sausage. We make our Merguez 3½ to 4 inches but do whatever you like/whatever works best for you. Do a couple twists for each sausage, twisting each in a different direction so that they don't come undone.

Prick the sausage. Once the Merguez is twisted, prick them all over with a casing pricker and squeeze the sausage a little while doing so in order to force any remaining air out.

Dry and store. Put the Merguez uncovered over paper towels in the refrigerator overnight to tighten up. They'll shrink a little, darken, and be dry to the touch after about 24 hours. Snip the sausages apart at the twists the next morning and then wrap them tightly (they keep 4 to 5 days in the fridge) or cook them. They freeze well for up to a month. If you vacuum seal them, they will keep much longer.

Coppa Steak
10–12 STEAKS

As a kid I hated steak. By now you've probably gathered that my mom was a horrible cook. Pot roast was fine but for love of good food, please not steak. My mom could cook anything decently enough that took a long time to stew. If she could throw it in the crockpot it would turn out decent but anything panfried she burned without fail. We had these family friends that moved to Tybee Island, off of Savannah. The summer between eighth and ninth grade, they invited me to come out for two weeks. I remember my friend's dad going and getting four rib-eyes from the market that were perfect. He seasoned them just right, cooked them to medium-rare and served them up. I thought, *That's steak! It's not chewy, it's not uniformly brown, it's got moisture. I love steak!*

There are a lot of steps to this recipe, but it's not too difficult. Yes, it takes time but in terms of hands-on time—versus curing and drying time where all you have to do is set the timer—it's the equivalent of roasting a chicken. Basically you take an economical but very flavorful cut of beef, salt and dry it, cold smoke it (you can hot smoke it too, see below), wet age it, and finish it off in the oven before serving. If you can't find chuck eye roast at your market then substitute strip loin. And don't hesitate to ask your butcher to trim your roast to get rid of the excess fat, as well as truss it.

One of the most important steps to our coppa is keeping the seasoned meat unwrapped in the refrigerator for one or two days before smoking it. This dries the meat and allows the salt and pepper to penetrate it ensuring a nice crust when grilled. Open-air salt curing also brings out more of the steak's awesome, beefy flavor. We dry off all of our protein this way before service including chicken and pork.

NOTE: *If you substitute strip loin for this recipe always ask for the positive side of the strip loin—the side without the connective tissue—because there is nothing you can do to make that connective tissue any good.*

You can also hot smoke the coppa after salt-curing it in the refrigerator all the way until it's ready to serve in a Weber or gas grill with wood chips. It will read 118 to 120 degrees when it is finished cooking, after about 20 to 30 minutes at 300 to 350 degrees.

5 pound chuck eye rib roast (makes about 10 steaks)

2 tablespoons salt and pepper mix (5 parts salt, 1 part pepper)

More salt and pepper for grilling

2 cups Salbitxada (page 282)

Truss. You don't need to trim the meat unless you see bone fragments. If you don't truss the rib roasts then you won't get an even cook or that nice even medium rare all the way through. We take a length of string and make tight circular loops with slip knots all along it. Basically you want it to look like the photo to the left. You can find all sorts of videos online that will teach you how to truss.

Salt and pepper. This cut is very forgiving and it's hard to overdo the seasoning so err on the liberal side. The larger and thicker the cut of meat the more salt you want to use. Once the meat is trussed liberally season the chuck eye with the kosher salt and pepper mix. Chuck eye rib roasts vary greatly in size so adjust your seasonings accordingly. When the coppas go on the grill, they get salted and peppered again.

Chill. Refrigerate the meat uncovered in the fridge overnight so that it air dries properly.

Cold smoke. The next day remove the meat from the refrigerator and smoke it in a 70 to 80 degree smoker for 30 minutes. Our smoker is out front 5 out of 7 days a week here.

Cure. After smoking let the meat sit refrigerated and wrapped in plastic for at least a week and up to 10 days. During this time the meat cures. This technique is a lot like brining meats.

Portion and grill. Slice the roast into 10 or 12 1½-inch thick steaks. Give each of the steaks another hit of salt and pepper and throw them on the hot grill for 10 to 15 minutes per side, until nice and caramelized. Put them in a 450 degree oven for 35 to 40 minutes. You are shooting for an internal teperature of 120 degrees. When I cook the coppa steak at home I usually cook it all the way on the grill over very low-heat coals for 1 hour to 1½ hours until the steaks are 120 degrees internal temperature. No matter how you finish the steaks, always let them rest for 10 to 15 minutes before carving them. Serve with Salbitxada (page 282).

193

Squid Ink Pasta
SERVES 6–8

When Toro first opened, a purveyor brought me an Italian anchovy syrup called colatura, which is basically a fish sauce made in Italy that's similar to Thai fish sauce. This was around the time Kasey was on a real pad thai kick. We had some squid ink pasta lying around so for staff meal we made a bastardized version of pad thai with it—using hazelnuts instead of peanuts and the colatura instead of fish sauce, plus chilies, sprouts, and onions. It was so good that we made it again the next day. Over several weeks we perfected it, and it's been on the menu ever since.

3 tablespoons + 2 teaspoons olive oil

1 medium yellow onion, julienned

Salt and pepper

9 ounces squid ink pasta (Get it online if you can't find it locally. We love the brand Rustichella D'Abruzzo. The family that owns the company bought old abandoned pasta mill and got it back up and running. The pasta is relatively mild in terms of the squid ink. Most Americans prefer that flavor tamed down a bit.)

2 cloves garlic, sliced

1 heaping tablespoon Mama Lil's Mildly Spicy Peppers in Oil (or 1 teaspoon of red chili flakes)

1 cup roasted hazelnuts, lightly crushed in a mortar and pestle

4 egg yolks

1½ to 2 tablespoons fish sauce (we use Red Boat fish sauce)

1. Put a large sauté pan over high heat with 1 tablespoon olive oil. Once hot add the julienned onion and cook it to caramelize. After about 5 minutes add the salt (it will leach out the water) along with the pepper. Lower the heat to medium for 5 minutes, then to low to finish cooking, about 10 to 12 minutes. Remove from heat.

2. Set a large pot of sea-salty water (¼ cup salt, 1 gallon water) to boil for the squid ink pasta. Cook the pasta for 10 to 12 minutes.

3. In a large sauté pan heat 2 tablespoons olive oil over high heat. Cook the garlic, about 30 seconds. Add the Mama Lil's Peppers and cook for another 15 seconds. If the peppers get too hot they like to pop, so be careful.

4. Add the caramelized onions to this pan and then add the lightly crushed hazelnuts and remove from heat.

5. Divide the 4 egg yolks between 2 ramekins (2 yolks in each ramekin). Stir 1 teaspoon of olive oil into each ramekin.

6. Strain the cooked pasta and put the colander over the hot pot to allow it to continue steaming for about 1 minute. Meanwhile, return the hazelnut/chili mix back to high heat.

7. Combine the pasta with the hazelnut sauté, and add the fish sauce a little bit at a time. Using tongs, toss until all of the ingredients are well distributed. Taste and adjust fish sauce. Remove from heat.

8. Serve the pasta divided into 2 medium serving bowls. Make a divot in the center of each bowl slide the 2 yolks with oil onto each bowl. Serve immediately and toss once at the table to incorporate the yolks.

Spicy Octopus and Prawn Stew

SERVES 6–10

There was a point, in the early days of Simpatica, when I really geeked out on coastal Mexican food. Snapper Veracruz is a spicy, saucy, tomato-based braised dish from the namesake town in Mexico. It occurred to me that it could be even better if I replaced the snapper with octopus—octopus is big enough in bite and flavor to stand up to the sauce—and added a piece of grilled bread to soak up all the good stuff. The base here is the pickled jalapeños and spicy tomato sauce—all common ingredients in Veracruz cooking. At Toro, we layer in clove, bay leaf, and cinnamon—making for a lot of subtle, building heat that makes this stew a comfort food, especially in the winter.

When we opened Toro we were playing around with octopus for several different dishes but always grilled it. At the time we were using these baby Mediterranean octopuses that looked like squids and fit in your hand. They were so small that we could cook them to order. They were good, but one problem was that when you blanched these baby ones, they'd get too soft. Grilling them over a ripping-hot grill would have been the ideal way to cook them, but most grills—including ours at Toro—aren't hot enough to grill them properly. A few years down the line, we hooked up with a Spanish fisherman and started sourcing larger deep-water farmed Spanish octopus. It's a far superior product. The size of your octopus really makes a difference and we prefer the medium-sized ones that take a single blanch, usually of an hour to an hour and a half. The really large ones, which are much cheaper, take several blanchings to tenderize.

NOTES: *When sourcing octopus you want the most tender and fresh ones that you can find that don't have a ton of ink in them and aren't too mangled from being caught. Spanish grandmas think that if you put a cork in the water while cooking your octopus that will tenderize it. I don't know if there's any science behind it, but it's an Old World belief.*

Spicy Stew

½ red onion, thinly sliced

2 cloves garlic, thinly sliced

2 tablespoons olive oil

¼ cup Pickled Zucchini (page 279), chopped

5 pickled jalapeños, julienned

1 tablespoon capers

1 28-ounce can tomatoes, blended in a food processor

¼ cup pitted arbequina olives or other good quality green olive, chopped

¼ cup paprika

¼ cup Pickled Zucchini brine (page 279)

2 tablespoons pickled jalapeño brine (from the can)

2 tablespoons parsley, chiffonaded

Spice Bouquet

2 bay leaves

½ cinnamon stick

1 clove

Octopus and Prawns

5 pounds octopus (we use high-quality, deep water farmed, sustainable Spanish octopus)

1 lemon, halved and juiced

1 yellow onion, chopped

1 tablespoon salt

1 tablespoon olive oil

8 wild Gulf prawns (under-15), peeled, cleaned, head and tail

removed, and halved

½ baguette, sliced on an extreme bias into 7½-inch pieces

Salt and pepper

___

For Spicy Stew

1. In a large pan over medium heat sauté the onion and garlic in olive oil, stirring occasionally until the onions are translucent.

2. Add the chopped pickled zucchini, julienned jalapeños, capers, blended canned tomatoes, chopped olives, and both pickle brines, and stir to incorporate. If you put your nose directly over the pan at this point, you're going to cough. It should smell very briney and vinegary.

3. Use a small piece of cheesecloth to tie a small spice bouquet. Break up the bay leaf a bit so that it's a small, tight bouquet.

4. Once the stew is boiling, lower the heat to a simmer, add the spice bouquet and chiffonaded parsley, and lightly simmer for 30 minutes. Remove from heat and take out the spice bouquet.

For Octopus

1. Thaw your octopus.

2. Fill a large pot three-quarters full with water, add the halved lemon into the water, the chopped yellow onion, 1 tablespoon salt, and the octopus and bring to a boil. Once boiling, lower the heat to a simmer and cook the octopus for about 1½ hours.

   NOTE: *Boiled octopus tends to want to float so use a plate that's slightly smaller than the diameter of your pot to keep it submerged as it simmers.*

3. The octopus is cooked when it wants to come apart at the tentacles. Test for doneness by pulling up one tentacle with tongs. When the tentacle starts to feel like it's just about pull apart from the body, it's finished cooking. Remove from the pot, place on a dish to cool and either discard the broth or use it for another purpose. If you're blanching any vegetables, the broth is great for that.

4. Once the cooked octopus is cool enough to handle, remove the head and discard it. (I don't think the head is very good, although others use it to stretch out their octopus. I think it's kind of grainy and doesn't have great flavor.) Slice apart the tentacles and remove the skin and most of the suctions by hand. Toss the skin. It's slimy and stinky and there's no good use for it.

5. Reserve 1 cup of the best-looking cooked octopus tentacle, slice it on a bias into 2- or 3-inch pieces, and skewer it to grill for the Octopus à la Plancha (page 108). Slice the remaining tentacles on a bias into about 2- or 3- inch long pieces for the spicy stew. Skewer these pieces for the grill and reserve the extra thin bits for the sauté pan.

Finish the Octopus and Prawns and serve.

1. Put a large sauté pan over medium-high heat and add 1 tablespoon of olive oil. Once hot add the prawns and any of the octopus that was too small to skewer. Cook for about 2 minutes, tossing the contents.

2. Drizzle all of the skewered octopus with olive oil and season with salt and pepper. Do the same with the sliced baguette. Grill both, turning them regularly for 2 to 3 minutes until they're both nicely charred.

3. Add the stew to the pan with the octopus and prawns, turn off the stove, and let the residual heat finish cooking the stew, about 1 minute.

4. Serve the stew, topping each bowl with the larger 3- to 4-inch slices of octopus, and a slice of grilled baguette. (Remember to reserve the 2-inch grilled pieces of octopus for Octopus à la Plancha.)

Scallops

SERVES 4–6

The first time I had scallops in romesco was at Cal Pep in Barcelona. I really dug them: the sweetness of the scallops against the sweetness of the almonds and the peppers and pimento.

We're sticklers for quality, and you should be too. Make sure when you buy scallops that they're whole and not broken, that they smell sweet and not too fishy, and that they're dry enough that when you squeeze them water doesn't come out (that's a sign that they've been frozen). You also don't want slimy scallops. Slime equals bacteria.

At Toro, we get dry-packed U-10 (fewer than ten per pound) scallops. We use the larger scallops for this because you can get a really good sear on them but still keep them mid-rare on the inside. We also like the larger ones because, generally speaking, the larger the scallop the sweeter the meat.

This dish goes really well with Txakoli or any other bright, acidic, dry, and slightly effervescent white. The scallops and romesco are so rich that it's nice to cut through them with a crisp wine.

---

10 dry-packed, U-10 scallops

Salt and pepper

1 tablespoon butter

1 tablespoon olive oil

10 tablespoons Romesco (page 281)

---

1. Put the scallops on a paper towel to dry (it's very important to dry them well so that they get a good sear). Season a plate with salt and pepper and stick the scallops onto the seasoned plate. Meanwhile, preheat the oven to 400 degrees.

2. Put a large cast-iron pan on high heat and add the butter and olive oil. Heat until the foam of the butter subsides and you don't hear any more sizzling, right as the butter is beginning to brown. No sizzling means that the water has been cooked out of the butter, which is what you want.

3. With tongs, place the scallops into the pan one by one, seasoned side down, being careful not to crowd them. Give them a lot of room, leaving at least an inch between each scallop. Season the unseasoned sides of the scallops with salt and pepper. Cook them on high heat for 2 or 3 minutes, flipping them once. Do not mess with the scallops while they're searing—at ALL. Don't move them or pull them up to check on them or you will break open the skin and release water, which is the opposite of what you want. I always like to say, when it seems like you should flip them, wait another minute.

4. Put the cast-iron pan with the scallops in it into the preheated oven. Cook them for 2 minutes or until the sizzling ceases.

5. Remove the pan from the oven. Transfer the scallops to a new, clean paper towel on a plate to rest and drain.

6. To serve, spread Romesco (page 281) into a circle on the bottom of a cazuela or serving platter, the way you'd spread red sauce on a pizza. Put the scallops on top. At Toro, we mound some Fennel Salad (page 120) around—but not directly on—the scallops.

Moroccan Tuna with Couscous
SERVES 6–8

During Bill's Moroccan period at Zenon, we came up with a Moroccan-style marinade for chicken. That marinade was still kicking around in my head when we got some really nice albacore at Toro. I marinated it, grilled it, and served it over some couscous. People went nuts.

There are a good number of steps in this recipe and I recommend that you start by preparing your marinade and the tuna sauce. You can make the sauce up to a couple days in advance and you want to marinate the tuna for three to twelve hours. Once the tuna sauce and marinade are ready you can quickly and easily prepare your couscous. While the couscous absorbs the spiced water, grill the tuna and reheat your sauce.

Tuna

1. Mortar and pestle the cinnamon, cumin, coriander, paprika, chili, and saffron with a slow and circular grind for about 30 seconds, or until the spices are roughly ground.

2. Combine the mortar and pestle spices with all of the other marinade ingredients in a blender and blend into a loose paste. Add salt and pepper to taste.

3. Using your hands, mix the marinade with the cubed tuna in a nonreactive bowl (glass or ceramic) making sure that all of the pieces are well coated. Cover and refrigerate for at least 3 hours, but no longer than 12 hours.

4. Remove the marinated tuna from refrigerator and put 5 to 6 pieces onto each skewer, not leaving any space between the pieces. You should have enough tuna for 12 to 16 skewers.

5. Grill the tuna over high heat, turning the skewers often and seasoning them with salt and pepper to taste for about 4 to 5 minutes, or until medium-rare.

Tuna sauce

1. Pour the stock and cherries into a small saucepan over high heat, bring to a boil, then lower to a slow simmer, uncovered. Reduce the stock by half (it should take about 45 minutes unattended).

Tuna

2½ pounds albacore tuna, skinned and cleaned, and cut into one inch cubes.

12 to 16 wooden or metal skewers (if the skewers are wooden, soak them in warm water for 10 minutes so that they don't splinter on the grill)

Marinade

1 tablespoon cinnamon, ground

1 tablespoons whole cumin, toasted

1 tablespoon whole coriander, toasted

1 tablespoon paprika

1 teaspoon chili flakes

Pinch of saffron

½ Preserved Lemon, skin chopped (page 275)

½ cup olive oil

Salt and pepper

Tuna sauce

1 pint Chicken Stock (page 291)

1 cup dried cherries

1 tablespoon rose petal harissa, or substitute any other harissa

Juice of ¼ lemon

1 tablespoon butter

Salt and pepper to taste

Couscous

2 cups couscous

2 cups dried cherries

2 tablespoons dried apricots, finely diced

2½ cups water

2 tablespoons salt

1 teaspoon coriander seeds, toasted

1 teaspoon cumin seeds, toasted

1 tablespoon butter

Garnish

¼ cup green onions, julienned

1 lemon, cut into wedges

2. Strain the sauce with a fine sieve or chinois and push all of the liquid from the cherries through. The cherry juice will add flavor and give the sauce a nice, slightly cloudy ruby color.

3. Before serving, bring the sauce to a boil, add the rose petal harissa, lemon juice, and butter. Stir until the butter is melted and incorporated. Season to taste with salt and pepper.

Couscous

1. In a large bowl, mix couscous with cherries and apricots.

2. Pour water into a medium saucepan with salt, coriander, and cumin seeds, over high heat. Bring to a boil and remove from heat.

3. Strain off the spices with a fine sieve or chinois while pouring the hot water directly into the bowl with the couscous and fruit. Stir the couscous to incorporate the water and then cover the couscous tightly with plastic wrap. Let it sit and absorb the spiced water for 20 minutes.

Serve

1. Before serving, add the butter and fluff the couscous with a fork. Add salt and pepper if needed.

2. Serve the couscous in a large shallow platter, drizzled with the hot tuna sauce, topped with the grilled skewered tuna, and garnished with julienned green onions and lemon wedges.

Harissa-Stewed Butternut Squash
SERVES 6–8

This is our all-time most requested recipe and it's also one of our simplest—a hybrid Spanish/Southern casserole. Note that I didn't say *easy*, I said *simple*. Yes, you have to peel all of the butternut squash, deseed, and dice it. No, you can't cook it and then peel it.

1 medium butternut squash, 2 to 3 lbs

4 tablespoons butter

Salt and pepper

1 tablespoon olive oil

1 medium yellow onion, julienned

5 cloves garlic, thinly sliced

2 tablespoons rose petal harissa, or more to taste

1½ cups heavy cream

⅔ cup fresh sheep cheese or fromage blanc

1. Slice the squash in half, peel it, scoop out the seeds and chop it into a ½-inch dice.

2. Put 2 large sauté pans over medium-high heat and put 2 tablespoons of butter into each. Get the butter just to the beginning of browning.

3. Split the squash between the 2 pans, and season each pan with salt and pepper. Let the squash cook, untouched, for 3 minutes. The squash's caramelization in the hot sauté pan is super important to the final flavor. You want it almost charred and just slightly burnt.

4. After 3 minutes—once it's nicely browned—spoon the squash into one pan, discarding the butter that remains in the emptied pan.

5. Put 1 tablespoon of olive oil in the emptied pan and add the onion and garlic and sauté, stirring regularly, until they get a bit of color, about 1 or 2 minutes.

6. Spoon the squash back into the onion/garlic pan, leaving a lot of the butter behind.

7. Add the rose petal harissa and heavy cream and stir to incorporate. Cook for 1 or 2 minutes.

8. Make sure that the squash is cooked through, the sauce is a good consistency, and the seasoning is to your liking, and remove it from the heat.

   NOTE: *At this point you can put the recipe on hold, refrigerate it, and finish it the next day.*

9. Divide the squash mix into 2 cazuelas or other shallow baking dishes.

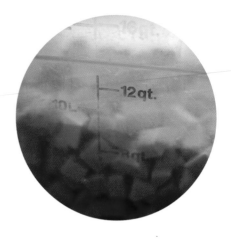

10. Take half the fresh sheep cheese and put 3 evenly placed scoops on the top of one dish. Do the same for the other dish.

11. Broil the squash for 3 or 4 minutes or until the cheese is nicely browned. Serve right away.

Hand-Cut Noodles
1 POUND, SERVES 6

These noodles took a lot of inspiration from *The French Laundry Cookbook*. Before I encountered Thomas Keller's recipe I was making noodles the classic way: flour, eggs, water, oil. Keller's noodles are big and rich and have depth, and don't just taste like flour. They're silky, smooth, and a beautiful yellow. His recipe has been the backbone of my rolled-out pasta ever since.

The most important thing when making pasta is getting a feel for how much flour to use. You want the dough to be dry, but not so dry that it cracks. Practice will make perfect. This is Toro's classic noodle recipe that we use for Ruby's Noodles (page 214), Noodles with Pimentón Dulce (page 212), and alongside our Braised Lamb. These noodles are nice and dry, well kneaded/rolled, and toothsome.

NOTE: *Both our Noodles with Pimentón Dulce and Ruby's Noodles are ridiculously simple pasta dishes. The key with them both is to use fresh pasta: either ours, another recipe, or store-bought. And you have to use manchego for both. Once you start using manchego for pasta I guarantee you'll never go back to Parmigiano-Reggiano.*

6 egg yolks

¼ cup milk

1½ teaspoons salt

1½ teaspoons olive oil

1 teaspoon champagne vinegar (or any white wine vinegar that you like)

2 cups + 1 cup all-purpose flour

With Pimentón Dulce

5 ounces of our noodles or another fettuccine width or wider pasta

1 tablespoon butter

1 tablespoon olive oil

3 cloves garlic, thinly slivered

1 heaping tablespoon pimentón (can substitute espelette pepper or another high-quality paprika)

1 cup manchego, finely grated and divided

1. In a blender, blend all of the ingredients except for the flour, about 10 seconds, until combined.

2. Pour this into a mixer with the dough hook attachment and add the flour a ½ cup at a time. Mix for 5 to 8 minutes and scrape the dough down a couple times during. You want the dough to be pretty tight and not at all sticky.

3. Tightly wrap (vacuum seal it if possible) the dough and let it rest in the refrigerator for 30 minutes to an hour so that the gluten relaxes and the moisture evens out. You can leave the dough up to 2 days in the refrigerator or freeze it for up to a month well wrapped or vacuum sealed.

4. Roll the rested dough out to the width that will fit in whatever pasta roller you are using. The dough should be dry and dense and take 5 to 10 minutes to roll out. Most home cooks have the Atlas pasta roller and that works great for this.

5. Flour your dough and machine whenever necessary so that it doesn't stick while you're passing the folded pasta through. Roll the dough through the pasta machine until you get it down to a medium-thin width (the #4 setting if you are using an Atlas machine) and then cut it in half. Fold each half in on itself, in thirds, until it's the same width of your roller, then feed back

each piece through the pasta machine that you've set back to the previous setting. (This is the final part of the kneading process. Folding the dough and passing it through again gives you clean edges and also works the dough a little more to make a more toothy pasta.) Keep passing the dough through the machine at thinner and thinner settings. In the end, you want to wind up with pasta that's thin enough that you can see your hand color and shape through it when you hold it up to light. We roll ours to the equivalent of the #6 setting on an Atlas machine, but really this is to your personal taste. Some want thicker and more rustic noodles, and others thinner and more refined.

6. Cut the pasta into squares and dust the pieces with flour before stacking them so that they don't stick. Using the cutter on your pasta machine, slice the dough into 1-inch wide pieces (or whatever width you want). Or fold the squares into thirds and then slice the dough with a knife. Once the pasta is sliced toss it to separate the pieces.

7. Boil the pasta in a large pot of sea-salty water (¼ cup salt, 1 gallon water) for about 2 minutes (or until it's as done as you like), stirring occasionally so that the noodles don't stick. We like our noodles to be just cooked and have some chew to them. Strain.

With Pimentón Dulce

1. As the pasta cooks put a large sauté pan over medium-high heat and add the butter and olive oil. Once it is melted and bubbling add the garlic and the Pimentón Dulce and let it bloom out with the garlic for about 30 seconds.

2. Once the pasta is finished cooking strain it and add it to the sauté pan along with ¼ cup of the pasta water and braise it while tonging it around until the pasta is dry or for 1 minute. Add a ½ cup of the grated manchego and toss the noodles around. Cook for 30 seconds to 1 minute.

3. Serve topped with the remaining ½ cup of grated manchego and a pinch per serving of the Pimentón Dulce.

Ruby's Noodles
SERVES 2–3

Katrina Zito was one of Toro's first cooks, and she was one of the fastest/slowest cooks I've ever had. What I mean by that is: she worked at a really steady-as-she goes clip, but somehow always pulled it off. At times we'd get a big pop and you'd look at her and think, *Oh shit, we're going to go down*, because she just didn't ever seem to have that sense of urgency. But her food would always be up before anyone else's, and it'd be perfect. She's one of the most talented cooks I've ever worked with. Katrina always made these noodles with butter and manchego for my daughter Ruby when she dropped by. Ruby was three years old when Katrina started making these for her, and to this day Ruby always wants Katrina's noodles. She absolutely loves them. So does everybody else. For a long time, whenever I'd bring Ruby in to eat everyone else at our table would want a bite of Ruby's noodles. That's how good they are. We never charge kids under eight years old for these noodles. It's on us.

5 ounces of our Noodles (page 212) or another fresh fettuccine width or wider pasta

1 heaping tablespoon butter

1 cup manchego, finely grated and divided

1. Bring a large pot of sea-salty water (¼ cup salt, 1 gallon water) to boil and once boiling add the noodles.

2. As the noodles cook (our fresh noodles usually take about 2 minutes to cook) put a large sauté pan over medium-high heat and add the butter. Once it is melted and the noodles are finished cooking, strain the noodles and add them to the butter pan along with ¼ cup of the pasta water.

3. Tong the noodles around in the water and butter for about 1 to 2 minutes and then add ½ cup of the manchego and tong it around for about another minute until it is fairly dry and well coated with butter and cheese.

4. Serve topped with the remaining ½ cup of manchego. If your cheese and pasta water weren't salty enough you may want to add salt, but most likely you won't need it.

Braised Lamb with Apricots and Coriander
SERVES 6

This is one of my favorite Toro Bravo dishes and just like a lot of my favorites it's largely inspired by Moorish cuisine: savory, sweet, and spicy, well balanced, and layered. We serve our braised lamb with fresh pasta sautéed with oil-cured Calabrian chilies, parsley, and butter. You could serve it over couscous—we sometimes do—but I like it better with the noodles.

NOTE: *I keep saying stews are better the second day and this one follows suit. No one's stopping you from serving it the same day you make it but it'll be better and potentially better for you if you serve it the next day. A great habit to get into—an easy way to make food healthier—is to refrigerate braises and stews overnight so that the fat rises and solidifies. You can just peel it off. Yes, fats transfer flavor, but once that flavor is transferred you don't need it.*

3½ pounds lamb shoulder, boned and cleaned

Salt and pepper

1 tablespoon coriander seeds, ground

1 tablespoon cumin seeds, ground

4 teaspoons oil blend (page 93)

2 tablespoons olive oil

1 cup dried apricots, halved

2 red peppers, cut into 1-by-1-inch cubes

1 yellow onion, julienned

5 cloves garlic, sliced

2 tablespoons honey

1 stick cinnamon

3 cups Chicken Stock (page 291, or use another; ours really works best for this, though)

¼ cup water

1 pound hand-cut noodles

2 tablespoons butter

2 cloves of garlic, sliced thinly

2 tablespoons parsley, chopped

6 oil-cured Calabrian chilies

1. Rub the lamb with 2 teaspoons salt, 1 teaspoon pepper, coriander, and cumin and let it rest uncovered in the refrigerator overnight to cure.

2. On day two, preheat the oven to 400 degrees.

3. Trim the fat off the lamb (not excessively though, you want some fat) and remove any glands (they taste like asshole) and connective tissue. Cut the shoulder into 1-inch cubes.

4. Put 4 medium sauté pans (French steel works best for this but cast-iron works too; you can also sauté in four rounds, in 1 pan, discarding the rendered fat after each round) over medium-high heat with a teaspoon of the oil blend in each pan. Once the pans are hot add the meat to each pan and season with salt and pepper.

5. Flip the lamb after 2 or 3 minutes and shake the pans periodically. Sear the lamb for a total of 5 minutes until it has a nice sear but is still rare. Remove the pans from the heat. At Toro, this is the point when we take a piece, slice it, and try it.

6. Put a large, ovenproof steel pot over medium-high heat and add the olive oil. Once heated, add the apricots, red peppers, onions, and garlic, and stir. After a minute reduce the heat to medium and cook for another minute until the onions are translucent.

7. Add the honey, cinnamon stick, lamb (but not the rendered fat in the pan; discard that fat), and stock, and stir. Bring to a simmer, then remove from the heat.

8. Cover the top of the braise with crumpled parchment paper to fit the diameter of the pot and pour ¼ cup of water over the paper to keep the paper on top of the lamb and keep the paper from getting brittle. Bake at 400 degrees for 2 to 3 hours or until the meat is fork tender but still keeps its shape.

9. Refrigerate the lamb braise and once fully cooled remove the fat and discard it.

10. To serve, reheat the braise. Sauté the cooked noodles with the butter, garlic, and parsley. Serve the braise evenly over the noodles, and top each serving with a chili.

Smoked Pork Shoulder Sandwich

SERVES 20–30, 15–20 SANDWICHES

At heart, I'm still a **Southern** boy, and this is my American-South-meets-Spain sandwich. The basics: salt your pork and let it cure for a few days, cold smoke it, roast it in beer until it's falling apart, and serve it with our Euro-spin on Carolina-style vinegar sauce: cabernet sauvignon vinegar with honey and chilies. In the summer we serve this sandwich with an arugula or mesclun mix and tomato salad, in the winter with a celery root slaw, and in the spring with a horseradish slaw. Make it for a party, and don't be afraid to make too much. Know that the leftover pork freezes really well. Know that there probably won't be any leftover pork.

7 pounds boneless, skinless pork shoulder

Salt and pepper

2 bottles low-hop lager

½ cup honey

½ cup cabernet sauvignon vinegar (or another high quality red wine vinegar or cider vinegar if you want it to be more of a southern sandwich)

1 tablespoon chili flakes

2 loaves of whatever bread you like

1½ cups Aioli (page 289)

¼ pound mesclun mix

5 heirloom tomatoes

Mama Lil's peppers (optional)

1 cup Pickled Zucchini (page 279)

1. Massage the salt and pepper into the pork shoulder for 1 to 2 minutes. Be sure to get into all of the areas including under the flap.

2. Truss the pork shoulder and put it uncovered in the refrigerator to cure for 2 to 4 days.

3. When the shoulder is done curing remove it from the refrigerator, preheat your oven to 350 degrees and start your smoker.

4. Cold smoke the shoulder at the lowest temperature that you can smoke at for about 1 hour. We smoke it at 250 degrees.

5. After smoking the shoulder put it in a roasting pan deep enough to hold the meat and beer. Braise, covered with a sheet of parchment paper, for about 5 hours. When the meat is fork tender and falling apart it's done. Remove it from the oven and let it cool.

6. With gloved hands, pick apart and shred the meat. Break up the fat and crispy pieces into bite-sized pieces.

7. Toss the pulled pork in the honey, vinegar, chili flakes, and as much salt as you like, and gently mix it.

8. Use ½ cup of meat per sandwich. If you're serving it straight from the refrigerator heat ½ cup of the pulled-pork mix per sandwich in a sauté pan.

9. Grill the bread to your liking and then slather the pieces with Aioli. Put ½ cup of the pulled pork onto the toasted bread and then top it with the mesclun mix and sliced heirloom tomato (sometimes we add Mama Lil's peppers too), and serve it with Pickled Zucchini. The pork keeps for a week in the refrigerator or for a very long time in the freezer, either in tightly sealed containers or vacuum sealed.

219

Drunken Pork

SERVES 6–8

Before I got to Café Zenon, I hadn't cooked with a lot of juniper. I'd just come out west from the East Coast, and because it's a a West Coast, high-desert kind of spice, I just hadn't encountered it much. I wasn't a big gin drinker when I was younger, either (though I've since come to like it). At Zenon, Bill loved cooking with it and I grew to love it, too. It goes really well with pork and bacon as it's paired here.

Our drunken pork recipe has evolved, over the years, but it's here to stay. My favorite way to serve it is with a cold avocado salad, which is what we do in spring and summer. In the winter, we serve it with braised beans. It's really important to use pork tenderloin for this, so make sure that the butcher cleans it well and gets all of the silver skin off for you (or you'll need to do that yourself).

We use Nueske's double Applewood-smoked bacon. If you can't get ahold of Nueske's, go for another thinly sliced Applewood-smoked bacon. And you don't have to use Tanqueray, but we do. It's a readily available gin that's good and junipery. When picking a gin, you want the perfuminess, so choose a juniper-rich one. We often do huge batches of drunken pork because it's what the people want. We'll sell 400 pieces in a single night.

Drunken pork is great for a big party because you can do a lot of the work a day or two ahead, and getting work done ahead of time is the key to enjoying any party you throw. The marinade is light but it will eventually cook the tenderloin with the acid and salt. This dish is seriously better the second day so if you can, prep the meat and marinate it overnight. We always try to do it a day in advance.

---

2 pork tenderloins, roughly 1½ pounds each, silver skin trimmed and meat cut into 1-inch cubes

½ yellow onion, julienned

¼ cup gin (Tanqueray works well)

¼ cup olive oil

6 dried juniper berries

2 cloves garlic

1 teaspoon whole coriander

½ teaspoon chili flakes

Salt and pepper

20 pieces of thinly sliced, double-smoked bacon cut on a bias at one end, each piece about five inches long

8 8-inch wooden skewers, soaked

---

1. Start your grill. I like to use charcoal but stoke up whatever you've got to a nice medium heat.

2. In a large bowl combine the onions, gin, and olive oil. Using your hands, mix everything together, squeezing and mashing the onions for about a minute to mellow them.

3. Place all of the remaining spices, seasoning, and garlic in a mortar and pestle and grind into a paste. It should be fairly smooth but still have some grit to it. Combine the paste with the onion, gin, and oil mixture.

4. Add the cubed pork to the marinade and stir with your hands or a spoon to coat.

Braise the oxtail

1. If the oxtail is really fatty, trim it and chop it into 6 to 8, 2- to 3-inch cross sections. Rub the oxtail with the salt and pepper and leave it uncovered in the refrigerator overnight to air dry.

2. On day two, put 3 sauté pans over medium-high heat and add 2 teaspoons of oil to each pan. (French steel is best but cast iron is fine. You can also sauté in 3 rounds in 1 pan, discarding the rendered fat after each round.)

3. Once the pans are hot add the oxtails evenly into each pan. Flip them with tongs occasionally until you get a good sear on all sides, which should take 3 to 5 minutes. Remove the oxtails from the heat.

4. In a large, ovenproof, steel pot over medium heat add 1 tablespoon of oil blend. Once hot add the onion, carrot, and celery and sauté for about a minute. Add the oxtail to the pot, but not the rendered fat in the pan, which you should discard, and cook with the vegetables for another minute.

5. Add the stock, bay leaves, cinnamon, and chocolate to the pot and once it's brought up to a simmer remove it from the heat.

6. Cover the top of the braise with crumpled parchment paper to fit the diameter of the pot and then pour ¼ cup of water over the paper to keep the paper on top of the meat and keep the paper from getting brittle. Bake this at 400 degrees for 2 to 3 hours. You want the meat to fall off the bones when you've finished cooking it and you want the braising sauce to be reduced by half.

7. Remove the oxtail braise from the oven and cool it. Once slightly cooled separate out the vegetables and discard them. (If you don't get rid of the vegetables this will taste like a cheap pot roast.) Cool the oxtails.

8. Refrigerate the braising liquid and once fully cooled skim off the fat and discard it. Once the oxtail is cool enough to handle, pick the

meat off of the bones. Discard the oxtail fat, sinew, and tendon. You can easily feel when the oxtail is still slightly warm what is edible and what is not. You should have about a pint of meat. Return the oxtail meat to the refrigerator and let it continue to cool for 30 to 60 minutes.

Make the croquettes

9. Cook 2 cups of béchamel (page 295) and let it cool.

10. Boil the peeled and chopped russet in sea-salty water (⅓ salt, 1 gallon water) for about 15 minutes, until the potato is fork tender. Strain the cooked potato and let it air dry for 10 to 15 minutes. This dries it out a bit because you want a dry potato for croquettes. Mash the potato with a hand masher.

    NOTE: *When boiled potatoes are finished cooking don't ever let them sit in the cooking water. Once cooked, they're porous like a sponge and will continue taking in water.*

11. In a large bowl, using your hands, mix together equal parts béchamel, mashed potato, and oxtail meat (reserving ½ cup of oxtail meat nicely handpicked apart for your sauce) until everything is well mixed. A little more oxtail is never a bad thing. There's always residual sauce on the oxtail so as you mix you'll start to see a

change in color from that. It gets a little pinkish. Taste the batter and adjust the seasoning if necessary.

12. In a small sauté pan simmer the ½ cup of reserved oxtail along with a ½ cup of the reserved oxtail stock for 3 to 5 minutes. There will be a little bitterness to the sauce because of the chocolate but that's okay. It will all blend together nicely when served with the croquettes.

Roll out the croquettes

13. You want your mix to be a little warm from the béchamel when you roll it out. Get a sheet pan and cover it with parchment paper and then put a couple tablespoons of oil blend in the corner and use that to oil your gloves in the beginning and periodically while rolling so that the oxtail batter doesn't stick to them. Roll the mix into cylinders that are about 1½ inches long and ½ inch wide. Tap the ends so that they are cylindrical. You can make your croquettes into balls too, but I like the way the cylinders cook and look.

14. Once the croquettes are rolled out refrigerate them for 30 to 45 minutes uncovered before breading them.

15. Set up the flour (2 cups), 3 cups bread crumbs and egg wash (1 egg and ½ cup of milk whisked together) in 3 medium-large bowls side by side. Most people put their breading bowls in the order that they dip, so flour first, egg wash next, followed by bread crumbs. I find that with the egg wash in the middle you always end up getting egg in your bread crumbs. So I always go wet on the end and cross over and back so that that doesn't happen. I have the flour on my left, the bread crumbs in the middle, and the egg wash on the right. I use my right hand for the egg wash and my left for the flour and bread crumbs. Do the breading however is most comfortable for you and place the croquettes on the parchment when you are done and don't crowd them.

Fry the croquettes

16. Fry the croquettes either in a home FryDaddy or in 280-degree rice oil. (You can also use peanut or canola. At Toro we use rice oil because it has a high frying temperature and people don't usually have allergies to it.) Don't overcrowd and only fry about 10 or so at a time. Fry them for 1 to 2 minutes until they are golden and crisp on the outside and hot in the center. Remember that everything is fully cooked already, so all you are doing when frying them is getting them crisp on the outside and hot all the way to the middle.

17. Remove the croquettes with an Asian spider strainer or something slotted onto paper towels and salt the croquettes with ½ teaspoon per 10 croquettes. NOTE: *Croquettes are everywhere in Spain, but they can suck. Many places fry up their croquettes and fritters all at once and then let them sit and get mushy and cold before microwaving them to serve. See, that sucks. You'll want to eat these not long after frying.*

18. Serve the croquettes over the hot sauce with a few scoops of jalapeño mayonnaise (about ½ cup) on top and ice water–blanched scallions.

Ice water blanched scallions:
Ice water blanching scallions takes out the negative, harsh onion flavor. Once blanched these will last about a day in the refrigerator.

1 bunch scallions

1. Slice off the upper green part of each scallion where the white part begins and then slice the remaining green portion in half. Lay the green sticks out and julienne them as thin as possible.

2. Put the julienned scallions in a bowl of ice water. After 30 minutes, take them out and let them dry until they get curly.

Jalapeño Mayo | 1½ cups

1 jalapeño, roasted on a grill or on a gas burner

1 egg yolk

1 lime, juiced

1 to 2 teaspoons salt

1 tablespoon water

1 cup oil blend

1. Blend everything except for the oil in a blender or food processor for about 30 seconds. NOTE: *With aiolis and mayonnaises, it's always important to salt the liquid so that it dissolves before you add the oil.*

2. Slowly drizzle the blended oil and allow the mayonnaise to emulsify. If it looks to be getting too thick and like it's going to break, add either 1 tablespoon of water or 1 tablespoon of lime juice to loosen and stabilize it. If you're happy with the acidity, use water, if it's not acidic enough use lime.

3. Use the jalapeño mayo immediately or store tightly wrapped and refrigerated for up to 2 days. It dies quickly.

Squash Dumplings
SERVES 6–8, 3–4 DUMPLINGS PER PERSON

The first summer we opened I was doing this dish that I called Eight
Pepper Braised Lamb with Shanks. One day we had a few shanks at
the bottom of the pot that over-braised to the point that the meat had
fallen off of some of the bones. We removed that fallen-off meat and
cooked it into a ragout for staff meal. I made a squash variation of Italian
drop-gnocchi to go along with it; the dumplings packed a lot of squash
flavor, and paired with lamb, it was perfect. Squash and lamb is a classic
combo. Dumplings were one of the few things that my mom actually
cooked well, so they'll always be comfort food to me.

When winter came along and I was cooking lamb necks (I really
like lamb necks for their big flavor; even though American lamb
tends not to be as flavorful, you'll still get a ton of flavor in the neck),
I decided to serve them with those staff meal squash dumplings. It had
been such a great lunch that the combination was still there, in the back
of my mind. The lamb and dumplings were a hit and they've been on our
menu ever since. (In the summer, we do an apricot-braised lamb with
fresh noodles.)

---

1 butternut (or other winter) squash,
1 ½ pounds

2 egg yolks

⅔ cup flour

1 tablespoon olive oil

Salt and pepper

---

1. Preheat oven to 400 degrees.

2. Slice the squash in half from top to
bottom and scoop out the seeds.
Place both halves skin side down on
a baking sheet and drizzle with olive
oil and season with salt and pepper.

3. Place the seasoned squash flesh side
down on a baking sheet and bake for
45 to 60 minutes, until the squash
skin and flesh are so soft that your
finger easily goes through the neck
of it.

4. Once the squash is roasted, let
it rest for at least 15 minutes, or
until the flesh is cool enough that
it won't cook the egg yolks that
you're going to add to it. (As it
rests, the squash is also releasing water, which is important for
attaining the right dumpling consistency. You want the dumpling
batter to be the consistency of a
really loose pasta dough. It should
be a little looser than a gnocchi dough since squash isn't as
starchy as potatoes.)

5. Once the squash has cooled, peel
and discard the skin. Pull it off
with your fingers starting at the
neck. It should come off easily.

6. Put a large pot of sea-salty water
(⅓ cup salt, 1 gallon water) over
high heat and bring it to a boil.

7. Combine the squash flesh, egg
yolks, flour, and 2 teaspoons of
salt in an electric mixer with
a paddle mix and blend for 15
seconds or until everything is

blended and feels like a very loose pasta dough.

8. When the salted water is boiling, use 2 spoons to make a test dumpling. Scrape a heaping amount of the dumpling mixture onto the spoon and then scrape it off into the boiling water with another spoon. After boiling for 3 minutes or so, the dumpling will rise in the pot so that it is cresting the water. Once it is floating like this, cook it for another minute and then remove it gently with a slotted spoon. If the dumpling falls apart as it cooks or is removed from the water then you need to either add more flour or work the flour into it a little bit more.

9. Salt and pepper the test dumpling to taste and try it. The consistency should be like gnocchi, soft and chewy but not doughy or raw. You don't want to taste any flour in these dumplings; that's why the recipe calls for such a small amount of it. If you put too much flour in these you'll taste it and you're fucked. Start over.

10. Once you have the right consistency cook 6 to 8 dumplings in the salted boiling water at a time. (You should be able to cook the entirety of the batter in 3 batches;

don't do too many dumplings in 1 batch.) Jostle the pot now and again so that the dumplings don't stick to the pot or to one another.

11. Once the dumplings have crested at about 3 minutes, cook them for another minute, then remove them with a slotted spoon and salt and pepper them to taste.

Note: *You don't need to change the water unless you cook more than this recipe calls for. Your goal is to keep the dumpling water as clear and as unmurky as possible.*

These never turn out that pretty, so don't sweat it if yours aren't. You're going to throw sauce on top, anyway.

Lamb Ragu with Eggplant
SERVES 6–8

My first meal in Spain was in 2007, at Barcelona's La Boqueria, a huge historic market packed with food and drink stalls. At a stall called Pinotxo (Catalan for "Pinocchio"), I noticed a Spanish family eating an eggplant dish that looked amazing. When I tried to order it, the server said something to the tune of, *You're not Spanish so you probably don't want that.* I had to convince him I did. It was so flavorful and comforting that I went back and had it three more times that week.

Toro's version borrows a lot from Pinotxo's: it's basically roasted eggplant topped with slow-cooked meat and melted mahon cheese, a sharp and tangy cow's milk cheese from the island of Menorca. We've always gotten shit for this dish. People say things like, *It's just an eggplant parm!* They think it's not Spanish enough.

Ragu

1. Preheat the oven to 375 degrees. In a large sauté pan over medium-high heat, brown the lamb and onion in the oil blend. Stir for about 5 minutes, until the lamb is cooked and has released its fat. Drain the fat and discard it.

2. Transfer the lamb to an ovenproof casserole dish. Stir in the rest of the ragu ingredients except the fresh herbs. Braise in the oven uncovered for 2 hours, until reduced by half. (If the ragu is still too wet, finish it by simmering it on the stovetop.)

3. Add the herbs and return to the oven for another 5 minutes. Adjust the salt and pepper but don't overdo it: remember you're also going to salt your eggplant and then top everything with salty mahon.

Eggplant

4. Preheat the oven to 350 degrees. Rub a large sheet pan (lined with parchment paper if you've got it) with olive oil and sprinkle with salt and pepper. Place the eggplant halves face down and roast for 60 to 75 minutes until tender. They should be soft all the way through, almost like deflated tires, but not black or burning.

5. Flip the eggplants over to their flesh sides. Put a ladleful of hot ragu onto each half and cover evenly with the sliced cheese. Broil until the cheese is bubbly and melted. Eat as soon as you can without hurting yourself.

Ragu

2 pounds ground lamb shoulder

1 yellow onion, julienned

1 tablespoon oil blend (page 93)

2 cups roasted red pepper, peeled and finely chopped

2 cups canned tomatoes

4 cups Chicken Stock (page 291)

1 tablespoon fennel seeds, toasted and ground

Salt and pepper

½ tablespoon parsley, finely chopped

½ tablespoon rosemary, finely chopped

½ tablespoon sage, finely chopped

½ tablespoon oregano, finely chopped

Eggplant

3 medium eggplants, sliced in half lengthwise (you want a slightly firm eggplant with no bruises and no mushy spots, that gives when you push it)

2 tablespoons olive oil

Salt and pepper

6 slices mahon cheese (We use one that's aged for 6 months. You don't want a cheese that's aged any longer because you want it to be relatively soft and melty. Substitute mozzarella or fontina if you can't find mahon.)

Moorish Lamb Chops
10–20 LAMB CHOPS

At Café Zenon we served something called Shashlik with lamb ribs. We'd score the ribs, bake them to lose some of the fat, then grill them. They were delicious and really flavorful, but kind of tough. Only other chefs would order them, because customers usually thought that they were too tough or burnt, even though that was how they were meant to be.

In the beginning, at Toro, we'd get inch-thick lamb chops, marinate them for a day or two, and grill them. People loved them, but I didn't think they were quite right. Then, on a trip to Spain a few years ago, we were in Seville at a small tapas restaurant near our hotel in the Jewish district where they served "whiskey lamb chops." They cut theirs on a band saw to about one-inch thick, Korean bulgogi style. Suddenly I realized that that was what our lamb chops needed.

Back in Portland, I talked to lamb farmers and all but one of them said, *There's no way that we'll slice your chops that thin.* A lot of them said, *You're going to have to buy a band saw and do it yourself.* We lost one lamb farmer but gained one in Anderson in the Willamette Valley.

It'll be hard to convince your butcher to cut your chops this thin but I bet if you ask nicely you can get them cut to a quarter-inch. Since this marinade is so strongly flavored and the chops are so thin we raw baste with it rather than marinate with it. We put the marinade in a squeeze bottle and every time we get an order, we shake it, squeeze it over the chops, and let them sit for a couple minutes before grilling them. Since they're so thin two to four chops is good for a serving.

10 to 20 lamb chops (we use ⅛-inch thick chops but you can use chops that are as thick as 1 inch depending on your preference and how accommodating your butcher is)

Marinade

½ cup soy sauce

¼ cup Scotch (we use J&B Scotch Whisky but you can use whatever you like)

1 tablespoon sesame oil

6 tablespoons honey

3 tablespoons garlic, minced

2 tablespoons ginger powder

2 tablespoons ground cumin

1 tablespoon ground coriander

2 teaspoons chili flakes

1. Mix your marinade ingredients in a squirt bottle or jar and shake until combined. NOTE: *Make this marinade a few hours before using it. It keeps 4 to 5 days.*

2. If using ⅛-inch thick lamb chops, toss them in the marinade for 1 or 2 minutes before grilling them on a very hot grill. You want the lamb flavor to stick since the marinade is so strong. Flash grill them until they're marked, for about 20 seconds on each side, then serve right away. NOTE: *If your chops are ¼ inch thick, toss them in the marinade and marinate them covered in the refrigerator for 1 hour. Basically, the thicker your chops, the longer you'll want to marinate them. Try your best to get your hands on the thin chops, but if you can't, marinate ½-inch chops at least 3 hours and 1-inch chops overnight.*

233

Chicken with Jamón and Manchego
SERVES 4–6

Our Chicken with Jamón and Manchego was born out of my desire to eat chicken with jamón and manchego. We used to cook a jamón-wrapped chicken at Fratelli in the Bay Area. I ate a lot of of manchego and chicken dishes in Barcelona. Putting those together resulted in this.

For this and all other chicken recipes: get a good chicken and break it down yourself. We use free-range Draper Valley chicken that's been slaughtered two days before we cook it. Chickens are treated horribly in our industrialized food system and when you buy chicken parts rather than the whole chicken you're contributing to the problem. Shitty chickens often have broken bones—legs, ribs, breastbones—from slaughtering. Conventionally slaughtered chickens get dipped in a disinfectant which adds water to the skin and creates more opportunity for cross-contamination. We use air-dried chickens, and they're worth seeking out. They go through an extreme chill as they're dried that makes for a beautiful skin that isn't waterlogged in the slightest.

4 skin-on chicken breasts with the first joint of the wing on

Salt and pepper

2 tablespoons olive oil

1 tablespoon butter

4 slices manchego, cut into 4-inch squares, about 1/16-inch thick

4 slices jamon, about 1/16-inch thick, 4 inches long, and 2 inches wide

4 cups Pisto Manchego (page 288)

1. Preheat the oven to 425 degrees.

2. Clean the chicken, pat it dry, let it come to room temperature, and season each piece on both sides with salt and pepper.

3. Put a large cast-iron pan over medium heat. Add the olive oil and butter to the pan and once the butter has melted and is lightly bubbling add all the chicken pieces to pan skin side down.

4. Sear the chicken for 6 to 8 minutes or until the skin is nicely browned, then flip each piece onto the other side and cook for 2 more minutes.

5. Remove the pan from the heat and place the chicken on a plate or cutting board.

6. Place one piece of manchego on top of one piece of jamón and place the still-hot chicken breast skin side down on top of both and wrap it in the jamón and cheese. Repeat with the other 3 breasts and place all the wrapped chicken back in the cast-iron pan with the seam side of the jamón and manchego down.

7. Put the pisto manchego in a pot over medium heat and heat until warmed through.

8. Place the skillet containing the chicken in the preheated oven and bake for 7 to 10 minutes. Remove the chicken from the oven and let it rest for 3 to 4 minutes before serving it whole or cutting each breast at a bias into 3 or 4 pieces. Place the chicken in a family-style platter, top it with the warmed pisto manchego, and serve.

234

HOW TO BREAK DOWN A CHICKEN

At the restaurant, I can butcher a case of twenty-four chickens in ten minutes. At home, take your time. You'll get faster the more you practice. Chickens are great practice for whole-animal butchering: getting a feel for the way meat and muscles pull apart. When I was at Zenon and first starting to butcher, that was the advice Bill gave me. He said to me, *Here's a chicken. Start with this. Get good at this.* In the beginning I'd make my incisions, put my knife down, move the chicken, put my knife down, move the chicken again. Eventually, you learn how to do all the steps while holding your knife; you learn how not stab yourself or the chicken. I like using 2½ to 3 pound birds because the flesh is tender, but they still have enough meat on them to be satisfying. Make sure you're using a very sharp knife. I like using a 6-inch boning knife with a slight curve. (Forschner makes a great one.)

1. Put the bird down on a flat surface, and take off the first 2 sections of the wings (the wingtip and the wingette), leaving only the drumette. You're gliding right between the joint. You should never hit resistance. If you're hitting bones, move your knife a little bit. You'll run into a little cartilage here and there, but if your knife is sharp, it should be sliding right through that stuff.

2. Moving on to the breast, take your finger and feel from the very top of the opening, from the legs, and feel your way up to where the neck used to be. Make a ¼-inch incision from the legs to the neck. Don't cut too deeply into the flesh. You just want to be able to see the bones inside. Repeat this on the other side, for a total of 2 cuts.

3. Turn the chicken so that the wing side is facing you, and follow those initial incisions to make deeper ¾-inch incisions following the wishbone down to the drumette on both sides. These incisions are just to open the chicken; you shouldn't be cutting too deeply into the breast. Now you should be able to see the cavity and the bones of the chicken.

    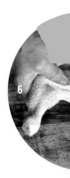

4. Disconnect the drumette, which should be easy now that you've freed the breast from the carcass. Again, all cuts should be easy.

5. Starting back up at the legs, using a little more pressure, start taking your knife down the breastplate to disconnect the breast. You can feel the end of the breast with your hands and follow with your knife, making sure not to cut your finger. Follow slowly with your knife to disconnect the entire breast. Again, there shouldn't be any resistance. You're barely even using your knife, at this point. The meat really just wants to separate. Take the skin off the carcass, and set it aside to use later. Now you've got 2 breasts.

6. To take off the leg and thigh, just glide your knife lightly along where the leg connects. Give it a little twist and pop so the thighbone disconnects from the carcass.

7. Now you have an extremely clean carcass: breasts, legs, thighs, and drumettes for cooking, wingtips and a carcass for stock.

Prepping Chicken for Paella

8. Here's how to break down the leg and thigh for paella. We used to take the chicken leg and thigh and pre-grill, marinade, and serve it in the paella still on the bone, like they do in Spain. I really liked those big pieces, but not everyone did. I figured out this method on a camping trip with Renee and her family. I wanted to grill chicken in a hurry, and thought to myself, *I'm just gonna butterfly the legs and thighs and marinate them. We'll grill the chicken that way, and it'll be really fast.* After I did that, I thought, *Oh my god, this is perfect.* We've been prepping our chicken for paella that way ever since.

9. Lay the chicken leg/thigh skin side down. Make 2 incisions along each side, as close as you can to the thighbone. Put your boning knife right underneath and, tilting it toward the bone, make another incision and pop out that bone. It's still connected to the leg bone at this point, but now it's loose.

10. Make an incision beside the bone along the drumstick, and butterfly the drumstick open. What you have now is a thighbone that's disconnected from the end of the thigh, but still connected to the drumstick bone. Once you've made these 2 incisions, make 1 incision between the thighbone and the legbone, through the cartilage area, and take out the thighbone.

11. What you'll be left with is a perfectly butterflied piece of thigh that only has a semi-exposed drumstick bone. You can marinate and grill that for our paella, or for anything else you'd like. When cut like this, the meat grills very evenly.

Chicken and Clams Cataplana
SERVES 6–8

I've loved steamer clams since I was little, growing up in the Southeast, along the coast. This is a hearty stew that I came up with during a phase of reading obsessively about Portuguese food. A cataplana is a type of Portuguese cookware usually made out of copper or metal that's shaped like a clam, with a hinge. When it's clamped shut it's really airtight, like a pressure cooker, so whatever's inside braises. Like a tagine, the cookware and the resulting dish cooked in it share the same name. At Toro, we make a cataplana with two sauté pans—one to hold the food and the other to cover it—but you can just use a lid and a pot.

For most Portuguese cataplanas, the sauce is prepared and then put it into the cataplana along with the clams and other seafood and often sausage. The whole shebang is cooked until the clams open, at which point the cataplana is unclasped, releasing all kinds of steam, and the dish is served. We prepared ours this way at first—we regularly find ourselves with a lot of scraps like ham, bacon, and chorizo ends, and we're always looking for recipes to make the most out of them—but eventually we started searing chicken and adding that to the mix as well. That's when people went apeshit over it.

Sauce

1. In a medium sauté pan over medium-high heat sauté diced bacon, chorizo, and jamón in 1 tablespoon of olive oil for 5 to 10 minutes, stirring occasionally, until they begin to render their fat and brown slightly.

2. Add the onion and garlic to the pan and cook until they are translucent, about 5 minutes, stirring occasionally.

3. Add the spices and minced chili and cook them for about a minute.

4. Add the wine and continue cooking, stirring occasionally, for about 10 minutes or until reduced by half.

5. Add the tomatoes along with their juice and break them up with a spoon. Once boiling, reduce the heat to a slow simmer and cook for about 1 hour, stirring occasionally.

Sauce

1 cup bacon, diced (we use Applewood-smoked slab bacon)

½ cup chorizo, diced

½ cup jamón, finely diced

2 tablespoons olive oil, divided

2 tablespoons butter, divided

1 yellow onion, sliced

2 cloves garlic, thinly sliced

½ tablespoon paprika

1 teaspoon pimentón

1 oil-cured Calabrian chili

½ cup dry white wine (I always cook with a wine that I like to drink, and prefer whites that haven't been aged in wood. Good cooking whites for our food include Vinho Verde, Verdicchio, Verdejo, and other young, crisp wines.)

1 28-ounce can of tomatoes

1 tablespoon parsley leaves, chopped

Chicken and Clams

1 chicken, about 2 to 2½ pounds

1 pound manila clams, cleaned

Salt and pepper

3 garlic cloves, slivered

¼ cup olive oil

1 dozen U-15 prawns

1½ teaspoons oil blend (page 93)

Paella

2 tablespoons olive oil

2 pounds + 3 ounces Carnaroli rice

2 pounds fresh chorizo (previous page)

2 medium yellow onions, fine-medium diced

1 quart roasted red peppers, julienned (about 8 peppers)

1 tablespoon saffron

⅓ cup Sofrito (page 283)

3 quarts Fideos Stock (page 291)

Salt and pepper

1 pound English peas

½ lemon, thinly sliced into half-moons

2 dozen mussels, cleaned

2 dozen clams, cleaned

1 tablespoon chopped parsley

Fresh Chorizo

1. Combine all of the ingredients except for the pork and refrigerate.

2. Cut the untrimmed pork into pieces that will fit into your grinder and then partially freeze it.

3. Grind the pork pieces with a ¼-inch plate.

4. By hand, mix the ground pork with the cold seasonings.

5. Use immediately, refrigerate, or freeze. Our fresh chorizo keeps in the fridge for up to 1 week, or in the freezer for up to 1 month.

Chicken and Prawns

1. Break down your chicken into 10 pieces with the skin on: legs, thighs, wings, and breasts each cut into 2 pieces. (I teach you how to do this on page 236.)

2. Combine the olive oil, paprika, lemon juice, salt, and pepper in a large nonreactive bowl and toss the chicken pieces in it to coat. Cover and refrigerate for 3 to 4 hours. If you plan on marinating overnight cut the lemon juice in half so that the acid doesn't cook the meat.

3. Clean the prawns and remove the heads. Use scissors to cut along the back of the shell to devein them. Leave the rest of the shell intact.

4. Combine the prawn marinade ingredients in a medium nonreactive bowl: the Calabrian chilies, lemon zest, lemon juice, slivered garlic cloves, and olive oil. Add the cleaned prawns, toss to coat and cover and refrigerate for 3 to 4 hours.

5. Once the prawns and chicken are marinated you're ready to start cooking the paella. Start your charcoal Weber grill.
   NOTE: *You want a very hot grill for paella—so hot that it will boil liquid in a pan placed on it. You also want evenly distributed heat, so make sure that the coals are spread out nicely.*

6. When the grill is very hot put the marinated chicken pieces on it, season them with more salt on the grill, and cook them for 5 minutes total, turning them regularly so that they get a good char on the outside but are still pinkish in the middle. Remove the chicken from the grill and set it aside.

7. Flip the grill grate of the grill over so that the handle parts of the grate don't get in the way of the paella pan.

8. Put paella pan on the grill grate over the hot briquettes. Once the pan is hot add the oil blend and grill the marinated prawns for 2 minutes

while moving them around with tongs so that the shells get nice and crispy. Remove the prawns from the pan and set them aside. Don't clean the paella pan at this point; you want to keep that prawn flavor and the residual oil in the pan.

Paella

1. Add 2 tablespoons of olive oil to the paella pan. Add the rice and sauté it for about 2 minutes while moving it around constantly to coat it in the oil and toast until it's sizzling. Be very careful not to burn the rice because even a few pieces of burnt rice can ruin paella.

2. Add the chorizo to the pan and with a large spoon break it up into small chunks and blend it in while stirring continuously. Cook the chorizo with the rice for about 3 minutes.

3. Add the diced onions to the pan and continue stirring them with the chorizo and rice until the onions are translucent and the chorizo is fully cooked, about 8 to 10 minutes.

4. Add the roasted red peppers, saffron, and sofrito, and stir to incorporate.

5. Add 2 quarts of fideos stock to the pan along with generous salt and pepper. Stir to incorporate and let it come to a boil.

   NOTE: *Do not stir the paella again after incorporating the stock. You want the paella to gently do its thing so that you end up with a nice crust on the bottom of the paella and around the edges. You can satisfy your desire to stir by gently shaking and spinning the pan and making sure that the contents are in an even layer. Also keep in mind that you don't want the paella to scorch. If at any point the grill is not hot enough or too hot, there's no shame in moving the paella onto a burner on the stove to finish cooking it there.*

6. Once the stock is boiling, add the remaining pint of fideos stock to cool the paella down, so that it doesn't boil too hard.

7. After about 30 minutes of cook time from when you put the rice in the pan, add the partially grilled chicken pieces skin-side up so that you don't lose the crispy skin. Evenly distribute the pieces throughout and push them slightly into the paella.

8. Add the peas and push them into the paella. Usig a large metal spoon, scrape the bottom of the pan here and there to check for sticking.

9. About 2 or 3 minutes later, when the paella is a little more dried, add the marinated and partially cooked prawns to the top of the paella, evenly distributing them.

10. Scatter the lemon slices over the top of the paella, then distribute the mussels and clams, taking care to place them hinge side down onto the paella. This way when they open they will open up and out.

11. Sprinkle the parsley on top of the paella and rotate the chicken pieces a bit if it seems that parts of them aren't almost fully cooked.

12. About 40 minutes after you first put the rice in the pan, you should start to get sticking at the bottom of the pan. That's the saccaret. Sprinkle more salt over the top.

13. The paella should be getting a nice crust around the edges, the stock should be almost gone, the clams and mussels should all be opened, and you should be hearing a good sizzle from the rice crisping at the bottom of the pan. Remove the paella from the grill, and let it rest for 5 minutes before serving.

Rabbit Fideos
SERVES 10–15

Before I ever traveled to Barcelona I did a lot of reading on paella and fideos and had played around with both. When I finally made it there, I went to Cal Pep and asked the locals sitting next to us where to go for the best fideos. They said that on Sundays everyone goes to Can Costa in the Marina district—that it was a really popular family affair. Can Costa's fideos was fantasic: loaded with sea snails, pork chorizo, and vegetables. Toro's fideos took a lot of inspiration from Can Costa's: it's cooked and served like paella, in a paella pan, but with noodles instead of rice. It's also drier.

For this seasonal version of our fideos we take housemade rabbit sausage with anise, fennel and garlic, and sear it with squid ink noodles. Right before serving we cut some corn off the cob and create a fresh corn milk glaze to finish the fideos with. It's that sweet corn glaze that forms on the top—along with the heirloom tomatoes, fresh tarragon, and everything else—that makes this a really special fideos. NOTE: *You need a Weber grill and a paella/fideos pan.*

Corn Cream Glaze

3 cobs corn

1 pint heavy cream

Salt

Fideos

4 medium-sized heirloom tomatoes

2 pounds dried squid ink spaghetti

¼ cup + 2 tablespoons olive oil

3 pounds bulk rabbit sausage with anise and fennel (You can use whatever nicely spiced bold bulk sausage you want. Spicy Italian works well here.)

2 yellow onions, finely diced

4 quarts Fideos Stock (page 291)

Salt and pepper

½ cup Sofrito (page 283)

1 pint Tomato Sauce (page 294)

5 oil-cured Calabrian chilies

1 bunch tarragon, stemmed and minced

Corn Cream Glaze

1. Cut the kernels off of the corn cobs, reserve them, and chop each stripped cob into 5 pieces.

2. Put the heavy cream, chopped corn cobs (reserving the kernels), and a pinch of salt in a medium-sized pot over medium heat, and bring it to a simmer. Simmer uncovered for 15 minutes.

3. Remove the corn glaze from the heat, set it aside to cool, and remove the corn cobs. Discard but reserve the heavy cream.

Fideos

4. Start your charcoal Weber grill. Flip the grill grate over so that the handle parts of the grate don't get in the way of the paella/ fideos pan.

5. Cut around the core of the tomatoes, leaving out the majority of the seeds and the cores. Dice the tomatoes and set aside.

6. Using your hands, break the squid ink noodles into 1-inch pieces.

7. Put your fideos/paella pan over the hot briquettes on the grill. Once the pan is hot add ¼ cup of olive oil and the rabbit sausage, using a spoon or spatula to break it up. Add the onions and broken squid ink pasta and sauté for 5 to 8 minutes. You want the pasta to get nicely toasted.

8. Put a large pot with the fideos stock over medium heat until it is hot and ready to add to the fideos.

9. Add the sofrito and stir to incorporate. Add the tomato sauce and Calabrian chilies and stir to incorporate.

10. Pour in 3 quarts of the heated fideos stock and let it come to a simmer. This should take 2 to 3 minutes. Continue to lightly simmer the fideos for about 30 minutes total. You want to end up with a nice crust on the bottom of the pan and around the edges, but you don't want the fideos to scorch. If it's not hot enough or if it is too hot on the grill, move it onto a burner on the stove and finish cooking it there.

11. After about 20 minutes, or as the fideos gets fairly dry, add the last quart of stock along with the corn kernels, 2 tablespoons of olive oil, and salt and pepper.

12. Sprinkle the tarragon and tomatoes over the top of the fideos. Do not stir. Pour the corn cream into the fideos in a spiral. Cook for 3 to 5 more minutes, then remove from heat once the fideos has come together and is fully cooked and not too dry. The total cook time should be about 30 minutes. Let the fideos rest 5 to 15 minutes before serving.

Jerez Negroni

Whenever we put an ad out for a bartending position it's insane the number of resumes we get. We always ask whomever wants the job to create a drink for us: whatever they want. Mindy's the only person who's ever put a Spanish twist on her stage cocktail. Most people do wacky or fruity shit but she made this perfect Jerez Negroni—which everyone loved immediately.

Mindy's been working front-of-house since she was fourteen (she's thirty-three now), and bartending since age nineteen at a brewery in Cedar Rapids, Iowa, where she made a lot of Long Island Iced Teas and Sex on the Beaches.

She'd read about a version of this cocktail *in The Wine Bible* by Karen MacNeil in a section about Jerez de la Frontera in southwestern Spain, where sherry is from. Typically negronis are made with gin but this one substitutes cream sherry. In Spain cream sherry is called *oloroso dulce*, which essentially means "sweetened sherry." We use Primitivo Quiles Vermouth Rojo, a red vermouth made in Jumilla on the southeastern coast of Spain, where really good Monastrell grapes come from. Most red vermouths get their color from burned caramel. This one doesn't, though, so it's nice and clean.

1. Combine and stir all of the ingredients over ice for 30 or so seconds, strain over new ice in a rocks glass, and garnish with an orange twist.

1 ounce Campari

1 ounce Primitivo Quiles Vermouth Rojo

1 ounce cream sherry

Twist of orange

Flor de Caña Fix

Mindy loves to travel, scuba dive, snorkel, and spend as much time as she can on the beach in Mexico and Central America. She was scuba diving for the first time in Honduras when she fell in love with Flor de Caña, a rum made from sugarcane (it's all produced in Nicaragua, but a little is bottled in Honduras). There's a light rum that's aged for four years—Flor de Caña 4—and also Flor de Caña 7, 10, 25: all these different types of the rum aged for different amounts of time.

Flor de Caña 7 is Mindy's favorite, so she always has a drink made with it on the menu. She wanted a summery, tiki-like cocktail, and this is it. Our Flor De Caña Fix is most popular when it's hot and sunny outside. The big rum pairs really well with the big, bold foods that we serve too.

2 dashes Angostura bitters

2 ounces Flor de Caña 7-year rum (There are many different year Flor de Cañas but 7 year is the best. It's aged in the barrel and has great flavor.)

¾ ounce mint syrup

¾ ounce freshly squeezed lime juice

1 bar spoon Domaine de Canton (ginger liqueur made with brandy)

1½ ounce ginger beer

Sprig of mint

Mint Syrup

1 large bunch mint

2 cups sugar

2 cups boiling water

1. Put the bitters, rum, mint syrup, lime juice, and ginger liqueur into a Collins glass (a cylindrical glass tumbler that holds 10 to 14 ounces) with ice, stir for 1 to 15 seconds.

2. Top with ginger beer, garnish with mint, and serve.

Mint Syrup
You can make mojitos, mint juleps, or any other minty cocktail with this versatile syrup.

1. Place all of the ingredients in a quart container that can withstand high heat, stir, and let cool to room temperature. Once cooled, cover, transfer to the refrigerator, and let sit for a minimum of 24 hours. The longer you let the mint infuse the deeper the flavor and color.

2. Strain and serve. Keep tightly covered and refrigerated for up to a month.

Toro Martini

I always wanted to have a martini on the menu—one made with local products. For our Toro Martini, Mindy decided to use local gin—she's a firm believer in the classic martini using gin, never vodka—and for a Spanish twist, she incorporated Manzanilla sherry and those poached, salted almonds that we use in so many dishes. The sherry used here is low in alcohol, like a vermouth, but because of the way it's aged it has a slight saltiness that you'd normally get from an olive.

The Manzanilla sherry we use is actually a Fino sherry but it's aged in Sanlúcar de Barrameda in southern Spain, near the sea, so it has a little bit of ocean saltiness. It's subtle, but you can definitely taste it. The yeast that sits on the sherry is what gives it that flavor and special thing. Use an extremely dry and very cold sherry for this. We use Aviation gin that's distilled here in Portland but use whatever gin that you like.

1 ounce Manzanilla or another very dry variety of Fino sherry

2 ounces local gin

1 Poached Almond (page 97)

1. Take a chilled martini glass (chill the glass in the freezer or fill it with ice right before serving) and rinse it with chilled sherry, making sure to cover all of the interior surface area of the glass.

2. Stir the gin with ice in a shaker or pint glass for about 30 seconds. (The larger the ice the longer you'll want to stir because that ice melting into the gin is part of what makes a martini a martini. And stir, don't shake. If you shake gin you'll bruise it. As a general rule: any drink that's mostly juice you can shake, anything that's primarily alcohol you'll want to stir.)

3. Strain into a chilled martini glass, drop in the Poached Almond, and serve.

Pepino

"Pepino" is slang for "penis"—more specifically, Kasey Mills's penis— but it also means "cucumber." This cocktail is very specific to the summer when cucumbers come in, which is usually in July here in Portland, and we usually run it for a month and a half to two months when the cucumbers are tastiest. This is a nice, light, not-super-alcoholic cocktail that pairs well with our summer foods: the gazpachos, cucumber salads, and other light fare. When Mindy came up with this cocktail, she pressed the cucumbers for each drink. Now we use a cucumber syrup to save some time. If you're just making a few of these, go ahead and muddle fresh cucumber with syrup for each one to get that really fresh, cucumber flavor. Be sure to strain before serving, and don't forget the salt: it's what brings all the flavors out.

1. Shake all of the ingredients over ice for several seconds and strain and serve over ice in a Collins glass (a cylindrical glass tumbler that holds 10 to 14 ounces).

2. Garnish with a skinny cucumber spear and serve.

Cucumber Syrup

This syrup is great in all sorts of gin cocktails, including martinis.

1. Use a quart container that can withstand high heat to muddle the cucumbers and sugar with a muddler or another blunt object until all of the juice is released and you have a cucumber-sugar mush. If the cucumbers are fresh, it should take you 3 to 5 minutes; when they are drier and/or it's later in season, this will most likely take 5 to 8 minutes.

2. Add boiling water to cover the muddled cucumber, stir, and let cool to room temperature. Once cooled, cover, transfer to the refrigerator, and let sit for a minimum of 24 hours.

3. Strain and serve. This syrup keeps for up to 2 weeks tightly covered and refrigerated.

2 ounces Pimm's #1

1½ ounce cucumber syrup

½ ounce lemon juice, freshly squeezed

Pinch sea salt or kosher salt

Skinny cucumber spear

Cucumber Syrup

2 to 3 large cucumbers, peeled and cut into ½-inch cubes, enough to fill a quart container ¾ full (if you don't peel them your syrup will be bitter)

About ¾ cup sugar (add enough sugar to coat the cucumbers)

The Basque Kiss

Mindy likes to go into the pantry, harvest ingredients the kitchen's using, and incorporate them into her cocktails. (Using ingredients you're cooking with is an easy way to make drinks that pair well with whatever you're serving.) She'll take apples that the kitchen is using in a dessert, for example, and make a cordial out of them. Early on, she came up with the Basque Kiss out of dried apricots she found in the pantry. As is, the apricots were way too dry. She'd already started using peach bitters in the Basque Kiss so she decided to make a peach-bitters simple syrup, soak the apricots in that so that they'd reconstitute, and use that as a garnish.

Mindy came up with this cocktail for the 2009 New Year's Eve menu. She wanted to incorporate Txakoli, an effervescent sparkling wine from the small region of Basque country right on the Atlantic. It's made from Hondarrabi Zuri grapes that are only cultivated in that tiny part of Spain, so it's got a very distinctive terroir. Mindy favors low-fruit cocktails—they go better with food—and this one follows suit. Since 2009, the Basque Kiss has been one of our most popular cocktails—our quintessential vodka drink for vodka hounds.

1 ounce Vodka Monopolowa (or any other vodka that you like as long as it isn't bottom shelf)

½ ounce Rothman and Winter Orchard Apricot Liqueur

2 dashes peach bitters

½ ounce lemon juice

1 bar spoon orange liqueur

2 ounces Txakoli (Use an effervescent one. You'll want it to be a Getariako Txakoli which is made in a region right on the coast. There are three regions and the Txakoli from this one is the bubbliest. If you can find a wine aerating pour spout use it because that really helps to jump the effervescence.)

1 soaked apricot

Soaked Apricots

1 quart dried apricots

1½ cups sugar

10 dashes peach bitters

1. Pour the vodka, apricot liqueur, bitters, lemon juice, and orange liqueur into your bar shaker, shake, and strain it into your chilled martini glass. Top it with 2 ounces of Txakoli.

2. Spear a soaked apricot with a toothpick, drop it in the drink, and serve.

Soaked Apricots

These reconstituted apricots are great to use in this and other cocktails, but they're also great with dessert. The staff likes to pop them plain at the end of a long night.

1. Fill a quart container that can withstand high heat with dried apricots and sugar.

2. Fill the container with boiling water, add 10 dashes of peach bitters, and stir.

3. Once cooled to room temperature, cover and refrigerate for at least 24 hours. The apricots will absorb most of the water and sugar during this time.

4. Serve the apricots chilled or at room temperature. They will keep for a very long time tightly covered and refrigerated, at least a month.

To Your Health

The same New Year's Eve that she came up with the Basque Kiss (page 256), Mindy came up with To Your Health, which uses dry and funky Basque cider and has an herbal quality to it. We use Trabanco dry cider which has a very limited production and is made with wild yeast and heirloom apples. The cider we use is very dry and fermented for a long time—very different than cider you'll find anywhere else.

For this apple cordial, you'll want to use apples that are fresh and as local as possible. This cocktail is only on the menu for about half of the year. It starts in September or October when apples come into season and it stays until the spring when rhubarb and strawberries take over.

1. Shake the Pimm's, Apple Cordial, and lemon juice with ice, and strain into a pint glass or large cocktail glass filled with ice.

2. Top with the Basque dry cider and garnish with a twist of lemon.

Apple Cordial

Since this cordial's base is Applejack you can use it with all sorts of bourbon drinks, including hot toddies. It works really well with the latter with cognac, brandy or apple brandy, and cloves, cinnamon, and lemon.

1. Place a large pot over medium-high heat and stir together the apples, honey, cinnamon sticks, Applejack, water, and lemon juice. Cook, stirring occasionally, for about 15 minutes or until the apples are soft and the room smells like apple pie.

2. Remove the pan from the heat and remove the cinnamon sticks with tongs.

3. Purée the mix in a blender on high until smooth and then strain it through a fine sieve using a spoon or spatula to push it through.

4. Let it cool, then cover and refrigerate for up to a month.

---

2 ounces Pimm's #1

2 ounces Apple Cordial

½ ounce lemon juice, freshly squeezed

1½ ounces Basque dry cider (We use Trabanco, an organic cider made with all heirloom apples. Use what you think is delicious.)

Twist of lemon

Apple Cordial

9 apples seeded, peeled, and chopped (use whatever is in season as long as it's a tart and sweet apple)

¾ cup honey (Use whatever is local and good; we use Wessels Family from Forest Grove, Oregon.)

6 cinnamon sticks

1 cup Laird's Applejack (this is an apple brandy made with grain spirits from the oldest distillery in the US in New Jersey)

1½ ounces water

¾ cup lemon juice

Limoncello

Limoncello typically takes about two months to make, but at the restaurant we can speed it up a little bit in our warmer curing room, which extracts the lemon a little faster. It's a simple recipe, but you do have to keep your eye on it to make sure that you don't get any mold.

I like to drink it straight as shots right out of the freezer. It's an awesome digestif but it's also a great component in cocktails. It's nice to float on a martini. I also like to make a drink using equal parts grappa and limoncello.

Limoncello Start

1¾ liters grain alcohol

1¾ liters Gordon's vodka

30 lemons

3 empty 1¾-liter bottles

Limoncello Finish

8 cups water

8 cups sugar

Limoncello Start

1. Mix the grain alcohol and vodka in large plastic container.

2. Zest all the lemons, being careful to avoid the pith, which will make the limoncello bitter. The lemons should be mostly white when finished.

3. Divide the zest into 3 equal parts and distribute among the 3 empty bottles.

4. Evenly distribute the alcohol mixture between the 3 bottles, apply the tops, then shake to incorporate all of the zest into the alcohol.

5. Wrap the bottles completely in foil and store in a cool space for 30 days.

Limoncello Finish

1. Mix hot water with sugar in a plastic container, stirring to dissolve. Allow to cool to room temperature, then refrigerate.

2. Strain the lemon/vodka mixture.

3. Mix the lemon/vodka mixture with the cold simple syrup and divide this between the clean bottles. Freeze for at least 2 weeks. We like to serve and drink it right out of the freezer. Freezing limoncello give it a slightly syrupy consistency and mellows it a bit.

Casa Rita

I hate the Casa Rita and I've asked Mindy take it off the menu more times than we can count. It's a chili-infused tequila margarita that was put on the menu when we first opened. To this day, we still get a lot of people who come into Toro Bravo thinking we're a Mexican restaurant, expecting chips and salsa. The fact that we've got a drink called the "Casa Rita" doesn't help.

Don't get me wrong—the drink is delicious, and it's one of our most popular cocktails. It's also a great recipe to make for a big party because you can mix up a large batch of it and serve it quickly and easily. For the record? WE'RE NOT A MEXICAN RESTAURANT.

2 ounces Chili Tequila

1 ounce orange liqueur (we use Patron Citronge)

1½ ounce lime juice, freshly squeezed

¾ ounce orange juice, freshly squeezed

½ ounce Simple Syrup (page 267)

Salt for the rim (or other flaky salt)

Chili Tequila

1 bottle Sauza Hornitos Tequila Reposado

2 dried guajillo chilies, seeded

1 dried arbol chili, seeded

1. Shake all of the ingredients on ice for several seconds and strain over ice in a tall chilled glass with a salted rim.

Chili Tequila

1. Put the chilies into the bottle of Hornitos and let them infuse it for 48 hours at room temperature. Strain out the chilies and serve. This will keep for months.

ITO
EN
LA
COL
LA COLONIAL
MOJITO
5€
PIÑA COLADA
DAIQUIRI
LIMON, FRESA
MANGO, GUAYABA
CAIPIRINHA
RON COLLINS
CUBANITO
SORBETE CAVA
CUBA LIBRE

Venus 75

One day we got these really cool grapes as a gift from Viridian Farms: these tiny, beautiful, purplish grapes called Venus grapes. The kitchen was throwing the grapes on salads, and Mindy wanted to use some too, so she came up with this cocktail: a sort of twist on a French 75. It's got the gin, the lemon, the bubbles, and then these grapes, which add another dimension—an elegance that makes for a very pretty cocktail. You definitely don't want to use the green grapes that you get from every American supermarket year-round. If you can't find Venus grapes use another beautiful heirloom varietal.

10 heirloom Venus grapes (or any pretty heirloom grape)

1½ ounces Bombay Sapphire gin

½ ounce elderflower liqueur (we use St. Germain, which is widely available)

½ ounce lemon juice, freshly squeezed

2 ounces cava (don't substitute with prosecco or sparkling wine if you can help it)

1. Press 7 grapes into the bottom of your mixing glass with a muddler or any blunt kitchen tool.

2. Add the gin, elderflower liqueur, and lemon juice to a glass filled with ice and shake for several seconds.

3. Strain into a chilled martini glass.

4. Top with cava and garnish with 3 grapes. Mindy thinks they look really cute resting at the bottom of the glass.

Botellazo

The name of this drink comes from where a few names for our cocktails come from—Ernest Hemingway's 1932 non-fiction book *Death in the Afternoon* about his travels around Spain and an up-close look at bullfights. The book has a glossary of Spanish words in it and the definition for Botellazo is "A stroke on the head with a bottle; avoided by not arguing with drunks."

Kasey and I call this drink the "crack drink" because you've got three really potent spirits that give you a fierce buzz. If you have too many, yes, you'll feel as though you've been struck on the head with a bottle.

¾ ounce Grand Marnier

¾ ounce Domaine de Canton (ginger liqueur made with brandy)

½ ounce Fernet-Branca

½ ounce lemon juice, freshly squeezed

Peel of ginger (optional)

1. Shake all of the ingredients (except for the peel of ginger) with ice, strain, and serve up in a chilled martini glass.

2. For a fun, optional garnish, take raw ginger and peel a piece of it with a vegetable peeler, loop it on a toothpick, and put it in the drink.

265

Red Sangria
1 LARGE PITCHER

The first sangria I ever had was made by Cressida Hatch, Bill's wife and Zenon's wine buyer. Our recipe is based on hers. Sangria's a summer thing—everybody knows that—but our red sangria is great any season. It's not too sweet or juicy and people are often surprised by how balanced it is. It's punch with alcohol—who doesn't love punch (and alcohol)? A lot of people add sparkling water or soda before serving to give it a bump of effervescence. When Renee and I were in Spain we had sangria sparkling more often than not and really liked it. Toro Bravo's used the same sangria recipe since the beginning, and we probably won't ever change it. That said, there is a little variation with the sangria depending on who makes it. Make it how you like it but I like red wine in the front, fruit in the back, and sweetness underlying that.

We make huge quantities of sangria and use boxed wine for it. You have to take the bag out of the box and cut it just so while holding it by the corner and twisting the top off. The first time a server makes sangria they often end up sticky with fruit and covered with wine and juice. And no matter how often you've made it, sangria is going to be messy and sticky, so consider an apron and have a couple towels at the ready.

To serve our sangria, we use traditional ceramic sangria pitchers (though in Spain sangria is usually served in glass pitchers). Our ceramic pitchers are gorgeous and sentimental—we've had them since day one—but they have a downfall. Literally. They break easily and usually break at the handle first. We've had more customers than we care to admit left holding onto just the handle, separated from the pitcher, as sangria cascades over everything.

My advice is to let sangria sit covered in the fridge overnight. The flavor of the fruit gets incorporated more, of course, when you let everything sit and steep overnight.

1 bottle affordable-but-decent un-oaked red Rioja, chilled if you're serving the sangria immediately (you can also use Tempranillo, grenache, or any other medium-bodied and not-too-strong, fruit-forward wine)

½ cup orange juice (preferably freshly squeezed; store-bought is okay)

2 tablespoons lemon juice, freshly squeezed

1 tablespoon lime juice, freshly squeezed

½ cup ruby port

¼ cup Framboise

½ cup simple syrup

2 small plums, rinsed and sliced (1 cup total of whatever fruit you prefer. Stone fruit is really good for red and white sangrias, and we love peaches and nectarines for both. Cherries and blueberries, cut in half, are good too. If the fruit is not bite-sized, slice it small enough so that it can glide into your mouth easily and so that it's not so big that it gets in the way of pouring the sangria from the pitcher. Your seasonal fruit can be whatever you want, but we recommend always using the suggested oranges because of the flavor and slight bitterness that the pith adds.)

1 orange, ends cut off (peels intact), quartered, and sliced into bite-sized triangles, about ¼-inch thick

1. Pour the wine into the pitcher along with the orange, lemon, and lime juice, and stir to incorporate.

2. To that, add about three-quarters of each of the remaining liquids: the port, Framboise, and simple syrup. The sweetness of your wine, as well as all as of all of the other ingredients, including the fruit, will vary so you don't want to add them all at once. It's much easier to add sweetness than to try to dilute sweetness. Taste.

3. Add your fruit to the pitcher. You can use 1 type of fruit or many, just make sure to use what's fresh, seasonal, and delicious. Taste again, and correct if necessary.

Correcting Sangria

If your sangria is ...
... too sweet: add more wine.
... too bitter from the tannins and orange rind: add more simple syrup
... too acidic and sour: add more port and/or a little more wine

4. Once you've gotten the sangria to a good balance of sweetness, acidity, and bitterness, and it's something you could picture yourself drinking a lot of—chill it, preferably overnight. When it's time to serve, pour it into glasses filled with ice. We use a large wooden spoon to keep some of the fruit back while pouring.

Simple Syrup

Our recipe is an easy standard: 1 part sugar, 1 part water. Combine the sugar and water and heat until sugar is completely dissolved. Cool to room temperature. Use. (Or refrigerate for up to 1 month.)

White Sangria
1 LARGE PITCHER

We serve our white sangria like classy ladies wear white, between Memorial Day and Labor Day. In the summer, we go through about three gallons of white sangria a night. It's a refreshing, fruit-forward sangria with a good balance of acid, wine, and sugar. Pros: it picks up more of the fruit flavors, especially if you let it sit overnight. Cons: the hangover's worse than the one you get from red sangria.

1. Pour the wine (chilled if you will be serving the sangria immediately) into the pitcher along with the orange, lemon, and lime juice, and stir to incorporate.

2. Add about three-quarters of each of the remaining liquid ingredients including the port, Moscatel, and simple syrup. The sweetness of your wine, as well as all as of all of the other ingredients, including the fruit, will vary so you don't want to add them all at once. It's much easier to add sweetness than to try to dilute sweetness. Taste and adjust.

3. Add your fruit to the pitcher. Taste again, and correct.

Correcting Sangria

If your sangria is …
… too sweet: add more wine.
… too bitter from the tannins and orange rind: add more simple syrup
… too acidic and sour: add more port and/or a little more wine

4. Once you've gotten the sangria to a good balance of sweetness, acidity, and bitterness, and it's something you could picture yourself drinking a lot of—chill it, preferably overnight. When it's time to serve, pour it into glasses filled with ice. We use a large wooden spoon to keep some of the fruit back while pouring.

1 bottle cheap un-oaked white Rioja (you want it to taste like fruit, not a tree)

⅓ cup orange juice, freshly squeezed

2 tablespoons lemon juice, freshly squeezed

1 tablespoon lime juice, freshly squeezed

⅓ cup white port

¼ cup Moscatel (or any sweet dessert fortified wine; we've used a lightly sparkling Muscat or Spumante in the past because a little bubbles can be pleasant)

⅓ cup + 2 tablespoons simple syrup (page 267)

1 orange, ends cut off and quartered and then sliced into bite-sized triangles, about ¼-inch thick (separate the sliced fruit as you add it to the pitcher). Your seasonal fruit can be whatever you want, but we recommend always using the suggested oranges because of the flavor and slight bitterness that the pith adds.

½ cup blueberries

½ cup raspberries

Breakside Brewery's Toro Red

5 GALLONS

I love beer and brewed a bit of it myself in my twenties. I'd been wanting to have a beer brewed especially for Toro Bravo for a while when I first started talking about it with Breakside Brewery's brewmaster Ben Edmunds. I like the classic, well-balanced beers that Breakside puts out, so I knew that Ben would be a good collaborator to work with. We had fun talking about flavor profiles and what would and wouldn't work with Toro's menu. Even though this smoky amber has espelette pepper in it and what seems like a shit ton of malt and very strong hops, it's very balanced. It's not too hoppy, barely spicy, and it's just a really clean, refreshing, flavorful brew.

9¼ pounds Golden Promise (or another pale) base malt, milled

1 pound German smoke malt, milled

8 ounces each Victory, Crystal 70-80L, and Crystal 135-155L malt, milled

2 ounces Challenger or Glacier pellet hops

.2 ounces espelette chili pepper

8 ounces slurry of American Ale yeast

1. In a large pot (big enough for 6+ gallons), bring 4 gallons of water to 160 degrees and remove from heat.

2. Place the milled grains and 1 ounce of the hop pellets in a loose, large mesh bag, and add to the water. Keep the bag loose so that there is good flow of water into the grain, moving it around to fully submerge the grains. Let sit 60 minutes off the heat.

3. In a second pot, bring 1½ gallons of water to 165 degrees. After 60 minutes, transfer the grain bag to the second pot. Let sit 45 minutes away from the heat.

4. While the grains are steeping in the second pot, bring the first pot slowly up to near boiling. Do not bring to a full boil.

5. After 45 minutes, remove the grain bag and add the contents of the second pot to the first. Bring to a boil, uncovered.

6. Boil 30 minutes and add the remaining hop pellets. After 20 more minutes of boiling, add the espelette chili pepper.

7. Boil 10 more minutes and remove from heat. Immediately place the pot of wort in an ice bath and cool as quickly as possible to 70 degrees.

8. Transfer the cooled liquid to a sanitized, 6-gallon glass carboy and add the yeast slurry. Cap the carboy with a rubber stopper and shake the vessel vigorously.

9. Replace the rubber stopper with an open stopper and airlock or blowoff hose. Leave to ferment in a temperature-stable environment (below 700 degrees) for 8 days.

10. After 8 days, or when fermentation has stopped, transfer to a second carboy and refrigerate for 3 days.

11. Bottle or keg the finished beer, as desired.

FUNDAM

Lemon Set 9/7

Preserved Lemons

1 GALLON

Every home cook should have a jar of preserved lemons. They're incredibly easy to make and add so much flavor to all sorts of dishes. Sometimes you don't want too much acid in a dish but you still want a lemony flavor. How do you put a lemon into your dish without the acid? You add preserved lemons. We use our preserved lemons in our Grilled Asparagus (page 146), Harira (page 144), and many other dishes. The best container for these is a wide-mouth gallon jar.

17 lemons

2 pounds + 6 ounces salt (roughly ¾ cup)

1 quart freshly squeezed lemon juice or a really high quality bottled lemon juice

1. Clean the lemons, cut off the ends, and quarter them.

2. Pour a ½-inch layer of salt into the bottom of your gallon container (glass, ceramic, or food-grade plastic) and then add a layer of lemons and enough salt to cover them. Do this until all of the lemons and 2 pounds of the salt have been layered.

3. Really pack the lemons into the container by pushing down on them. You want them to be entirely submerged in the salt. At the end of the curing process they should be soft to the touch, but they won't be if any are peeking out.

4. Pour in the lemon juice. I've worked at places that cheat and use water for this step rather than lemon juice, and those preserved lemons are never as good. You should have liquid coming up to the top of your container when you squeeze down. This is really important. Preserved lemons will mold if not fully submerged.

5. Add the remaining 6 ounces of salt at the end to cover the lemons. You don't want to see any lemons coming out at the top. Cover the container tightly and tightly wrap it in plastic wrap (otherwise juices might escape).

6. Date and refrigerate the container or store it somewhere cool for 6 weeks. We cure ours at 80 degrees, but you have less of a chance of mold if you keep it cooler. The cooler the temperature the slower the curing. Check on the lemons once a week. Mold can crop up, but if you've followed these steps it most likely won't. If you do get mold on the top of the lemons, just remove the affected lemons and keep the rest. Anything under the salt is protected.

7. After 6 weeks the lemons should have finished curing and be very soft. Refrigerate and store in salt for up to 3 to 4 months.

8. When you're ready to use them, rinse the lemons to get rid of the salt. All the recipes in this cookbook call for only the skin of the preserved lemon: never the pith or flesh, which are too bitter. Quarter your preserved lemon, lay it yellow side down on your cutting board, and flatten it. Using your knife, scrape the flesh and pith out. You'll end up with just the skin, which is all you want to use: it contains all that quintessential, clean lemon flavor.

275

Pickled Beets
5 POUNDS

I pride myself on Toro's balanced pickles. A balance of tartness, saltiness, sweetness, and spice is what I look for in a pickle. Growing up in the Southeast I've always loved pickles. Folks in the neighborhood would give jars as gifts, and as a young cook, I didn't realize it was something you could do in restaurants. Pickling was always something that neighbors did.

At Simpatica, Jason had this really hard-to-find, out-of-print pickling book called *The Complete Book of Pickles and Relishes* by Leonard Louis Levinson that he loved and guarded. He referred to that book a lot and when we opened Toro, I scoured the cookbook shelves at Powell's and tried to find myself a copy. I never did manage to find it, but I found old Fannie Farmer cookbooks instead. So we have the late Mrs. Farmer to thank for most of Toro's pickles. They're great books (especially for baking), even though they were written around the turn of the century. Fannie Farmer and her compatriots used white distilled vinegar for most of their pickling back in the day, and it was pretty harsh. We use champagne vinegar, which I prefer to white wine vinegar because it's more refined and mellow. We also take a light hand with the cloves, cinnamon, and other strong spices in our brines. We serve our thicker sliced pickled beets with Marinated Olives (page 293) as well as on charcuterie boards, with the Sherry Chicken-Liver Mousse (page 174), and in some of our salads. I really like them in the seasonal Groundwork Greens salad (page 114) with fromage blanc, pickled red onions, and hazelnuts.

NOTE: *If you get a bunch of beets that are really varied in sizes, you'll want to separate them and cook them at different temperatures and for different amounts of time. Roast the larger beets at a lower temperature; you want to cook them for a good deal longer and in doing so you don't want to burn their sugars. There's a really negative flavor that tends to come out with beets that cook at too high of a temperature. Normally I roast small- to medium-size beets at 350 degrees, but for the larger ones go lower and slower.*

5 pounds beets

1 tablespoon + 2 tablespoons salt

5 black peppercorns

2 bay leaves

1 cinnamon stick

½ cup water

2 cups champagne vinegar

¼ cup sugar

6 cloves

1 cinnamon stick

3 yellow onions, julienned

1. Preheat the oven to 300 to 350 degrees depending on how large your beets are. Small to medium beets should roast at 350 degrees and larger beets at 300 degrees.

2. Put the rinsed and trimmed beets (leave a ¼ inch of the tops on) in a roasting pan or 2 with enough water to fill the pan to one-third, along with the salt, peppercorns, bay leaves, and cinnamon. Roast covered for about 1½ hours or until the beets are a little tender and the skins rub off easily. Larger beets will take 2+ hours at 300 degrees.

3. Remove the beets from the oven, uncover them, pour out any remaining roasting juices, and let them cool. Once the beets are cool enough to handle, peel and cut them into bite-sized pieces and return them to the pan.

   NOTE: *At Toro we remove the beets from the oven and immediately put ice on top of them so that we can peel them sooner, while they're still warm.*

4. In a large nonreactive pot (NO ALUMINUM!), bring all of the brine ingredients to a boil. Once boiling, remove the pot from the heat and pour the brine over the peeled and chopped beet pieces. There should be enough liquid to submerge all the beets.

5. Cool to room temperature, then ladle the pickled beets and brine into your glass pickle containers and refrigerate. The pickled beets will be ready to eat in 1 day and will keep for up to 3 months.

Pickled Zucchini
5 POUNDS

A lot of chefs will get a brine down and then cook every vegetable in that same brine. That's why restaurant pickles are often too tart or too heavily spiced. It just doesn't work. Every vegetable needs the care and attention of a special brine and pickling techniques for its particular flavor profile.

The technique for this recipe—as well as for most of our pickles—is a quick two-step cooking process, and it really makes a difference. Almost everyone thinks that these are cucumber pickles because they're so crisp and flavorful on our Bacon Manchego Burger (page 240) and charcuterie board. We use zucchini rather than cucumber because it's a very consistent vegetable year-round, whereas cucumbers can be inconsistent in the winter and their water content changes throughout the year.

6 cups champagne vinegar

1½ cups sugar

½ cup salt

3 teaspoons celery seeds

3 teaspoons turmeric powder

1 teaspoon dry mustard powder

2 yellow onions, julienned

5 pounds zucchini, thinly sliced with a mandoline

1. In a large nonreactive pot (NO ALUMINUM!) bring all of the ingredients except for the zucchini to a boil; then remove it from the heat.

2. Put the zucchini into the brine, making sure that all of it is immersed, and let it rest for 1 hour at room temperature. If any of the zucchini is sticking out of the brine, use a plate or smaller lid to weigh it down.

3. Return the pot with the zucchini and brine to the stove uncovered and bring it to a boil. Boil the zucchini for 3 minutes—no more and no less.

4. Pour the zucchini and brine into a shallow nonreactive pan to cool. Ladle the cooled zucchini and brine into your favorite glass pickle containers and refrigerate. The pickled zucchini will be ready to eat in 1 day and will keep for up to 3 months.

Vanilla Extract

½ GALLON

When I was in my early twenties at Caffe Centro, we were using a lot of vanilla in our pastries and throwing the vanilla beans away afterward. One day Jean-Pierre Moullé said, *There's so much flavor still in these beans. You should put them in sugar.* Everyone was putting vanilla beans in sugar back then. I thought, *He's right; we should definitely use them.*

Around the same time, a friend of mine in Tahoe got a bottle of really nice dark rum and added her own vanilla beans to it. She brought it over one night when we were cooking and while we made cake for dessert, we had vanilla rum and Coke on the rocks. I put some of the rum in the cake batter and it was the best vanilla flavor I'd ever had in my desserts. Sold, I started making my own.

Making your own vanilla extract is easy, and turns out great every time. You have to carefully clean each bean off well, so that you don't contaminate the extract and ruin the entire bottle. We've lost a bottle or two over the years despite the fact that alcohol is strong enough to kill most things. If you have too much fat still on the beans when you add them you'll get a white surface mold. This recipe can be adjusted up or down easily; don't sweat it if the ratio isn't exactly right.

750 milliliters vodka (We use Gordon's vodka but any decent vodka will do.)

4 fresh vanilla beans

Up to 10 cooked vanilla beans

1. Divide the vodka into 2 food-grade bottles. Split the fresh vanilla beans and put 2 into each bottle.

2. Cover tightly and refrigerate for 2 weeks.

3. Begin adding any cooked vanilla beans to the vodka bottles after this point and put roughly the same amount into each bottle. Be sure to rinse them well and clean off the fat or butter before adding them to the vodka. Give the vodka a good shake every time you add vanilla beans.

4. After about a month and once the extract has taken on a nice amber color, it's ready to use. If you always clean all of your beans well before adding them, this vanilla extract will last up to 1 year.

Romesco

3–4 CUPS

There's nothing too complicated about this romesco. Romesco is another classic emulsification, so you've got the formula: protein, acid, motion, fat. Ours isn't too nutty or peppery and it's good, clean, and consistent. You can use it on meats, fish, and veggies. We serve it with our Scallops (page 202), Bacon Manchego Burger (page 240), Tortilla Espanola (page 126), Fried Anchovies, Fennel, and Lemon (page 130), and with grilled vegetables. It's good with eggs and sandwiches, too.

If you don't have the time or care to roast your own peppers then don't bother making our romesco. Canned roasted peppers don't even come close to fresh roasted. You also need to use a good sherry vinegar—none of that flavored crap. You want a sherry vinegar fermented from sherry, not a distilled vinegar flavored with sherry.

1 cup roasted red pepper, chopped

1 cup Poached Almonds (page 97)

1½ tablespoons paprika

1 teaspoon pimentón

5 cloves garlic

2 tablespoons sherry vinegar

1 egg yolk

2 tablespoons of olive oil + enough canola oil to make a cup

Salt and pepper

1. In a food processor with the blade set in place, add the peppers, almonds, paprika, pimentón, garlic, and sherry vinegar, and pulse for 30 seconds.

2. Add the egg yolk and pulse again for 10 seconds.

3. Turn the food processor on and slowly drizzle the oil in a slow, steady stream. As the food processor runs, the Romesco emulsifies. It should take about a minute to add all of the oil slowly. Once all of the oil has been added, let the sauce blend for an additional 30 seconds. Add the salt and pepper to taste, blend, and serve. Don't freeze Romesco; it'll break. It keeps for 3 or 4 days, tops.

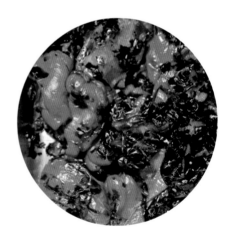

Salbitxada

2 CUPS

Salbitxada is the traditional sauce that grilled spring onions are dipped in during the spring calçots festivals in Spain's Catalonia region. For the festivals, called calcotadas, spring onions are grilled until blackened and then peeled and eaten with salbitxada. Salbitxada is basically a roasty toasty, bigger-flavor version of romesco, so use it the same way you use that, as well as with heartier foods. Because you toast the almonds, garlic, and chilies for salbitxada, all of them bloom out, and you get a little more heat than in a romesco. We serve salbitxada with grilled leeks and green onions but it's tasty with other vegetables, and with certain cheeses and meats. We really like it on burgers and roasts, and on our Coppa Steak (page 192).

1 cup Poached Almonds (page 97)

5 Arbol chilies, dried and stems removed

5 cloves garlic

¼ cup red wine vinegar

¼ cup Tomato Sauce (page 294)

¼ cup water

1 egg yolk

2 tablespoons parsley, chopped

1 cup oil blend (page 93)

Salt and pepper
(If the almonds have a lot of salt clinging to them, you won't need to add much salt; if the chilies are spicy, you won't need to add much pepper.)

1. Toast the poached almonds, chilies, and garlic in a dry medium sauté pan for 3 or 4 minutes over high heat until everything has a good char. It should get charry enough that standing directly over it makes you cough. (At Toro we sometimes take these smoky pans and wave them around the dishwasher's face if he's being a dick.)

2. Put these toasted ingredients along with the red wine vinegar, tomato sauce, most of the water, egg yolk, and parsley into your food processor and blend for about 1 minute.

3. Once blended, slowly drizzle in the oil for about 30 seconds. Don't over process this. You want some chunkiness to the almonds. Season with salt and pepper to taste and serve. Within 1 to 2 days salbitxada becomes dull and slightly metallic because of the vinegar, so eat it as soon as possible and always serve it slightly cool to room temperature.

Sofrito

ABOUT 1 PINT

Sofrito is basically a tomato-and-onion paste that's the base for paella and fideos and all sorts of other classic Spanish dishes. You caramelize the onions first, but after that you cook everything in one pot slow and low until it's nice and thick. A spoonful of sofrito adds a ton of depth and flavor, so put it in things like an already cooked pan of beans or throw a little cream at it and toss it with fresh-cooked pasta and you'll be happy.

We always use high-quality whole canned San Marzanos for ours, but you can use any stewed tomato as long as you check the sodium level. You don't want your tomatoes to be too salty, because that kills the flavor. And I love Arbequina olive oil for this but if that's too costly or difficult to find, use any good olive oil.

NOTE: *If you like to can, this is a great recipe to make a lot of and store. Sofrito keeps for 2 to 3 weeks in the refrigerator or 2 to 3 months in the freezer in small containers.*

1 tablespoon olive oil

10 yellow onions, julienned

10 cloves garlic, julienned

Pinch saffron

1 6-pound, 7-ounce can of tomatoes

1. Preheat the oven to 350 degrees.

2. In a medium-sized nonreactive, ovenproof sauce pan sauté the onion and garlic in olive oil over medium-high heat, stirring regularly, until they start to caramelize.

3. Add the saffron and tomatoes and bring back to a boil. Once boiling, remove from heat and put into the oven. Roast for about 2 hours, stirring every 5 to 10 minutes until reduced by half. As it cooks you will keep getting more and more caramelization on the top, which you want to keep stirring in so that it doesn't burn. It gets very thick, like a jam.

NOTE: *Be careful to pay attention to your sofrito as it cooks, because it quickly turns to lava and easily scorches. In other words, this is not a recipe to walk away from.*

4. Purée the sofrito in a blender while still hot and serve, or refrigerate or freeze.

Mojo Picon
ABOUT 1½ CUPS

While filming the *Endless Feast* in Phoenix, one of the farmers featured—Maya Dailey of Maya's Farm—fried up some squash blossoms stuffed with goat cheese. They were really simple and wonderful and not over battered and I remember thinking, *I bet mojo picon would go really well with these.* Mojo is a pop-in-your-mouth chili-and-olive-oil sauce that I'd been playing around with. I discovered it while reading about the outskirts of Spain, including the Canary Islands. Mojo picon is one of the region's primary sauces.

A month after we opened Toro Bravo, Viridian Farms came in with squash blossoms and I did a purée of onion and mint with fresh sheep cheese for them. I stuffed the blossoms with that purée and quickly fried them. At first we just squeezed lemon and salt and peppered them, but that wasn't right. That's when I remembered the mojo picon. We added it to the mix and fell in love. At the restaurant we also use mojo picon with our Butter-Braised Turnips (page 143), with seafood, and sometimes for a quick staff salad dressing.

½ cup Three-Chili Purée (page 286)

¼ cup red wine vinegar

6 cloves garlic

½ tablespoon ground cumin

1 tablespoon thyme leaves

1 tablespoon oregano leaves

1 tablespoon parsley leaves

½ tablespoon pimentón

½ cup olive oil

Salt

1. Combine all of the ingredients in a blender, and blend for about 30 seconds, until you have a smooth sauce.

2. Use right away, or store in a tightly lidded container.

Tapenade
ABOUT 3 CUPS

I hated olives until I was twenty-four years old. Another cook at Zenon said, *Hey, do you want to taste some olive bread?* I thought she said *challah* bread and I was really busy so I said, *Yeah,* and popped it in my mouth without looking. When I realized what it was I said, *Oh, gross.* She looked at me incredulously and said, *How the fuck are you going to be a chef and not like olives?* And I remember thinking, *You're right. How the fuck am I going to be a chef and not like olives?* Every day after that I'd eat five olives as soon as I got to work. I thought, *I'm just going to have to make myself like olives.* There was a day I thought, *Oh, I like this type, I like Picholines.* And next I thought, *Oh, these are good. I like Niçoise.* When you get to the point when you like kalamatas, you know you've arrived at fully loving olives. You can definitely train yourself to like foods. I did.

Get a jar of anchovy-stuffed Manzanilla olives for our tapenade. Manzanillas have such a unique flavor, and that combined with the anchovy really makes this tapenade special. If you don't have them, then make it with regular Manzanillas and throw in a vinegar boquerone. I like tapenade on so many different foods. We use it on the toasts we serve with Radicchio Salad (page 116). People like our tapenade so much that they regularly order the toast on its own. It's that good.

2 cups anchovy-stuffed Manzanilla olives, finely diced

¼ red onion, finely diced (about ½ cup)

2 tablespoons parsley leaves, finely chopped

1 tablespoon chives, finely chopped

1 tablespoon tarragon, finely chopped

½ cup olive oil

1. Place all of the ingredients except for the olive oil in a bowl and mix.

2. Add the olive oil and stir to incorporate.

NOTE: *If you smash olives first with the blade of your knife it's much easier to finely dice them and you won't lose so many rolling off onto the floor.*

Three-Chili Purée
ABOUT 3½ CUPS

You won't find this three-chili purée anywhere but Toro Bravo. It's in our Paella (page 242) and much more. It's a sauce that we messed with a lot to get just right. When you reconstitute dried chilies, they can get very spicy as well as bitter. We tinkered for a long time to get just the right, not overpowering, amount of heat and depth. When reconstituted dried chilies aren't too spicy they can be bitter, too, so it's a fine line of bitterness versus heat.

You can use Three-Chili Purée when braising meats, or put it on sandwiches, or mix it into sauces and stews. Adding this purée to dishes is a really great way to introduce a surprising, extra layer of flavor that's hard to pinpoint.

NOTES: *I don't care how tough you think you are, put on latex gloves for this one. Some cooks make the mistake of thinking that dried chilies don't pack much heat. I've seen many cooks come back from the bathroom dancing from the heat of chilies.*

Dried guajillos, nyoras, and arbol chilies aren't too hard to find, but you can substitute other dried chilies of comparable heat if necessary. If you're only going to spend time seeking out one of the three, I'd say pony up for the nyora. It's a sweet, mild, really tasty chili. I love them all but it's one of my favorites.

This purée lasts about a month so make a big batch and use the hell out of it. It also freezes well. I recommend using a freezer-safe bag and freezing it flat.

10 dried nyora chilies

5 dried guajillo chilies

2 dried arbol chilies

3 cups water

1. Wearing latex gloves, stem and seed the dried chilies and break the skins into pieces. It's okay if some seeds make it in and it doesn't matter how big or small the pieces of chili are.

2. Pour water into a medium saucepan over high heat. Once the water is boiling, lower the heat to medium-low and add all the chilies. Cover them and simmer for 30 minutes.

3. Remove the saucepan from the heat and keep the lid on it for at least another 20 minutes.

4. Pour the chilies along with the water into a blender and purée until smooth, about 30 seconds.

Piperade
ABOUT 5 CUPS

Piperade is a Basque sauce that's basically onions, peppers, and tomatoes. This is one of the easiest recipes in this book. Basically you sauté everything in quick succession, then simmer for twenty minutes. When the tomatoes start to fall apart you're done. And it's versatile: we use piperade with our Octopus à la Plancha (page 108) and with baked eggs. At my restaurant Tasty n Sons, piperade goes in the frijado, which is a Jewish tortilla. It's great with seafood, too. Most home cooks remove bay leaves from dishes before serving but in my family, whoever gets the bay leaf gets to kiss the chef. When we tested this, Renee's twenty-one-year-old brother, Dustin, got the bay leaf, and so he got to kiss our friend and recipe tester, Josh.

½ cup olive oil

1 yellow onion, julienned

6 cloves garlic, minced

1 pint roasted red bell peppers, julienned

1½ teaspoon sugar

1½ teaspoon paprika

1 28-ounce can tomatoes

1 bay leaf

1 tablespoon salt

½ teaspoon pepper

With eggs

5 cups piperade

6 eggs

1 loaf good crusty bread

¼ cup olive oil

Salt and pepper

1. Put a stainless steel or other non-reactive medium pot over medium heat and add the olive oil.

2. Once the oil has warmed, add the onion and garlic and sauté for 2 minutes, stirring occasionally.

3. Add the peppers and sauté for 2 more minutes, continuing to stir occasionally.

4. Add the sugar and the paprika and cook for 2 minutes, or until the paprika blooms.

5. Add the tomatoes and bay leaf, stir, and bring to a boil. Simmer slowly, uncovered for 20–30 minutes or until the tomatoes have broken down. Add salt and pepper to taste and serve.

With eggs

1. Preheat the oven to 425 degrees.

2. Place the warmed piperade in a cazuela or casserole. Break the eggs into the dish, being careful not to puncture the yolks, and leaving a few inches between each egg. Using a fork or spoon, break up the whites a bit and push them into the piperade so that they'll cook well.

3. Slice the bread to about a ½-inch thick, drizzle it with olive oil, and season it with salt and pepper. Grill it, toast it in a toaster oven or broil it until golden just before serving the baked piperade and eggs.

4. Bake the piperade and eggs for 7 to 10 minutes or until the egg whites are set. Serve family-style with the oiled, toasted bread.

287

Pisto Manchego
5–6 CUPS

The first time I had pisto manchego was when I was finishing my shift at Café Zenon, and a cook was trying his hand at it. The whole kitchen smelled of stew, so I had to have a bowl. I loved it, and still do. A big bowl of pisto is one of my favorite staff meals. Pisto manchego has a lot in common with ratatouille, which I've always been a fan of. But ratatouille can sometimes be bitter—because of the eggplant—and when it's not prepared properly, the texture can be off. This pisto was perfect. It was sweet and soft and really rich. No water had been added. It was just the essence of good summer vegetables at their purest form.

In Madrid, pisto manchego is everywhere—especially as a base for baked eggs. When we were in Madrid there was a taverna that Renee and I frequented that served pisto manchego in a sort of Spanish nacho kind of way. They fried slices of these little round potatoes until they were crispy and served these homemade chips with pisto manchego, jamón, and cheese. At Toro Bravo, we use it mainly with chicken and pasta. It's super easy to make: throw everything in the stock pot and simmer for a couple hours. Done.

¼ cup olive oil

2½ zucchinis, chopped (quarter them lengthwise and cut into 1-inch pieces)

1 yellow onion, chopped

3 red bell peppers, chopped

6 cloves garlic, slivered

1 28-ounce can tomatoes

Salt and pepper

With eggs

5 cups pisto manchego

6 eggs

1 loaf good crusty bread

¼ cup olive oil

Salt and pepper

1. Place a large pot over medium heat and add all the ingredients, including generous pinches of salt and pepper. Reserve some and taste after an hour or so before adding the remainder.

2. Bring to a boil and then lower the heat to medium-low and simmer, uncovered, for about 2 hours. Stir regularly until the vegetables have released all of their liquid and the consistency has turned more saucy. At that point you can leave the pisto largely unattended (keep stirring occasionally.) After 2 hours of simmering, taste. Add more salt and pepper if needed, and serve.

With eggs

1. Preheat the oven to 425 degrees.

2. Place the warmed pisto manchego in a cazuela or casserole. Break the eggs, being careful not to puncture the yolks, into the dish, leaving a few inches between each egg. Using a fork or spoon, break up the whites a bit and push them into the pisto manchego so they'll cook well.

3. Slice the bread, drizzle it with olive oil, and season it with salt and pepper. Grill, toast, or broil it until golden, just before serving the pisto manchego and eggs.

4. Once the oven is preheated, place the dish in it and bake for 7 to 10 minutes or until the egg whites are set. Serve family-style with the oiled, toasted bread.

Aioli

2½ CUPS

I'm a big believer in the mortar and pestle. When it comes to spices and garlic, it does a much better job than a knife or food processor. For our aioli you can either do it all in the mortar and pestle or just part. At the restaurant we only use the mortar and pestle for the first two steps, but feel free to go all the way.

Aioli doesn't like to be manhandled, so you've got to be gentle. The metallic flavor that you get in many aiolis is the result of the food processor or blender's fast blade. When you blend garlic with a blade, it breaks down the structure and water in a weird way that makes it taste metallic.

The other key to killer aioli is the freshest garlic and lemon. Always peel your own garlic and never buy the pre-peeled or minced shitty garlic. At Toro we probably go through two or three quarts of peeled garlic a day, and we peel every single one of those cloves. If you don't know what makes either fresh, ask someone in the produce department at your grocery store. If they don't know, find a new grocery store.

4 cloves garlic

1½ teaspoons sea salt (not kosher), divided

¼ lemon, zested

¼ lemon, juiced

1 egg yolk

1 teaspoon pepper, divided

3 tablespoons water, divided

2 cups oil blend (page 93)

1. Mortar and pestle the garlic and 1 teaspoon sea salt into a paste, then add the lemon zest, lemon juice, egg yolk, ½ teaspoon of pepper and incorporate.

2. Set up a mixing bowl with a towel wrapped around it at the base to keep it somewhat stationary. Robustly whisk the mortar and pestle contents into it, adding 1 tablespoon of water and then slowly drizzling in a cup of the oil for about 1 minute.

3. The aioli should be getting pretty tight at this point. If it is, add the remaining 2 tablespoons of water and whisk again while drizzling in the remaining cup of oil. If it isn't, whisk until it is, and then drizzle in the remaining water and oil.

4. Add the remaining ½ teaspoon of salt and ½ teaspoon of pepper and whisk to incorporate. Taste and adjust the seasoning to your liking.

NOTE: *You want aioli to hold its shape but still be loose and jiggle if you put a spoonful on a plate and shake the plate. It should react a little like Jell-O. When aioli cools, it tightens up.*

5. Serve immediately or store tightly covered for 3 to 4 days. At day four or five, aioli gets metallic tasting because the acid starts having its way with the garlic.

Salsa Verde
ABOUT 1 CUP

This sauce is all about fresh herbs, so please don't destroy one of my all-time favorite sauces by reaching for your spice rack. Yes, it takes time to pick all the leaves off the stems and finely mince them in batches, but the big, green flavor is what defines salsa verde. And it's so worth it. Think of it this way: once you've prepped the herbs, the only thing left to do is to stir. So many people add acid to their salsa verdes, but I think acid kills it. This one gets better the next day because we don't add any. It's always bright.

At Toro Bravo we serve salsa verde on our polenta and with our Seared Cauliflower (page 138). This sauce is freaking incredible to have in your refrigerator because it goes well with so much: a piece of toast with some cheese, a grilled steak, tossed in pasta. It's incredibly versatile and the epitome of fresh.

2 tablespoons parsley

2 tablespoons mint

2 tablespoons tarragon

1 tablespoon chives

2 tablespoons sage

2 tablespoons fennel fronds
(can substitute 1 tablespoon dill)

1 shallot

2 tablespoons salt-packed
capers, rinsed

½ cup olive oil

1. Clean, dry, and stem the herbs, then finely mince each herb separately with a sharp knife. Be careful not to bruise the herbs and mince them in nice swift and clean chops.

2. Finely dice 1 medium shallot and finely dice the capers.

3. In a small mixing bowl, combine all of the ingredients with olive oil. If you adjust anything in this recipe you can adjust the shallot, capers, or olive oil to your preference, but always be sure to use equal parts of all of the herbs. Serve immediately or allow to sit overnight refrigerated.

Chicken Stock/Fideos Stock

8 QUARTS

Stocks are the foundation of any kitchen, and our chicken and fideos/paella stocks are Toro Bravo's main stocks. Stocks require quality ingredients. A lot of kitchens use shit for stocks and expect to get something great in return. That just doesn't make any sense. At Toro, we're not making stock from frozen blocks of mystery bones. We use chicken parts—often leftover from breaking down chickens for our other dishes—always from quality, healthy chickens. At home I'll often make stock out of a whole chicken. Once it's been poached I'll take the chicken out, make a meal out of it, and then return the bones back to the stockpot to simmer.

That's the number one rule when making stock: simmer. Never let your stock come to a rolling boil; always keep it to a low simmer. At the restaurant, we like clean stocks so we don't let ours cook overnight. We start them at ten in the morning and they come off the burner at five in the evening, right before we open.

When Toro first opened, we put our walk-in together ourselves with rickety 18-inch wire Metro racks. As we got busier and busier, those shelves had to sustain more weight and movement than they should have. Even still, for years we'd put two 22-quart containers of heavily iced stocks on the racks right by the walk-in fans to cool quickly. One day during a rush, somebody bumped into the shelf. The shelf quaked and the broth, still boiling hot, cascaded like a waterfall right onto the foot of John Shucks, one of our cooks. Shucks had to do about six weeks of skin grafts after that and the poor guy is still limping around from that one. Moral of the story: be careful with hot stocks.

Chicken Stock

4 or 5 chicken carcasses

1 yellow onion, roughly chopped

2 carrots, roughly chopped

4 celery ribs, roughly chopped

2½ gallons cold water

Fideos Stock

2 tablespoons olive oil

1 pint diced bacon

1 yellow onion, roughly chopped

2 red bell peppers, roughly chopped

1 head of garlic

2 bay leaves

1 teaspoon saffron

8 quarts chicken stock

It's such a great stock for various soup bases; you could even add salt to it for a great broth alone.

Chicken Stock

1. Put all the ingredients in a large stockpot, fill with cold water, and turn up the heat.

2. Watch the stock as it heats. Right before the stock begins to boil, turn the heat down to a simmer.

Let it simmer all day, uncovered, about 5 to 7 hours.

3. After 5 to 7 hours, strain the stock. Cool and refrigerate overnight, removing the fat once it's cold. You can easily freeze it too.

Fideos Stock

1. Heat olive oil in a large stock pot. Sauté the bacon, onion, bell peppers, garlic, and bay leaf at high heat, until everything gets a little caramelized. Add the chicken stock and saffron.

2. Simmer for 5 to 7 hours. Strain the stock. Cool and refrigerate overnight, removing the fat once it's cold. You can easily freeze it, too.

Orange Marmalade
1 QUART

At Simpatica we would make orange marmalade in the winter and add 50-percent maple syrup to it for our French toast and waffle syrup. Straight up, it goes really well with our Pork Rillettes (page 184): the perfect combination of citrusy sweet plus smoky salty pork.

7 navel oranges

1½ cups orange juice, divided

1 cup water

2 cups sugar

1 vanilla bean, halved and scraped

1. Halve the oranges top to bottom and thinly slice them into half-moons.

2. Put the sliced oranges into a large pot and fill the pot with enough water to cover them. Place over high heat.

3. Bring the water to a boil and, once boiling, drain the water (keep the oranges in the pot). Fill the pot with water to cover the oranges again and repeat. These two blanchings take some of the bitterness out of the skin and pith and help break the oranges down. If you have especially bitter oranges (it happens from time to time), do a third blanching.

4. Add 1 cup of the orange juice, 1 cup of water, the sugar, and the vanilla bean to the pot and return to high heat. Bring the marmalade to a rapid boil and allow it to boil, uncovered, for about 35 minutes.

You want to cook all the liquid out and allow the marmalade to caramelize.

5. Stir only every 5 to 10 minutes or so. Begin stirring regularly during the last 10 to 15 minutes, so that the marmalade doesn't scorch. At this point you should hear a crackly sound as the marmalade cooks since most of the liquid has released.

    NOTE: *Be careful of spitting marmalade. It's extremely hot and sticky and can really burn you.*

6. Do a taste test. If the marmalade isn't sweet enough, add more sugar. Once it's to your liking, remove it from the heat, place it in a new pan, and put plastic wrap over the surface of the marmalade so that it doesn't get a film on it. Once fully cooled, contain it and refrigerate. It keeps for up to a month.

Marinated Olives

1 QUART

We go through a lot of olives at Toro, and this is a really simple mix of mostly Spanish, pits-still-in olives with olive oil that we use in everything from our Seared Cauliflower (page 138) to Grilled Asparagus (page 146) to Halibut Cheeks (page 204). We use Arbequinas, Castelvetranos, Talledes, and Moroccan dry-cured olives for our mix, but you don't need to hunt down those exact ones. Source a good mix of tasty green and black European olives and you'll be good to go. Niçoise olives are always a tasty addition. If you were going to use just one olive for most of Toro's recipes I'd choose the big, bright green Castelvetranos. They're versatile, delicious, and are becoming easier and easier to find.

NOTE: *Here's a trick for pitting a lot of olives all at once. Spread them out on a cutting board, put a towel over them, and then whack them with a rolling pin or wine bottle—just enough so that they slightly smoosh and you can then easily pick out the pits. You obviously don't want to whack them so much that you break the pit and/or pulverize them.*

1. Mix all of the pits-still-in olives with the olive oil to coat.

2. Use immediately or store for up to 1 month. Use the leftover olive oil for dipping bread in, making dressings, or sautéing.

1¼ cup Arbequina olives

1¼ cup Castelvetrano olives

1¼ cup Tallades olives

¼ cup Moroccan dry-cured olives

¼ cup olive oil

Tomato Sauce
2 QUARTS

Cook our tomato sauce just like you cook our piperade—at a low temperature, just until the tomatoes break down. Don't crush the tomatoes and don't overcook them because you don't want to caramelize the sugars. Normally I'm all about caramelization, but in this case, it takes away from the delicate brightness of the tomatoes. This is a good, reliable tomato sauce that you can use for anything that calls for a red sauce.

4 cloves garlic, minced

¼ cup olive oil

¼ cup parsley

1 6-pound, 6-ounce can tomatoes

Salt and pepper

1. In a medium nonreactive saucepan over medium heat, cook the minced garlic in olive oil for 3 or 4 minutes.

2. Add the parsley and sauté for 1 minute.

3. Add the tomatoes and bring to a slow simmer. Simmer for 1½ hours until the tomatoes are nicely broken down.

4. Whisk the tomatoes to break them down further. Simmer for another 15 minutes.

5. Season with salt and pepper and serve, or refrigerate for up to 1 week.

Béchamel

2 CUPS

There's not much to say about this recipe other than it's a classic, dependable béchamel. Béchamel is a slightly thick white sauce made with a roux of butter and flour cooked in milk. Feel free to use any béchamel recipe that you love, as long as it's not too loose. Croquettes need a tighter béchamel so that they don't fall apart. My only other advice is if you use a different recipe—though why would you?—don't get too crazy with the cloves or nutmeg. We don't have either in ours because they'd be a little heavy for the croquettes, which already have cinnamon (which is what we want to highlight).

¼ cup butter, cut into chunks

⅓ cup all-purpose flour

1½ cups milk

1 onion pique (This is a fancy French name for a peeled half onion with a bay leaf pinned onto it with 2 cloves.)

Salt and pepper

1. In a medium sauté pan over high heat, create a blond roux by melting the butter, adding the flour, and stirring with a wooden spoon until evenly mixed and slightly nutty after 35 to 45 seconds. Remove from the heat.

   NOTE: *Roux loses gluten as it cooks and darkens, so brown roux has way less gluten and therefore tightening powers than a light roux. We want a light roux here, but we also want a little of that toasty flavor.*

2. Place the milk and onion pique in another medium-sized pot and bring to a simmer while stirring occasionally for 10 to 15 minutes.

3. Strain half of the milk through a sieve (leaving behind the onion) into the roux (still not on heat), slowly whisking, then add the other half. Put the pot back over high heat, bring to a boil, season with salt and pepper, and cook while stirring with a wooden spoon (you don't want to scrape up any milk film from the bottom of the pan) for 1 or 2 minutes until it's a gluey consistency with no lumps and looks like wet mashed potatoes.

4. Strain the béchamel and use, or cool and refrigerate covered for up to 1 week.

Chocolate Almonds
3 CUPS

Scott Weider is a wild card kind of guy who was always getting hurt doing crazy things like getting in scooter accidents in Mexico and jumping off cliffs. We cooked together on the line at Citron for a year, until he left for Chez Panisse. He threw a going-away party at his house, and there was a bowl of perfectly cooked almonds on the table. I remember trying them and thinking, *Fuck, these are so good.* When I asked how he made them, he told me that his family had a California almond farm and they were his family's almonds toasted in olive oil with a little sea salt. Simple as that. At the end of the night he brought out white almonds coated in chocolate that were incredible, too. I asked again, he told me, and I've been making these chocolate almonds ever since.

If it's someone's birthday and they're celebrating at Toro Bravo, we'll put a candle in the cazuela and send chocolate almonds out. It's a really great dessert to share or give out in little bags as Christmas gifts.

10 ounces 55% semisweet chocolate

3 cups Poached Almonds (page 97)

5 cups powdered sugar, divided

1. Melt the chocolate in a double boiler.

2. Place the poached almonds into a large bowl, pour the melted chocolate over them, and mix them with gloved hands until the almonds are covered in the chocolate.

3. Add some of the powdered sugar to the chocolate-y almonds and continue to gently mix by hand. Keep mixing and adding more sugar as needed, but don't mix too vigorously or the chocolate will rub off the almonds. When done, the almonds will be separated from one another and coated in white.

4. Pour the almonds onto a parchment paper–lined sheet pan and refrigerate them uncovered for 1 to 1½ hours to cool.

5. Using a sieve, gently shake the excess coating off the nuts. Serve or put them in a tightly covered container and refrigerate. They'll keep for 1 to 2 weeks, but they never last that long. They're too good.

Olive Oil Cake
1 CAKE, 6–8 SERVINGS

I learned to make coffee cake when I was in third grade, and it was one of the first foods that I got good at making. I think I chose coffee cake because all of the ingredients were usually in the cupboard. I remember making coffee cake for my mom and finding joy in that: in sitting at the table and giving someone something that you made that was really good. Since then I've loved slightly sweet, almost savory coffee cakes. Our Olive Oil Cake is exactly that. Six years since I first started making it (thanks to Jason Owens for giving me the original recipe, which we've changed up over the years), I still have a slice every day in the morning with my coffee. We serve the cake at room temperature, with seasonal sauces: rhubarb sauce in spring, strawberry and blood orange caramel in the summer.

NOTES: *At Toro, when you start to prep the olive oil cake you tape your oven shut as a way to say, Don't fucking touch my oven, because this is a needy and delicate cake. Once the cakes are in the oven you tape it shut again. You want a very stable 450 degrees at the beginning or the cakes won't set. Steer clear of rubberbandy olive oils, too. Most Spanish olive oils aren't like that, but sometimes Italian and French ones are.*

1 tablespoon butter, room temperature

2 eggs

1⅔ cup sugar

1 cup milk

1 cup olive oil

½ lemon, zested

½ lemon, juiced

1¾ cups + 1 tablespoon all-purpose flour (and 1 tablespoon for dusting the cake pan)

1 teaspoon baking powder

½ teaspoon baking soda

¾ teaspoon salt

1. Preheat the oven to 450 degrees.

2. Butter a 10-inch cake pan and then top it with parchment paper cut to fit the pan. Butter the top of the parchment paper as well. Dust the pan with flour and set it aside.

3. In a mixer, mix the eggs and sugar on medium, about 10 minutes.

4. In a bowl, combine the milk, olive oil, lemon zest, and lemon juice, and whisk. Return the mixer with the eggs and sugar to medium and slowly pour your liquids into the mixer. It should take about 30 seconds to do so. Once these wet ingredients have all been added, mix for another 30 seconds.

5. In another bowl combine the flour, baking powder, baking soda, and salt. Add this to the mixer and mix on medium for about 1 minute.

6. Pour the batter into the cake pan and bake for 10 minutes. NOTE: *DO NOT open the oven.*

7. After 10 minutes reduce the heat to 400 degrees and bake for another 20 minutes.

8. After 20 minutes lower the heat to 350 degrees and bake for 5 to 10 minutes, until the cake is golden brown on top.

9. Test doneness by inserting a toothpick into the middle of the cake. If it comes out clean and the cake looks firm around the edges and cooked in the middle, it's done. Let it cool completely, then serve at room temperature or wrap tightly in plastic wrap. It keeps for 4 to 5 days if wrapped well.

Baked Fruit Clafoutis

6–8 PEOPLE, MAKES TWO 5-INCH CAZUELAS

We made a lot of clafoutis in culinary school. This is a traditional French clafoutis, baked to order in a Spanish cazuela. I think that clafoutis is best when it's ugliest and hottest although no one usually serves it that way. We do, and you're welcome. My favorite clafoutis is the strawberry rhubarb in the late spring and early summer. After that we have clafoutis with marionberries, blueberries, raspberries, and wine grapes. When berry season's over we use roasted apples and pears. There's always something different you can do with this custardy batter. The berries go in raw, but for apples and pears and other more dense fruits, you'll want to sauté them first. We like to do apples and pears with a little cinnamon, brown sugar, and nutmeg. We sear rhubarb with butter and vanilla. Use whatever fruit you like, but always use two pints of whatever is fresh, tasty, and seasonal.

2 ounces butter

½ vanilla bean, split lengthwise

4 eggs

4 egg yolks

1 cup heavy cream

1 cup sugar

½ cup brown sugar

½ cup all-purpose flour

1 teaspoon nutmeg

½ teaspoon salt

1 pint pitted cherries

1 pint sliced strawberries

1 pint good vanilla ice cream

1. Preheat your convection oven to 400 degrees or a non-convection oven to 425 degrees.

2. In a medium sauté pan on medium-high heat, brown the butter with the split vanilla bean for 2 minutes. Inhale, because this step smells great.

3. Strain the butter and scrape the bean into it. Discard the shell (after rinsing, we use the shell for our Vanilla Extract, page 280) and set aside.

4. Place the wet ingredients (eggs, egg yolks, heavy cream) and butter into a food processor and pulse to combine.

5. Add the dry ingredients (sugar, brown sugar, flour, nutmeg, salt), except for the fruit, and blend until smooth.

6. Place a layer of fruit in whatever baking dish(es) you use. You can do all of this in one pan as long as it's just under 2 inches deep. (Any deeper and the clafoutis won't bake properly.)

7. Pour the blended batter over the fruit and use a fork to move the fruit around a little bit so that the batter gets distributed. Don't mess with it too much— just a few pushes here and there will do.

8. Bake the clafoutis in a convection oven for 25 minutes or in a non-convection oven for 30 to 35 minutes. Once you see the fruit bubbling up out of the batter and the top of the clafoutis is golden, remove it from the oven. It should be really firm around the edges and a little soft in the middle but not wet.

9. Let it rest for 10 minutes (it's like lava right out of the oven), then serve it topped with a good vanilla ice cream. If you have any extra clafoutis batter, it keeps in the fridge for 4 to 5 days.

303

Panna Cotta
SIX 6-OUNCE CONTAINERS

I was at LuLu and twenty-seven years old when Steve Duggan, their pastry chef at the time, made this panna cotta. I told him it was the best panna cotta I'd ever had and he chuckled, like he was in on a secret. He said, *This is the simplest recipe known to man. You can't fuck it up. You can't make it not amazing. It has four ingredients and takes five minutes and is foolproof so long as you pay attention.*

But, contrary to Steve's assertion, it *is* fuckupable, especially if you're unfamiliar with sheet gelatin. People tend to soak it too long or not long enough. You have to activate it correctly. If you soak it too long or in warm water it disintegrates and you don't get as much gelatin. You have to get it soft and wring it out without losing any of the gelatin. Also, if you don't whisk it when you put the gelatin in, the gelatin will go right to the bottom of the pot and it'll stick and burn.

When I first came to Portland, I made this panna cotta a lot because pastry chefs at Paley's Place and other restaurants wanted me to. The next thing I knew, it was on a lot of menus in town—or renditions of it. The trick to this panna cotta is using those gelatin sheets. You won't get close to the same results with gelatin powder. Gelatin sheets are much smoother. They don't clump up, there's no graininess, and it's way more predictable than the powder.

Our panna cotta goes well with so many things: berries soaked in grappa, our caramel sauce (which we've included here), roasted apples, and walnuts. Trust your instincts when it comes to topping. Use whatever's delicious and in season.

---

1 quart heavy cream

½ vanilla bean, split and scraped

½ cup sugar

4 gelatin sheets

---

1. In a heavy, medium saucepan over medium heat, add the cream, vanilla bean, and sugar, stir to incorporate, and bring to a boil. Lower the heat to a very low simmer, about 45 minutes.

2. Remove the cream from the heat and discard the vanilla bean. (Or rinse it and add it to your Vanilla Extract, page 280.)

3. Soak 4 gelatin sheets in cold water for 30 seconds to a minute, until they turn limp. (If you leave a sheet in water for too long, it'll start to disintegrate and lose some of its thickening power.) Once limp, remove the sheets from the water, squeeze out the remaining water, and add the sheets to your cream, whisking until they're fully dissolved.

4. Strain this mixture through a fine sieve and then put it in a dish in an ice bath. Stir the panna cotta, still in the ice bath, until it starts to thicken. Once it is thick, put it into whatever serving containers you want. We use 6-ounce ramekins or flaneras.

5. Cover each panna cotta with plastic wrap while it's still a little bit warm, so it doesn't get a film. Refrigerate until cool and serve topped with caramel sauce or another topping to your liking. Panna cotta keeps for about a week refrigerated.

Caramel Sauce
FOR 6 PANNA COTTAS

1. Put a small sauté pan over medium heat and add the sugar, water, and lemon juice, then leave it alone as it comes to a boil. Let it boil for about 5 minutes. You want this to turn a little darker than amber. If you move the pan around too much as it boils, crystals will form at the rim of the pan and mess up the clarity of the sauce. The bubbles tend to come down as the caramel gets hotter and caramelizes.

2. Turn off the heat and add the cream a little bit at a time. The caramel sauce is going to want to blow up, so add your cream little by little. Add the brandy and stir.

3. Bring the sauce back to a boil over medium-high heat. Once at a boil, cook it for 30 more seconds, then remove it from the heat and let it cool to room temperature. Pay attention, because if you cool the caramel sauce beyond room temperature it will get too thick. Spoon 1 tablespoon of caramel sauce on top of each panna cotta and serve.

½ cup sugar

2 tablespoons water

1 teaspoon lemon juice

¼ cup heavy cream

1 tablespoon brandy (we use Cardenal Mendoza, but use whatever brandy you feel allegiance to)

Crepes

15–20 CREPES

Savory crepes are what made Simpatica's brunch famous. Jason and I would come back from whatever event we'd just catered and make crepes until about two in the morning. Then we'd sleep for a few hours, come back again, and cook them for brunch service.

One day we had some crepes and lemon curd left over from a party, so I baked the crepes and served them with the curd and it was delicious. Lemon curd is one of my favorite desserts. It's so good and so easy. Making crepes, on the other hand, takes some skill. If you don't know how to flip without a spatula, then learn before making them, because crepes hate spatulas. There are all sorts of videos online to school you on how to make and flip crepes. At the restaurant we cover our burners in nonstick pans and do several crepes at once in many rounds. Once you get your perfect heat, don't adjust. The first couple crepes in the batch are always crap and it's not the batter's fault, it's the temperature. Go ahead and throw them away. If you don't use all your batter at once, freeze it, defrost it, and then blend it again quickly, and you're good to go.

NOTE: *If you're into making crepes buy a nonstick pan and dedicate it to them, because the newer the nonstick pan the better and the easier it is to make crepes.*

3 eggs

¾ cup all-purpose flour

1 teaspoon salt

¾ cup milk

4 tablespoons + ¼ pound butter (We like to use clarified butter when cooking crepes because it can withstand high heat without burning.)

½ cup water

1. In a blender, combine all the ingredients and blend until smooth, then transfer to the container that you'll be pouring the crepes from.

2. Put your medium nonstick pan or pans (at Toro we use 6-inch omelette pans) over medium-high heat and put a quarter to a half teaspoon of butter in. Move it around to coat the pan. Right when the butter is about to brown, pour in 2 to 3 tablespoons of batter.

3. Your goal is to get the crepes as thin as you can. Flip each crepe once it's browned on the first side and cook it for about 45 seconds to a minute longer. A lot of French chefs don't want any color on their crepes, but I think that that caramelization is delicious.

4. Stack the cooked crepes while they're hot. (Don't worry about them getting stuck. They'll separate because of all the butter.)

Serve with the lemon curd, powdered sugar, and whipped cream.

NOTE: *For a dinner party, cook all of your crepes, stack them while making them, then fold them into fours/triangles, and bake them in the oven at 350 degrees for about a minute to reheat before serving. Serve the crepes with butter, powdered sugar, and bowls of lemon curd and whipped cream, for folks to apply however they like.*

Lemon Curd

ABOUT 3 CUPS

1. Combine all of the ingredients except for the butter in a medium nonreactive pot and whisk over low heat for about 5 minutes, until the eggs are loosened up.

2. Add half the butter and whisk the curd periodically until it begins to thicken. Once the curd is slightly thickened, whisk it constantly and bring the heat up to 175 to 180 degrees. This part of the process should take 10 to 15 minutes. Don't ever go over 185 degrees. If you get warmer than that, your curd will break, you'll have scrambled eggs and there's no way to fix that. And if you cook this too fast, the eggs won't thicken properly. Eggs thicken the best at 180 degrees. So many cooks think that it'll just magically happen but if you get there too quickly and don't stay at that temperature long enough, it won't. Slow and low is the way to do it.

3. Once the curd is at 175 to 180 degrees and properly thickened (if you dip a spoon in the curd and then hold the spoon sideways, you should be able to make a line in the curd that stays; you want your curd tight, but not so tight that it's hard or grainy in the mouth), turn off the heat, add the second half of the butter, and whisk to melt it.

4. Pour the curd through a sieve that's not too fine into a non-reactive cooling pan and strain out the lemon zest by using a ladle to push the curd through. Cover the curd with plastic wrap right over the top of it and refrigerate. The curd will get a film if you don't put plastic wrap right on top of it. Once cooled, serve the lemon curd with warm crepes and any other crepe fillings that you like.

---

7 lemons, juiced and zested

1¾ cup sugar

6 eggs

9 egg yolks

1¼ cup butter, divided

Hazelnut Ice Cream

2.5–3 QUARTS

This ice cream with a shot of Pedro Ximénez sherry (P.X.) poured over the top is one of Toro Bravo's best desserts, and like many recipes it began with a fuck-up. One day—this was one of our early days—Ron had overcooked some hazelnuts (he truly just overcooked them this time, not like the "overheated" crostini coals on page 44). They were a little too bitter for our salad. By then I'd played around with some heavily toasted nut ice creams where the flavors came out big, bold, and interesting, so I made an ice cream base with those slightly burnt nuts. It turned out awesome. But as I was eating the ice cream my first thought was, *I need some P.X. to go with.* That's how we've served our hazelnut ice cream ever since: with a shot of P.X. over the top. It goes well with chocolate, too.

NOTE: *As far as home ice cream makers go, I really like the Cuisinart one with the removable freezer bowl. It's about fifty bucks and does a solid job.*

1 quart heavy cream

1 quart milk

14 ounces sugar, divided

1 quart of dark-roasted hazelnuts, crushed (throw in a food processor and hit pulse several times, leaving some fine and others more chunky; there's no need for them to be uniform)

20 egg yolks

1. In a large nonreactive saucepan over medium heat, bring the heavy cream, milk, 7 ounces of sugar, and crushed hazelnuts to a slow simmer. Once simmering, lower the heat and simmer for 15 minutes. Don't ever let the mixture get above a slow simmer, because you'll quickly have a hot, burnt-sugar, and frothy-cream mess on your hands. And the difference between simmer and boil can be a matter of seconds. Don't leave this unattended.

2. Put the egg yolks and the other half of the sugar, the remaining 7 ounces, into a large bowl and whisk that for 2–3 minutes until the sugar is incorporated into the yolks and the mix has a light, ribbony consistency.

3. Once the cream, milk, sugar, and hazelnuts have slowly simmered for 15 minutes, strain out the hazelnuts and discard them. Reserve the hot cream mix.

4. Take 1 cup of the hot cream mix and slowly add it to egg yolk/sugar mix while slowly whisking to incorporate it. If you add the hot cream mix too quickly, it will cook the eggs. You don't want that.

5. After you've slowly whisked 3 cups of the hot cream mix into the yolks whisk the rest in more quickly now that the danger of curdling has passed. You still want to continuously slowly whisk while adding the remaining hot cream mix in order to avoid any hot spots.

6. Once all of the hot cream mix has been incorporated, you basically have a hazelnut crème anglaise. Pour this back into your pot over medium heat.

7. Slowly, continuously whisk the mix over medium heat, making sure that nothing sticks to the bottom. The egg yolks are heavy, and will want to sink. Put a thermometer into the mix and watch it closely

until it gets to 180 degrees, and no higher. This should take 10 to 15 minutes.

8. As soon as the mixture reaches 180 degrees, immediately remove the pot from the heat, strain the mix through a fine-mesh sieve or cheesecloth, and pour it into a bowl that's sitting in another container filled with ice. After 15 to 20 minutes, wrap the cooled bowl in plastic wrap and place it in the refrigerator to cool completely for 1 to 2 hours.

9. Once the ice cream mix is cold, transfer it to your ice cream maker, churn, and freeze according to the manufacturer's instructions. This batch makes about 2 Cuisinart ice cream bowls' worth of ice cream. Eat it right away or store it tightly contained in the freezer for up to 2 weeks.

NOTE: *You can make the ice cream base and keep it refrigerated for up to a week if you want to break up your ice cream batches. I recommend doing that if you can't eat it all at once. Ice cream is always best freshly churned.*

ACKNOWLEDGMENTS

From start to finish this book took two and a half years to make, and I want to thank John Gorham, Renee Gorham, and the entire Toro Bravo crew, especially Josh Scofield, Kasey Mills, and Mindy Cook for enduring, sometimes enjoying, and almost always appreciating the long and winding process. John, some of my best memories of this book are from our many long lunches around Portland and its outskirts: you talking about Toro and cooking and your upbringing and Toro's recipes over noodles, sushi, curry, and more. So sweet and so special. Thank you.

Rachel Khong, editor extraordinaire, you know how much I love you and how grateful I am to have gotten to work with you on this. In the words of our favorite older, suited, Spanish male server: *thank you milady*. I will never be able to apologize enough for the fact that, during the writing of this book, you once had to crawl through my dog door to get into my house.

Thank you David Byrne for just so happening to send ice cream to the McSweeney's office the first time I visited and therefore elevating what was already an incredible moment for me to shooting-stars dreamy. McSweeney's, ice cream from David Byrne, and oh wait, a visit from Elizabeth Gilbert?! It all happened on my first visit to McSweeney's because that's the way they roll. I love all of you McSweeney's folks so much. And even though you're on the other side of the country now, Walter Green, I am so grateful that you carry on with the clan remotely. You made us such a strikingly designed, beauty of a book.

Thank you David Reamer for all of your kick-ass photographs and love of Spanish cats. Thank you Ron Avni for being one of my new favorite dining companions and for always taking notes and making special requests even when you drive the servers crazy. They still love you.

Thank you Kim Witherspoon (and Allison Hunter!) for taking John and me on and fighting for us.

Thanks to the many Portland cookbook authors who rallied for us and gave us all kinds of sound advice early on, including Ellen Jackson, Nick Zukin, Piper Davis, Julie Richardson, and Mark Bitterman. Thank you JJ Goode for your early words of wisdom and encouragement. Thanks to all of the solid, fun Sunday-night-dinner recipe-testing folks, particularly Rhonda and Josh Collier. Thanks to the McSweeney's interns, particularly Amanda Arnold, Aralyn Beaumont, Kylie Byrd, Naoki O'Bryan, and Vanessa Martini for cooking from the book and transcribing things like:

J: I think that he's chickenshit.
L: That would be reasonable, yes.

(And no, we were not talking about Mr. Kasey Mills.)

Thank you to all red-pants-wearing Spanish men. And as for all the golden ones—thank you to all of my friends and family and Portland for your endless love and support. Only one life. **—LIZ CRAIN**

Special thanks to all of the folks that have ever entered the bullring.

The biggest thanks ever to my wife and service manager, Renee Gorham. A woman who doesn't fuck around.

Big thanks to Kasey "Chicken-Shit" Mills aka "Sugar Tits." When this is done we will wear robes and hot tub together.

Josh and Sarah Scofield. You're both matadors! Toro wouldn't be what it is without you both.

Mindy Cook! Thanks for all the tasty beverages. You're one of the few who will push harder than myself.

Pat Manning. We set you free and you came back! True love. You know how to climb a ladder.

Ron Avni. One of my best friends. We're all on your team!

Café Zenon. Bill Hatch, Tim Washburn, Mitch Temple, David Counter. Four restaurateurs who forever shaped my beliefs in food and spirits. There is hardly a day I don't reflect on the magic that was in that building. There will never be another restaurant like Zenon again.

Matt Cartwright, Tim Lundholm, Brett Smith, Bob Ryan (even though you broke up with us, it took three guys to replace you). These are the men who helped build Toro Bravo, and keep it standing.

Viande Meats & Sausages and Simpatica. Thanks to the crew that helped launch these two crazy concepts! Breaking up with you two was one of the hardest and best things I've ever done.

Bergit Markus. My family wouldn't be the same without you. I'm so thankful you are in my children's lives.

Thanks to Kyle C., Jannika, Pat, Tomas, Kyle P., Jeff, Erin, Tynan, Morgan, Charlie, Prange, Juliette, Stacy, Rebecca, Catherine, Emma, Colyn, Josh, Blaze, Shawn, Adam, Sarah Marshall, Heather, Amanda, Katie Kelly, Jenn. These are the folks that run Toro Bravo, Tasty n Sons, and Tasty n Alder day in and day out.

Katrina, Alicia, and Drew. You're bulls for life!

Ruby and Royal. My beautiful girls.

Dave Harmsen. A good accountant is worth his weight in gold!

Virdian Farms, Provvista, Nicky USA, SP Meats, Your Kitchen Garden, Stumptown Coffee, Columbia Empire Meats, Laughing Stock Farm, Sunshine Dairy, Grand Central Bakery, Wildside, Groundworks, Creative Growers, PDX Wines, Lemma, Matello, Cameron, Oregon Brand Management, J. Christopher, Real Good Food, Alexis Food, Ocean Beauty, Newman's, Pacific Coast Fruit, Roses Restaurant Equipment, Breakside, Cana's Feast, Portland Farmers' Market, Galaxy, Mitchell, D'Vine, Vinum, Maletis, Uptown Liquor, Dinerware, Butcher Packer, McGraw Marketing, Patrick's Berries, Cheese Bar, Sammy's Flowers, Teutonic, Service Linen, Gathering Together Farm, Mary's Chickens, Autochlor, Wiley's Cooking Woods, Automatic Ice, Portland Candle, De Maison Selections, Phil Smith, Portland Paper, Kelly Paper, Ink Brigade, Columbia Distributing (even though you're the biggest pain in the ass of the bunch).

Bonnie, Emma, Holly. For educating our crew regularly.

Rhonda, Josh, Isaac, Ron, Jane. without these folks there would have been no Toro Bravo. Thanks for the dough!

Damien Baker. My two other hands!

Courtney Wilson, Rachael Donaldson, Jason Friend, Amber Ferguson. Toro's past managers.

Mike Wathen. Toro's house DJ, and lifelong best friend!

Get A Life Marching Band. Every restaurant should have a marching band!

Paul Klitsie. For introducing my food to Portland.

Mike and Joe. Our number one regulars.

Morgan Brownlow. Hcap plan master!

Dave Reamer. You're a good friend and a hell of a photographer!

Liz Crain. Thanks for helping tell the story of a bull. It's been awesome to get to know you.

Rachel Khong and the entire McSweeney's crew. Thanks for believing in our story.

To my family. I love you all.

Gene. Sorry I threw all your tools away. I love you, Pops.

Mom, RIP. I'm happy you never have to feel pain again.

Granddad Gordon. I wish you could be here now. I think about you all the time.

PORTLAND. I love this city. The only place that has ever felt like home.

Gallbladder. I miss you all the time. Sorry I worked you to death. Life isn't the same without you.

N.L.S. acknowledging I think you suck! Fold your damn towels.

—**JOHN GORHAM**

I would like to thank everyone involved in the creation of this amazing cookbook. John Gorham, one hell of a guy and a solid friend. They definitely broke the mold after you, dude. Thanks for having so much faith in me. Liz Crain, it's been great collaborating with you. You're gonna do Portland proud. I can't wait to open a bottle of cava and settle into some juicy stories. Rachel Khong, Walter Green, and all the folks at McSweeney's, thanks for bringing this story to life and letting us do it on our terms.

Thanks to Kasey Mills for having the patience of a Buddhist. (I would have punched me a long time ago.) You're a really good dude. Thanks to Josh Scofield. I'm happy you're finally getting the props you deserve for all your hard work, talent, and innovation. Thanks also to Renee Gorham for gracefully keeping the hull of a hectic ship steady through often rough seas.

A very special and heartfelt thanks to every line cook, prep cook, waiter, waitress, bartender, manager, and dishwasher at Toro Bravo who had to stop what they were doing or went out of their way to help me make a shot better. Sorry for the inconvenience. I couldn't hack doing what y'all do. I have endless respect for your hard work and dedication. Glad you're all finally getting health insurance!

On that note, thanks to the entire Portland restaurant scene for all the love and support over the past six years. Each and every one of you has helped me make my dream of being a professional photographer come true.

Thanks to all my friends and family who have encouraged me to be a better photographer and a better person. And of course, thank you most of all to my wonderful wife, Meredith, for always being there for me and putting up with all my crap. I love you.

—**DAVID L. REAMER**

INDEX: PEOPLE AND PLACES

INDEX: FOOD

REWARDS FOR STOLEN ART

- *Dinner for four with a reservation for the return of my framed Ferdinand illustration*
- *Dinner for two with a reservation for the return of either of my Boqueria plates*
- *No questions asked*

The real painful thefts at my restaurants over the years have always been of art. You steal a pepper mill, you steal a carafe, you steal a water glass, some money—that shit's annoying. But you steal my heirlooms, my art? That really hurts.

Years ago I bought a very hard to find oversized copy of *The Story of Ferdinand* by Munro Leaf and illustrated by Robert Lawson (pub. 1936). I had the last page of it—the one where Ferdinand is sitting under the old cork tree—framed and hung in Toro's bathroom. Someone stole it out from under us a few years ago, and I still see red when I think about it. At one point I even hired a private detective to look into it—no joke—but he couldn't manage to find anything.

I didn't hire a detective when my red-and-white Boqueria plate was stolen. I just went ahead and bought another one on a visit to Barcelona in late 2012. A few weeks after I hung the second plate, guess what happened? It was stolen. Again.